In Parallel

A YORKSHIRE CHILDHOOD

by Janet Barker

JEREMY MILLS
PUBLISHING LIMITED

Published by Northern Heritage Publications
an imprint of Jeremy Mills Publishing Limited
www.jeremymillspublishing.co.uk

First Published 2008
Text and images © Janet Barker

ISBN 978–1–906600-08-2

The past is parallel with the present.

(The playwright Dennis Potter, in interview.)

For my children, Thea and Patrick,
my grandchildren,
Lauren, Eleanor, Dominic and Samuel,
and all who come after.

*In writing this book, I have drawn heavily on my
mother's own stories of past people and events,
and the encouragement of my husband, Malcolm.*

CONTENTS

CHAPTER ONE – 1942:
FATHER AND MOTHER

IT IS MORE than sixty-five years since I saw my father, but I remember the night clearly. He had been ill at home for about a week. I had begged for the novelty of sleeping in a different room from my own, further down the corridor, where the pub bedrooms were set out behind numbered doors. I lay in a black iron, brass-knobbed bed.

The door opened and my father, a coat over his pyjamas, came in, followed by my mother, who murmured, 'Don't wake her, Harry. It's a shame – she'll be asleep.'

But he could not leave without saying goodbye to me, he said. (He had always taken pains to explain things.)

He told me he was going to a nursing home in the doctor's car with my mother. I sprang up, white-faced as I later learned, and blurted, 'You're not going to have an operation, are you, Dad?'

My grandfather had died three years before, following an operation, and since then the word had been synonymous with death. I cannot recall my father's reply but he must have reassured me, and I think he told me to look after my mother. He would come back soon, he said. Then he and my mother both kissed me and left the room.

I felt a need to prolong his nearness, and pattered across the lino, which struck chill even though it was June, reaching the narrow sash window in time to see Dr Singh's car pull away from the forecourt and disappear up the street. I remember the acrid smell of steamy glass, the lumpy old paintwork on the sill patterning my elbows as I leaned into the window and looked out. Then, the final farewell taken, I climbed back into bed in that neglected room smelling of cold dust, in the huge white elephant of a pub which my father had come to manage only three weeks before.

The next days moved slowly. Because my father had always kept his promises, I felt confident of his return, and, with my mother suddenly caught up in the myriad new duties of running the pub at the same time as paying visits to the nursing home, I entertained myself with reading, writing poetry, exploring the pub's enormous gardens, and getting to know Paddy, a rough-haired terrier we had acquired from my Greenwood cousins, who felt he needed more space than they could give him.

Paddy was a year old and had recently recovered from an abscess under his chin which had forced his head to one side and left him with a mouthful of evil-smelling teeth. He howled and barked shut up in the kitchen that first night, and my Sykes cousin Dorothy, who was staying, got up, despite my pleas, to give him a crack with her slipper. Paddy settled after that, and attached himself to my father, who, when he took to his bed, marvelled aloud at the hours the little dog spent on the mat outside his door.

Being an only child, I regarded a certain amount of loneliness as normal, but now I had Paddy for my boon companion. Mother, whom Dad had never admitted to the intricacies of stock-taking and book-keeping, although she had helped him to run our previous pub in Hull, and three grocery shops before that, had suddenly been plunged into full-scale management, answerable to John Smith's brewery. But although it was wartime, and there were many shortages, she still had plenty of staff: a live-in 'girl', bar-cellar man, part-time waiter, four or five cleaners, and a woman who reported on a Monday just to boil up the clothes in the set-pot in the garden wash-house. The garden was left to its own devices, apart from the vegetable section tilled by a local resident, who paid us with carrots, beans and lettuces (but never his prized peas). All the staff rallied round Mother, enabling her to delegate her duties in order to catch the trolley-bus, known as the trackless, and walk across town to spend time with my father at St. George's Nursing Home, a private establishment where he had been operated on for a perforated intestinal ulcer.

He was there for several days, and my mother believed, I think, that he would recover. He had suffered with stomach trouble for years, and she had grown used to his clenched jaw, his belches, his inability to digest her glorious pastry, which he loved, his leanness, his sharp retorts when the pain was at its worst, his reply of 'Just middling' when people asked him how he was, and the permanent supply of Rennies indigestion tablets in his waistcoat pocket. Sometimes, though, he felt 'badly', and after particularly severe attacks she would coax his 'system' back with arrowroot to 'coat the lining', poached fish, eggs whisked up in milk, and later on, shin beef strengthened with a pig's foot or cow heel. The ulcer had been a threatening force for most of the twenty years of their married lives and I suppose she thought that now it had finally burst, Dad was at last receiving the treatment he had always shied away from.

When it became obvious that he was very ill, as peritonitis had set in, she asked the surgeon, Mr Shepherd, 'Is there any hope?'

'We never give up hope,' he replied. 'Where there's life, there's hope.'

Clinging to this thread of encouragement, she would return to the alien world of the Big Drum, that forbidding edifice of grey pebbledash and cabbage-green tiles, full of strangers.

Meanwhile, I was revelling in my new life, for I was told little of events at the nursing home. Each day validated the excitement I had felt when Mother and Dad had first described the Big Drum to me. It was truly enormous, they had said, with a concert-room, complete with stage and dressing-rooms, and so many bedrooms I should have one for my toys, in happy contrast to our cramped temporary quarters in a shared semi-detached in Zetland Road, Doncaster. Dad had moved us there away from the Hull Blitz on his fiftieth birthday, September 10th, 1941, because, despite the excitements of watching familiar town buildings blazing against the night sky, late summonses from bed for communal singing in the air raid shelter, and jolly rivalries pursued at school in collecting lumps of shrapnel from surrounding streets, I had apparently started to fall on my knees and pray to God to save us from the bombs

***

OUR FIRST-FLOOR living quarters at the Drum consisted of two long kitchens, each with a huge, black-leaded range, each range furnished with two ovens which must have been considered essential when the Drum was built in 1913 as a commercial hotel, although it was no longer residential. Only the range in the first kitchen was ever lit, and it was the core of all our domesticity in what became our living-room, its black and silver body throbbing out heat as the fire leapt in the grate, with the sooted kettle singing on the hob, a few family treasures on a mantelpiece so high that even the grown-ups had to stand on the steel fender to reach the tea-caddy, and maybe a nose-twitching saucer of Cheddar (known in our household as 'toenail' cheese) toasting in one of the ovens for Mother's tea.

I was stretched out on the coconut matting before the fire late one afternoon, reading for the second time a storybook about a girls' boarding school, called *Sally Cocksure*, when Mother said she wanted to talk to me.

I remember feeling the usual resentment at having to put down a book, and, as always, used my index finger to mark the place. But my mother raised me on to her knee and, with her arms around me, told me through her tears that my father had died. I remember being gripped by a cold paralysis before finding myself suddenly riven with sobs. 'But he promised to come back,' I cried, juddering out the words as though on a ratchet of grief. Mingled with disbelief was outrage that such a solemn promise could have been broken.

Gradually, soothed by my mother's quiet words, I came to accept that he had been too ill to keep the promise, while in the armchair by the fire, Granmer Greenwood, his mother, wept her own tears for her second son. She had been summoned forty miles from Hull by taxi, but had arrived at the nursing home too late to see him before he died.

Dad, as he instructed Mother from his sick bed about to how to manage without him, had said, 'She's a good girl, Janet is.' This I never felt, but his faith in me, carried to the constancy of almost his last breath, spurred me to immediate action. I dried my eyes.

'So now there's just you and me, and we shall have to look after each other,' said Mother.

I slid off her knee, hugged Granmer, and resolved to set the tea-table. We had entered another dimension, but the comforting civilities of family life were still around us, waiting to be laid out with routine ceremony: a white cloth only big enough to cover one end of the table, odd white china cups and saucers, a square glass sugar-bowl, and a glass salt-pot inscribed 'Saxa' in flowing blue letters, a relic of an advertising campaign acquired when Dad and Mother were in the grocery trade.

Some sort of chronological order is achievable when I piece together my impressions of the days surrounding my father's death. Parts of the original mosaic may have slipped out of context, and huge chunks may be missing, but enough fragments remain to suggest a pattern. My father's horror when he came round from the operation to find a tube in his side, and his resultant conviction that, as in his father's case before him, this signified cancer ('I know what that means.') My mother's truthful protestations that this was merely a drainage tube (for no cancer had been found). His plea, 'Take me back to Northern,' (meaning Northern Cemetery, Hull). His repeated question of 'Where's our Jack?' (His older brother, Jack, who lived in Doncaster, had said he would call on his way from work, but, like Granmer, came too late. Mother believed Dad vainly tried to hold on until Uncle arrived to support her.)

All this she either told me later, or else I gleaned it in overheard conversations. I am able to quote my father word for word because, as with certain nursery rhymes, I can still hear his brief sentences in the cadences of my mother's voice. She described how, after Dad died, she left the nursing home to make her way back to the Drum alone, and in a daze approached a strange woman in the town, saying, 'I've just lost my husband.'

The woman was sympathetic and responded, 'Oh, have you love – I'm very sorry.'

But it was wartime, and many lives were being lost, so perhaps this did not seem an unusually tragic piece of information.

Arrangements were made to fulfil Dad's request to be buried in Hull. It was only years later that the true significance of this was borne in on me, perhaps when I was staying in Australia and suddenly recognised, admittedly on a bigger canvas, how profound was my own need, when my end came, to be on home soil. He must have loved the city, hated leaving, been so homesick, beset as he was by illness, with his hard-won savings draining away during eight months in a strange town, with nothing being earned but the tiny rents from three terrace houses.

Taking on the management of the Drum was to have been a temporary measure, a tourniquet to staunch the haemorrhage, as I see it now. Naturally he worried about his financial situation, brought about by the exigencies of war, for he was in his own way an ambitious businessman. How many times after fleeing to Doncaster did he ask himself, as he paced the footpath across Town Moor towards Elmfield Park, 'Have I done the right thing?' Yet the air raids and alerts continued in Hull, which most likely answered this question.

He took the Drum after a crushing disappointment. He had hoped to secure the tenancy of the Queen's Hotel in Pontefract, and arrived with the deposit to find someone else had beaten him to the prize. I have passed the hotel a number of times since, and find it hard to imagine us there, so mammoth is its structure, but to my father its loss was devastating.

He decided to apply to John Smith's for a manager's job until such time as he should find a suitable place of his own, and this was how, one fateful day, he and my mother came to catch a Woodlands bus to the end of Watch House Lane and walk over the railway bridge to inspect the Drum. Someone must have told them this was the best route to take and, although it was not the quickest, it gave my parents a long-distance view of the building, which at that time stood in isolation, surrounded by allotments.

Though locals knew it as the Big Drum, the pub's real name was the Bentley Hotel. I thought this a much more dignified address, and once we had gone to live there I used to get quite sharp with people who referred to our home as 'the Drum'. But long after we left, when the public rooms were gutted, refurbished, and given a new lease of life, the premises were renamed 'The Drum' by the brewery, and an appropriate sign was hung outside.

It pleases me now, this endorsement of the affectionate nick-name I once tried so hard to suppress. How it originated we were never quite sure, but some old customers recalled being entertained in the concert-room by a very popular drummer.

Mother always maintained that, even at a distance, she was seized by foreboding at first sight of the Drum. 'Don't let's take it, Harry – it gives me an awful feeling,' she said. But Dad, anxious to return to the world of work with money coming in, told her it would not be for long, that he would soon find them a pub of their own, and this would keep them going in the meantime.

5

***

SO IT WAS arranged, and we moved in on May 18th, 1942, Dad and I going ahead on the trackless, with me carrying my doll, Jeniffer. Before we left Zetland Road, Dad had displayed a rare flash of irritation with me, indeed, the only one I can remember: 'Why does she want to bring that doll?' Perhaps he was afraid I would lose her. He must have been frustrated, too, when we found ourselves on the wrong trackless, and were told by the conductor (luckily before setting off) that to get to Bentley we should dismount and make for the North Bridge terminus in a different part of town.

I remember this, but not alighting at the end of the journey. We must have walked together between the terrace houses along Broughton Avenue, and, as we turned the corner, seen the Drum loom up on its stony incline, filling the sky like a liner moored against a dock.

Things happened quickly. Dad became immersed in the handover from the retiring manager, and I was introduced to Georgina, the 'live-in girl' we were to inherit, who seemed very old at twenty-one to my eight-year-old eyes. She was kind but preoccupied, and I was left to my own company. No-one had thought to tell me the whereabouts of the lavatory and I was too shy to ask strangers. I held on for as long as I could, but suddenly, as I stood alone in the kitchen, the waters burst from me, making a large pool on the lino.

Thus voided, I filled instead with panic, and snatched a roller-towel from behind the door and tried to dissipate the puddle using flicking motions. When this did not work, I resorted to actual mopping-up, and hung the sodden towel back on its roller, hoping it would be dry by the time anyone used it. I never afterwards referred to the episode, and it passed into shamed limbo.

With sopping knickers, I walked wide-legged down the brass-edged stairs, along a marble-floored corridor, past the billiards-room and the concert-room, which really did have a stage with a painted backdrop of a balustraded terrace set against flowers and trees, and a dressing-room on either side.

There were two bars, one in the men's tap-room, where darts and dominoes were available and beer was a penny a pint cheaper than in the lounge, and another in the lounge itself, where tub-chairs and round tables were set out on a carpet, and Big Sid, the waiter, was on call at weekends. Here the bar was grander, a magnificent hexagonal structure of gleaming mahogany, with mirror-backed shelves, and screens of engraved glass, which could be (though seldom were) pulled down at closing-time.

Hatches behind the tap-room bar serviced the jug-and-bottle's outdoor sales, and the ladies' tap-room, venue for weekly meetings of a bizarre coven called the

Death and Dividing Club, whose members, if not called upon to pay for a relative's funeral, or their own, saved up for Christmas, and in summer chartered a coach for a day's junket on the coast once the war had ended. There was an office behind the lounge bar, containing precious bottles of rationed whisky, gin and rum for the optics, and big cardboard boxes of cigarettes – Capstan Full Strength, Gold Flake, Player's Navy Cut, and my Dad's favourites, Wills' Woodbines. An upper club-room, which could accommodate up to 400 people, ran nearly half the width of the building, but this could be reached only by an outside iron staircase, and was rarely used.

As with the attics, it was forbidden territory to me, although I was allowed to creep down the steep stone steps leading to a series of cavernous cellars, which smelled fruitily of beer and stagnant pools; for the pub was subject to coal-mining subsidence, and an electric pump hummed in the main cellar almost continuously to cope with several inches of flood water. In a boiler-room a fiery furnace, which heated the tap water and radiators, raged like a dragon, too fearsome for me to approach.

Back up on the ground floor, however, I found an accessible smoke-room with a piano open to a quick flourish of 'Oh can you wash your father's shirt?' Best of all, behold, a sitting-room, assigned to us. To this Mother and Dad waved in the removal men with the best china for stowing in our beautiful liver-coloured sideboard (bought by Mother for fifteen shillings from a second-hand shop on an impulse frowned on by my father) and our uncomfortable fawn, green-piped three-piece suite.

Unfortunately, the sitting-room did not overlook the garden. But it was there, a wind's breath away, in all its vast, quiet greenery and promise, every child's dream, a long-vanished Eden that haunts me yet. It had originally contained two bowling-greens with benches set around at intervals, and many of these seats remained, entwined in summer with white convolvulus we called 'milkmaids', their rotting planks for the most part still conveniently in place. The greens had now become a field of rough grasses, daisies, buttercups, sorrel, celandines and other wild flowers I could not identify.

There were further signs that the field had once been landscaped. Half-way along one side was a tall copper beech, flanked by two strange trees with swaying, down-curving branches that swept the ground, and four big laurels like green igloos. Their precise grouping was reflected by seven similar trees and bushes on the opposite side of the meadow, and another great beech stood at its centre.

The entire garden was bounded on three sides by barely penetrable shrubberies, where a narrow track twisted through dense undergrowth. Past a forgotten tulip bed, where a few striped specimens raised defiant heads, the path led among trees, some frailer ornamental varieties such as lilac, crab-apple and walnut, others more substantial and climbable, like the thick-branched willow in a clearing my cousins and I were later to christen 'Camp'.

***

AN INTREPID EXPLORER would come eventually to a yard. Here stood a stable with a loft above, which could be reached by a plank nailed to the wall, with crescent-shaped holes to take hands and feet. My young cousin Annette, when shown them, thought they were for horses. If we prised up a round metal cover in the yard, water gleamed on the surface of a well far below. A gate opened on to Pipering Lane, a rutted cart track leading to Pipering Wood, which in May and June was hazed with bluebells.

In summer, too, rising grove-like beside the vegetable plot, the unpruned soft-fruit bushes came into their own, never failing to yield vast amounts of gooseberries, blackcurrants, raspberries, loganberries and redcurrants despite being completely ignored for the rest of the year. We took the harvest for granted, and plundered it with Paddy in tow. Sheltering from the sun beneath the leaves, he would sometimes interrupt his panting to snatch a raspberry, and immediately spit it out in disgust. The nectar of the Drum's soft-fruit garden drenches my tongue afresh whenever I think of Christina Rossetti's *Goblin Market*.

To a child who had never owned a garden, all these were magical discoveries. Neither had my father really known one, I think, apart from a pocket-sized patch behind his parents' terrace house in Pendrill Street, Hull. He was thrilled by the verdant acreage at the Drum, and talked of the fruit pies Mother would make. Someone carried down one of the two big basket-chairs he had ordered from the East when he was a shipping clerk (its twin had been left in the Hull air raid shelter for an old lady who had taken a fancy to it) and Dad was assisted down, wrapped in a blanket, and sat gazing over his new domain. It was a sunny day, and Mother recalled afterwards how his face had developed a tan.

But June was too early for fresh soft-fruit pies, and on the twelfth of the month he died. When it came to choosing the funeral flowers I should send, Mother told me she had ordered pink and blue cornflowers. She thought I would like to do the card myself. What should I put? She left it to me, and I remember writing in careful, joined-up letters, 'To my dear Daddy with love from Janet'. I have the card still, along with all the rest.

John Smith's, through their District Manager, informed Mother that she could stay on at the Drum as manageress. This was a relief because, although the family had assumed she would return with me to Hull, she said my father had brought us away to make us safer and she would not go against his wishes.

His brother George and his wife Clara offered to have the funeral from their house in Anlaby Park Road, Hull, and the family undertaker, Mr Kemp, made the arrangements for a service in St. John's Church, Newland, where my parents had been married and I Christened, followed by burial at Northern.

***

MOTHER DID NOT want me to see Dad now he was dead. She wanted me to remember him as he was, and I agreed this was best. Neither did she wish me to attend the funeral. Father lay in the front room at 30 Anlaby Park Road and she told me he looked very peaceful. Part of me was relieved not to be taken into the room; part of me was curious enough to try to peer from outside the window through the drawn curtains. But they met too tightly for me to discern anything.

On the day of the funeral, my cousins Georgie and Brian and I were sent to the cinema to see 'Sergeant York', a strange decision in retrospect, but I suppose the grown-ups wanted us out of the house and there was nowhere else to send us. I had already seen the film once, and my attention wandered, although it would have done so anyway. I was aware that the cars would be passing the cinema as they made their way along Anlaby Road, and whispered to Brian, 'I wonder if they're there yet?' 'Shush', he hissed, a bit unsympathetically I thought, but he was only nine.

Two more memories survive of that time. After the funeral, my mother sat by the fire with Uncle Fred, Dad's youngest brother, talking. Uncle said, 'There's only one thing worse than losing a father, and that's losing a mother.' In my wretchedness I thought this remark unfeeling, perhaps a reference to his wife, Aunt Gwen, who I was given to believe had run off with a bus-conductor, leaving a note in a potato-basket, and my cousin Brian unintentionally motherless (she had tried to claim him later, but in vain). But I realise now my uncle had spoken nothing but the truth.

The other memory is of stepping off the number sixty-three trolley bus at the top of Cromer Street, where Aunt Nancy lived in Hull, with Mother, slender and smart in her fitted black bouclé coat and round, black 'pill-box' hat. She was deep in sad thoughts, and set off across Beverley Road with my hand in hers and little regard for her surroundings. A driver of a car or lorry, I cannot remember which, shouted to her to look where she was going 'with that kid' as he whisked seemingly inches by. She was startled, and grasped my hand even more tightly.

Once or twice, on return trips to Hull, we visited Dad's grave. There was no head-stone, for Dad would have rued spending money on one. Mother said that,

9

unlike Aunt Nancy, who made regular Sunday visits to the cemetery with flowers for family members, she could never draw comfort from visiting such a place. Her own preference, it transpired, was for cremation.

Although, standing by the piled-up clods of earth, I felt a reverence for my father's last resting place, I knew there was no comfort for me there either. Even so, sixteen years later, when Auntie suggested that she might take my wedding-bouquet to lay on Dad's grave, at such an emotional time I seized on her offer gratefully. By sending him the white roses, I was not only able to make a declaration of filial love; I could also make him part of the ritual which had symbolised such a radical change in my life.

**

WHEN WE RETURNED to Bentley, Mother knew that after weeks of liberty, during which no-one had had any time to enrol me, I must be sent to the local school. She asked Wyn, the barman, the way, and set off with me for Kirkby Avenue Juniors, two trackless stops off, although ever afterwards I walked along the 'backs' behind the houses, where the occasional spurt of hawthorn offered a nibble of 'bread and cheese'.

My previous school had sent a note for Mr Smalley, my new head, which Mother preserved, telling him, 'She is a quiet, careful worker, and takes a real interest in all her work. Her general knowledge is good and she is able to memorise very quickly. Her work and general attitude towards her work show great promise.' No mention, thank goodness, of my terrible handwriting, which always ended up festooned with blots.

Mr Smalley, tiny indeed, with shining pink crown and bright blue eyes, took me aback by requiring me to tell him the year of my birth, which I had never been asked for previously, but together we managed to work out it was 1933. Somehow he must have learned that my father had died, but I recall no direct reference to it. I was assimilated without fuss into Standard Two, where Mrs Mattox imparted to us some of the magic of the Greek myths at story-time. In September I moved to Standard Three, with delightful Miss Finney, brown-eyed, blushful, still only twenty. Some of us bought her cards when we got wind of her twenty-first birthday, and she blushed more than ever.

These school days I recall as largely happy, Dad's absence being absorbed into the background of classroom and playground activities. Perhaps it helped that many other fathers had been called up to fight or were away on war work. But whenever I remembered that I had 'lost' my own, I felt ashamed. I was desperate to prevent anyone knowing, and for years I dreaded being asked about him, although, strangely, I never was, apart from once being given a class assignment to write an essay on 'My Father'. I ignored this, and though fearful of being called to account, was never challenged.

It was at home, and usually at night–time, when I missed Dad the most, even though, had he been alive, he would have been down in the bar. He had rarely found fault with me, given me only the gentlest of reproofs; had been anxious for me to be happy, healthy, clever, honest, well-mannered and unafraid. I cannot remember him ever raising his voice to me, and certainly never his hand. He had spent hours talking with me, singing, telling stories, and, in playful pretence, rehearsing me in the formalities that were expected when we met his friends in the street. ('If they say, "Hello Janet, how are you?" what do you say?' 'I say, "I'm very well, thank you, how are you?"'– a reply that in those days caught adults by surprise, and is still automatic. For her part, Mother would emphasise that the 'How do you do?' used in polite society must never be taken as a query after one's health, and an introductory gambit of 'Pleased to meet you' was a sign of ill-breeding.)

Dad believed in me so trustingly that any major correction became, very unfairly, Mother's responsibility, and I certainly needed strong words and a smack now and then, for I was wilful. Even so, I dreaded disappointing my father more than any punishment.

Poor Mother. After he died, she had so much to do, to think of. Takings and stock to balance, wages to work out with a Ready Reckoner, staff to organise and 'fill in' for, customers to please during long hours behind the bars, John Smith's to satisfy, domestic tasks like shopping and cooking to fit in, and (when the laundry-woman left soon after our arrival) the washing and ironing to share with Georgina. In addition, she had me to bring up unaided, and the solicitors to negotiate with, for Dad, who I think had not liked to contemplate his end, had died without making a will. She found she was entitled to only the first £1,000 of his estate, plus half the income on the sum remaining. The other half of the income was available to her as maintenance for me if my guardian, Uncle George, signed for each withdrawal, but completing these legal arrangements took many months.

They would exist until I was twenty-one, when I would inherit three little rented houses in Hull and a few hundred pounds (I cannot remember exactly how many). This was scarcely just when she had spent twenty years working hard to help my father establish himself, but such was the law, and I was never made to feel guilty about it.

***

DESPITE ALL THE demands on her time and energy, Mother ensured that our outsize quarters at the Drum felt like home. At night we would curl up together in her feather bed, though she would come up late. For, once the last customers had reluctantly drifted away after closing-time, she and the staff had ashtrays to empty, tables to wipe, glasses to wash, barrels to 'tap', and the two ornately-chased brass tills to cash-up. Sometimes she was too tired even to unclip her earrings as she sank into bed.

She still loved to take me on her knee and sing, and talk about her school days, and my father, and family personalities. Little wonder, though, that at other times she was sharp or impatient with my moods, which swung between melancholy, bookishness, absent-mindedness, 'cheek', disobedience and sluggish introspection. Once, when she could not break my concentration, in desperation she flung a book I was reading into the fire. After such hurts I would sob to myself, 'Not fair, not fair,' as I lay in bed, willing Dad to walk through the door. If tears and prayers could have brought him back, we would have had a second Lazarus.

Why not? Jesus had promised, as I had I learned at Sunday School, that 'whatsoever ye ask in My name, I will grant your request', and 'Ask and it shall be given unto you.' The secret was to truly believe, and I knew in my heart that I did not, and that all my pleadings for a miracle were in vain.

Misery would creep up on me, too, in daylight hours. There were times when I was exasperated, even angry with Dad for not believing that he didn't have cancer, for then he might have tried harder to get better. I have a vision of huge, hot tears rolling down my nose and jaw-line and glistening on Paddy's rough head as I cradle his chin in my hands. He smiles up at me empathetically, releasing a wave of halitosis.

CHAPTER TWO – HARRY

SO WHAT DO I know of my father? He was tall (about five feet eleven, said my mother) and had the Greenwood blue eyes (what my mother called 'well opened', a description she had read in a book) and a dimple in his chin. He was fair when she met him, and she liked tall, fair, blue-eyed men, being tallish, dark-haired and brown-eyed herself. Father and his three brothers all married dark, brown-eyed girls, and I thought it natural that couples everywhere should admire contrasting colouring in one another. Two brown-eyed or blue-eyed people together seemed such a waste. Who wanted to look constantly at eyes the same as one's own?

Later, Dad's thick, springing hair began to turn grey, a mixture Mother called 'pepper and salt.' Sometimes he would let me play hairdresser's with it. He was shy, quiet and 'highly-strung', diffident yet dry-humoured, sparing with praise, careful with money. He bit his nails (he had his own bottom teeth), smoked quite heavily, scowled at times with dreadful stomach pain, worried about business. How much of all this was due to his experiences as a dispatch-rider across the French battlefields during the 1914-18 War, and how much was part of his character, I do not know, but Granmer Greenwood said he had clung to her as a small child, even to the extent of waiting for her outside the 'W.C.'. Of all her sons, I think he was emotionally the closest, and her welfare, especially after Grampa died, was always a strong priority with him.

As well as stomach trouble, he suffered with his feet, and would sit soaking them in an enamel bowl of hot water with his trousers rolled up, reading *The Daily Express*, whose Beachcomber column he relished. To stretch a tight shoe, he would insert a small rolling-pin. In the late afternoon he would take a nap in his easy chair with a newspaper over his head. He also, I gathered later, enjoyed the books of Edgar Wallace, then in vogue. In his younger days he had been a Hull City Football Club supporter, said Mother, but I never remember him going to a match.

He often lay in bed in the morning while I was got off to school, and I used to open the door at the bottom of the stairs at the Station Inn, our pub in Hull, and call goodbye. When I walked home at lunch-time from my first school, there was the busy Beverley Road to negotiate, and until my seventh birthday, when I spent the day importantly crossing and re-crossing the road, I was not allowed to dice with the traffic. I would stand on the pavement facing the pub, and yell 'Dad, Dad' very loudly, and he always heard me from his place behind the bar, and came over to get me.

At weekends I would join my parents in bed for conversation, constructing tents with the sheets, and singing. There was one special story Dad made up which I never tired of hearing, though Mother called it bloodthirsty. It was about a little boy from a very poor family, without food, clothing or fire, who was sent out to beg in the snowy streets, and was befriended by a rich lady, who accompanied him home, bearing every conceivable comfort.

In the end Dad got tired of repeating this saga, and decided to end it by having the boy fall beneath the wheels of a carriage, which chopped off his head. But I was so distressed by this turn of events that he hastily devised a rescue plan, describing how the rich lady felt so moved by the terrible sight that she bought a large cabbage, had holes cut in it for eyes, nose and mouth, stuck it on the lad's neck, tied a scarf around to hide the join, and made him perfectly all right again. This new version enchanted me, and he was not allowed to discard it.

**

UNCLE GEORGE HAD been in an amateur concert party, and had a reputation as a great wag. He would say things like (on a freezing, snowy day when all the family were walking to Granmer's to tea), 'I do hope Ma has a nice ... cold jelly waiting for us.' People fell about, holding their sides, and the story was regularly repeated, especially by Aunt Clara, with undiminished appreciation. On another occasion, when the womenfolk were complaining of low pressure in their gas ovens, he famously inquired, 'Is your gas bad, Clara?' which was regarded as another rib-tickler.

If a guest came to Granmer's for a meal, he would stare at their laden plate and ask, 'Are you going to eat ALL THAT?' Another episode that especially tickled my mother was when someone called unexpectedly for tea and he said to Uncle Fred, 'Go next door and ask Miss Rogerson if we can borrow her teapot and tell her she needn't empty it.' I cannot say I found all this very funny, but humour in the thirties and forties lacked edge.

Dad's humour was even less obvious, and Mother told me that sometimes his witticisms would not register with people until afterwards. I can only quote one, a reference to Uncle Fred's antics while pretending to shin up a broomstick. 'He's no need to climb it,' murmured my father ('meaning he was already up the pole,' Mother explained to me years later, still laughing). Mother laughed, too, when I told her that I had asked Dad what 'amen' meant, and he replied that he supposed it meant 'that's all'.

He taught me that Snowdon was the highest mountain in England and Wales, and Ben Nevis the highest in Scotland, and that a billion came after a million, and a trillion after a billion. When I asked what followed a trillion, he said, 'Don't know, a sillion, I expect'. He advised me to breathe in through my nose and not my mouth (so the air would be warm when it got to my lungs) and never to eat the white pith inside orange peel because it was indigestible. If there was a particularly noisy event taking place in the pub at night, he would warn me of it in case I awoke and was frightened. Such memories are, I suppose, unremarkable, the simple stuff of any loving father-daughter relationship, but they are few, and I cherish them.

Dad never felt he could leave the business for long, so although my mother and I went to Bridlington for a week every year, usually with my Great-aunt Jinny, he would come to see us there for only a day. He paid dearly for this brief visit one year, for he and I both caught impetigo. Mother had warned us not to use anyone else's towel in the bathroom shared by all the boarding-house guests, but we ignored her advice and made free with one we found hanging behind the door. Later we came out in the most hideous spots, which had to be bathed in red-hot water twice a day, and have their tops twisted off. I used to run away squealing when the steaming basin and squares of pink lint were produced by Mother or our live-in girl, Jessie, who took their duties as nurses far too seriously, I thought. The torture seemed to go on for days, but the knowledge that Dad was a fellow-sufferer helped considerably.

As well as joining us at Bridlington, Dad would take other days off occasionally to go to the races, maybe at Doncaster or Pontefract, perhaps treating himself to a plate of jellied eels, and bringing me back gifts of Royal Doncaster Butterscotch or Pontefract Cakes. Once he took me to a circus with Uncle George and his son Georgie. We travelled on top of a double-decker bus, and it was on this journey that I developed my recurrent, unspoken fear that if the top were nailed to the bottom, as I surmised, the upper deck might tear off as we went round a corner. Quite regularly, I accompanied him to Linsley's Brewery, threading through the network of narrow streets in the Old Town, by the wharves and warehouses and crumbling Georgian houses, both of us sucking Rowntree's Fruit Gums. If he went without me, he would return with a bar of caramel-centred chocolate squares in a wrapper marked out like dominoes. It was a delicacy surpassed only by the scraps of pre-war bacon and bread, coated in 'dip', fried egg and tomato, that he would hand me from his plate.

I still see him, unshaven, shirt with collar not yet attached, sharing his breakfast as I stand with my head just above the table-top. Then would come his preparations for the working day, with bar and cellar duties to be performed before the early customers came in at eleven, the men usually heading for the tap-room with its sawdust and spittoons, the funny, opinionated old women for the tiny snug.

Perhaps he would first make a visit to the lavatory. I was always puzzled as to why he flushed it as soon as he entered, but think this was for reasons of decorum. Stubble now shaved, he would stand before the mirror above the Yorkist range with a brush in either hand, and attack his hair with vigorous, alternate back-strokes.

He would sometimes sing before the glass, making a fair attempt at yodelling, another thirties fashion, with a hand controlling his epiglottis. I loved the 'straight' songs he knew, too: 'Daisy, Daisy,' 'Lily of Laguna', 'Sweet Rosie O'Grady', 'It's a long way to Tipperary', 'Pack up your Troubles in your Old Kitbag', and others from the Great War. His favourite was probably 'When it's Springtime in the Rockies', but he was also very fond of 'Mademoiselle from Armentières' (he pronounced it 'Armatears') and 'If you want the Sergeant-Major, I know where he is.' He would substitute another version: 'If you want to find our Janet, I know where she is, she's sitting on her Daddy's knee.' I was proud to think he spoke French, the one sentence he taught me being *'Voulez-vous promenade avec moi ce soir?'* (which came out as 'avec moy sisswar'). He knew German too, and it was years before I learned at school how to pronounce correctly his 'ine funderkatoffles' ('one pound of potatoes'), and that something I had thought sounded like 'ishvice-ishness' was really *'Ich weiss es nicht.'* Although he eschewed all pretence of domesticity, having, like his brothers, been thoroughly spoiled by Granmer, he was a success with a toasting-fork, and we enjoyed the results with thickly-spread strawberry jam.

We had a dog, Rap (short for Rapscallion), a surprise present whom I had one day ecstatically discovered warming his black rolls of puppy-fat on the hearth-rug. He made friends with Tiddles, the stray cat who had been found in the shed with a litter of kittens. Neither Mother nor Dad could bring themself to drown the new-born, but Jessie, who came from an orphanage, and had learned how not to be unduly sentimental in such matters, did the deed in a bucket. Like most unpleasant facts, including the troubling progress of the war, this was kept from me. Tiddles became part of the household, and although Dad purported to ignore her, he was really as fond of her as the rest of us.

I can't remember whether Tiddles ever sat on his knee, but in any case this was my special spot. I would lie with my cheek pressed against his tickly waistcoat, listening to the shifting of coals in the grate, fighting sleep as I rose and fell to the sound of his regular breathing. I would rasp his stubble with my fingers, and smooth his wrinkles. I knew every part of his face in those days, but although I could recall the separate features after his death, it was surprising how soon I was unable to form them into a complete image.

***

AFTER HE DIED, Granmer used to love to talk to me about him, and I loved to listen. But her stories always took the same well-worn track, and I lacked the initiative to branch out with fresh questions. Now I would know better and say, 'Tell me all you can remember from the minute he was born', and build up a chronological picture of his early life.

I discovered from sending for his full birth certificate that he was born at 2 Fern Grove, Northumberland Avenue, East Sculcoates, Hull, and that his father, George, was an iron-yard labourer. Dad had a brother, Jack, sixteen months older, and it was another ten years before Uncle George came along, with Uncle Fred following two years later. Dad was the only son given two Christian names, Harry Anelay.

Granmer had been Eleanor Anelay, and came from the village of Eastrington, near Goole. She was one of a big family, and her father had been a blacksmith. His horse knew the way home with him when Great-grandfather left the pub in a state of inebriation. They must have had money to spare, for Granmer was sent to school with a penny in her pocket to pay for the lessons, although I do not know what sort of period this covered, nor how regularly she attended.

Afterwards she went into service, but I never heard about this part of her life. She told me how Grampa 'asked me if I was willing, and I said yes, I thought I was.' They were married at St. Mary's Parish Church, Sculcoates, Hull, on April 20th, 1889, when Grampa, described as a labourer, of 6 Kate Terrace, Cave Street, Hull, was twenty-eight. His father, also called George, was dead, and had been a labourer, too.

Granmer was twenty-three, her father, John Anelay, is on the marriage certificate still described as a blacksmith, and Granmer's address is given as 10 Model Avenue, Hull. I wonder if this was her place of work. A James Greenwood (Grampa's brother?) signed as a witness, but I find it amazing that Granmer's sister, Henrietta Anelay (my Great-aunt Hetty) could only make her mark, for Granmer used to write newsy letters to Mother and me, although the spelling was erratic ('Dear Dorie Janat ...Yrs ever Ma Grma', complaining, poor old lady, about her 'rhumtic', or rheumatics, and referring to my cousin Brian as 'Brain'). She also, though more rarely, corresponded with her sister, Great-aunt Annie, who had emigrated with her husband to Sydney, Australia, many years before.

I know nothing of my Dad's schooldays, and have no photographs of him until he was a young man, apart from a small head-and-shoulders of a boy who I think might be he. I found it after my mother died, in a sugar-bowl packed away with a Chinese tea-set, and I feel sure from the features that it is my father at around twelve years of age. He wears a dark jacket, a stiff white collar and a flower in his button-hole, and looks as though he is dressed for a wedding.

Granmer's boys were mischievous, and up to many a tease. My grandmother's tiny frame would shake, her parchment face crinkle and her faded blue eyes water with mirth as she and I sat, united by a bond of love, talking of the old days. There was one trick of theirs she particularly enjoyed relating. They had an old aunt whose apron-strings they would tie to the back of her chair, so that when she stood up it followed on behind her.

Granmer was restless and loved moving house. In those days there were lots of little properties with 'For Rent' signs in the windows. The family legend went that she would no sooner be settled in one than she would take a greater fancy to another in a nearby street, and arrange a quick flit. Her boys used to jest that they could never be certain when they went home at tea-time whether they had arrived at the right house.

Dad became an apprentice grocer with the big Hull company of William Cousins. After he completed his time he took a little shop in Sculcoates Lane, and started his own modest business, stocking up with lucifers (matches) when a shortage seemed likely because of the war. He would be nearly twenty-three when it broke out in 1914, and was conscripted, I am not sure when. Possibly he was made a dispatch-rider because he was already used to a motor bike.

During this period he was seeing a schoolteacher called Ivy who was, I think, older than he. She was, according to Mother, very, very fond of him, and my father was urged by Granmer to marry her, and did so. From what Mother told me, they had very little life together, and poor Ivy died from tuberculosis. I have no idea of the timescale, or whether she was already ill when they married, but I believe he came home on leave to find her desperately sick. I knew none of this until long after Dad was dead, for my parents had decided not to mention Ivy to me, though of course he was described as a widower on their marriage-lines.

It was a jolt to all my romantic conceptions of my parents' relationship when at length Mother confided the truth, but now I feel only sadness for the ailing, clever young lady who loved my father. She gave him a silver cigarette-case inscribed 'From Ivy', and a silver match-holder. He always carried them, and after he died Mother wept to find a folded ten-shilling note tucked inside the match-holder for emergencies. I have the two cases (though not the note), and a small table delicately incised by Ivy with a classic design of flowers and leaves. Mother said this had been burned into the wood with a red-hot poker, a fashionable craft of the time, for Ivy had been artistic.

***

18

LIKE MANY OF his contemporaries, Father never talked about the war, his only reference to it being the songs. I don't know whether he and Uncle Jack ever compared notes, for Uncle had served with the infantry on the Somme and at Ypres, and been gassed. He recovered, but forever afterwards suffered from 'trench feet'.

Dad's Army papers showed he was in the Army Service Corps Motor Transport division and qualified to drive a lorry in April 1917. The one experience of his that I did hear of from my mother might well have led to his death. While he was serving in France he drove a motor bike through a pocket of gas which had collected in a dip in the road. He fell from his machine unconscious, but was rescued, and taken to hospital.

He remained a private, and stayed on with the Inter-Allied Rhineland Commission in Germany, chauffeuring diplomatic and military big-wigs in a Rolls-Royce. He kept some records of these journeys, and the first, dated January 8th, 1919, is some sort of pass written in pencil by a billeting officer. It says, 'Coblenz - Frankfort. To Helz Garage, Telegraph Barracks. Billet car & driver of General Clive, British Army, tonight. Dr. (Driver) Greenwood, 70026 Rolls Royce.'

There is an official card approving my father's purchase of subsistence stores at the Headquarters of the American Army at Coblenz, dated August 27th. On September 25th, No. 284381 Pte Greenwood, A.S.C.M.T., 'has permission to proceed with car no. 70026, carrying Mr. Wise and party of the Supreme Economic Council to Rotterdam.' It is signed by the A.D.C. to the Military Governor of Occupied German Territory.

On October 30th there is another pass issued by the British Department of the Inter-Allied Rhineland Commission, authorising him on behalf of the British Commissioner to take the Rolls to Cologne, returning to Coblenz the following day. There is also a 'British Department Circulation Slip', listing 'Sir Harold Stuart, Mr. Urwick, Mr. Harvey, Mr. Mackinnon Wood, Major Maxwell Thin, Capt. Lumby and Registry.'

On the back of two of these now fragile papers, Dad has set out his expenses. He wrote with a copying-ink pencil, and though his writing is strong, he indulged in a few fancy flourishes. He stayed at the Rhine Hotel, Andheim, in September, paying twenty-four Marks for two dinners, eight Marks for bed, six for breakfast, plus ten for breakfast at Rotterdam and 'one day's road allowance' of twenty-eight Marks.

At some stage he had a nasty accident when turning over an engine by gripping the starting-handle with two hands, though whether of a car or lorry I do not know. It sprang back, breaking both his arms. One wonders how on earth he coped with his twin disabilities, but the bare details are enough to conjure weeks of pain and inconvenience.

There is one photograph of Dad in an Army greatcoat, peaked cap and driving goggles, and another very dark one of a young lady in a large hat seated in an impressive car, presumably the Rolls. Apparently he was taking out a German girl at this stage, and had considered marrying her and staying in Germany, he told Mother. What happened to change his mind (or the young lady's) I have no idea.

In the end he came home, and got a job as a wages-clerk with the Hull shipping line, Macgregor, Gow and Holland. He had good references. One, from a captain in the Oberpraesidium, Coblenz, says: 'I knew the above-mentioned man for several months as a chauffeur on the staff of the Inter-Allied Rhineland Commission at Coblenz and have much pleasure in testifying to his capabilities as a driver and to his steadiness and trustworthiness as an individual.' Another, signed by a T.H. Urwick, says: 'H.A. Greenwood acted as driver of the car which I used for some months last year while he was in the Army. I found him always sober, obliging and trustworthy. He is a good and careful driver, and takes an interest in his car, and I can thoroughly recommend him.' From G.H. Thomas in Wales came another appreciative testimonial: 'I had Mr. Greenwood in my employ for a considerable period as a chauffeur-mechanic, and always found him all that could be desired in every respect.'

Later on, when he came to apply for licensed premises while at Doncaster, Dad was armed with more up-to-date references from Hull. Stanley J. Burtt, F.A.I., said: 'I have known Mr. Greenwood for many years, he having been the licensee of an important house in this city for some considerable time. I have always found him most reliable and straight-forward and will, I am sure, continue to maintain his splendid record.' G. Barker, who kept the furniture store next to the Station Inn, wrote that he had known Dad 'both socially and commercially for about ten years, during which time I have always found him straight-forward and strictly honest in all his dealings. I should have no hesitation in recommending him for any position of trust or responsibility.'

A third is more mysterious, for it is headed 'Crawford's Cream Crackers', signed by a J. Crawford, and with the address of 'The Modern Grocery Stores, Cave Street, Hull'. It says the writer has known my father for over thirty years, and describes him as 'a straight-forward businessman of the highest integrity.' He adds a P.S.: 'If he accepts the liability, he'll deliver the goods.'

I am very proud of my father's references, and that is why I have given them at such length.

**

DAD MUST HAVE been about thirty when he met my mother, and she twenty-four. Dad was such a keen dancer that he kept a pair of patent-leather dancing-shoes in his overcoat pocket. Mother was not an enthusiast, but her young Aunt Jinny persuaded her to go to an event in a hall somewhere, and Dad was there. He invited Mother on to the floor, and although he could not have been impressed by her proficiency, he went home and announced to his family that he had met a girl he was going to marry.

I am not sure whether it was at this dance or a later one when Dad excused himself and went out for a beer. Mother, whose childhood had been scarred by the evils of drink, as a result of which she had taken a vow of temperance, was disgusted, and told Dad on his return that she did not wish to see him again.

A day or so after this, she was walking along a street when she spotted my father a short distance in front of her. He bent to tie his shoelace until she drew abreast of him, they fell into conversation, and that was that. She must have come to terms with his partiality to a glass or two, and eventually, of course, found herself behind a bar; but her first and only time in a pub before their marriage was when he took her into the Haworth Arms, not far from her home, and bought her a port and lemon.

***

WHEN MOTHER AGREED to marry my father, she said she did not want a ring. She had already been engaged twice before and ended both love affairs, and perhaps she thought another ring might be unlucky, although Dad did buy her a sapphire half-hoop later. I once asked her why she had decided to marry him and she said, 'I suppose I thought he was ... different.'

She was a clever seamstress and made her wedding and bridesmaids' dresses, as she had done for friends before. Given the skin colouring that went with dark chestnut hair (though it always seemed actually black to me) she was warned by her father not to wear white. 'You'd look like a toad looking out of a snowdrift,' he said charmingly. So she walked down the aisle at St. John's in oyster satin, and afterwards there was a reception at the bride's modest home, 7 Inglemire Lane (the road is now renamed though the row of cottages is still there).

Among the wedding presents were a silver-plated tea service from the Greenwood family, fruit-knives in a blue velvet-lined case, two cut-glass pickle jars in a silver stand, and an oak mantel-clock bearing a brass plate inscribed 'Mr and Mrs H.A. Greenwood from the staff of Macgregor, Gow and Holland, on the occasion of their marriage', and the date – August 7th, 1922.

Like many of her generation, Mother harboured some superstitions, and she must have been appalled when she broke a mirror before she left for the church. My cousin Gladys, who was a small bridesmaid, remembered that it poured with rain that day. She also remembered Mother crying.

To my eternal regret, Dad, in a fit of parsimony, decided that there was no need to have wedding photos. But he was eager to take Mother on a good honeymoon, and booked a week at Blackpool, at that time being freshly marketed as the last word in sophistication. They spent only one night there, however. Mother said they were both terribly disappointed, it all seemed so brash and artificial, although from something I once heard her let slip to a friend when she did not know I was listening, I have since formed the view that her virginal first night of married life was traumatic.

They sailed the next day to the Isle of Man from Fleetwood, and spent the rest of their honeymoon in Douglas. I think this was the last holiday they ever had together. He did consent to Mother's plea for a snap by a sea-front photographer, and there they are in my one precious picture of that time, on the prom at Douglas, she leaning against the rail in a wide-brimmed hat, long coat and pointed shoes, he perched up on the rail beside her in a close-fitting suit and a trilby.

Mother, who was twenty-five, had given up her skilled, responsible job as the supervisor of a work-room making surgical appliances, near the old Infirmary. It was a specialised private company, and she was presented on leaving with a superb gold watch. She and Dad moved in with his parents in Pendrill Street, and furnished their bedroom with a Sheraton-style suite in inlaid mahogany. The house, one of a terraced row, looks small from the outside, and I wonder how they all fitted in. Uncle Jack, whose wife was away in hospital, lived there with his children, Gladys and Jackie, and Uncle George and Uncle Fred were unmarried, and still at home too.

That first year was hard for Mother. She got on well with Granmer and Grampa, but was plunged suddenly into unrelenting housework. Granmer was 'a scrat', who liked everything 'just so' and held to the stern regime that was a common observance at that period – Monday for washing, Tuesday ironing, Wednesday bedrooms, Thursday downstairs rooms, Friday baking, Saturday shopping.

Protocol was strict. The front doorstep had to be scrubbed and edged with donkey-stone by an early hour, and carpets beaten in the back yard before the other residents of the street were around to take note of the dust. When Mother swept the bedroom lino for the first time and went out to empty the dustpan, Granmer asked her to cover it so Miss Rogerson next door would not see the fluff.

Mondays and Tuesdays were particularly toilsome. Uncle Jack was a sugar-boiler at Needler's sweet factory, Uncle George was a grocer and Uncle Fred worked with paints as a sign-writer. All of them got through a lot of overalls, and then there were the bedding, clothes and table-linen to soak, dolly, scrub, boil, rinse (several times), blue, starch, mangle, hang on the line (inside-out to keep the exterior smut-free), take in, sprinkle, fold, iron, air, refold and put away.

The demands of wash-day made sparkling results a much more personal achievement than they are today, and housewives everywhere scanned other people's clothes-lines with baleful eyes. In later years Mum still tended to giggle if she spotted a line of fawn 'whites', and murmur her own version of an advertisement for Persil: 'Someone's mother's using Oxo.'

When wash-powders came in, rivalries arose between Rinso and Persil, and Mother and Granmer favoured Rinso. Not only had washing to be bright and flawless, it had to be pegged out correctly, another cause for criticism if badly done. There was a verse to help the nervous new exponent:

'A skirt up by the waist-band,
A stocking by its toe,
A shirt up by its tail-flap
When on the line they go.'

Mother was a light hand at pastry, and Granmer liked to get her to do a stint on Friday. Granmer was apparently a disinterested cook, and meals took a back seat where house-work was concerned. She ran up big bills for chops and expensive cuts, which she would throw into a hot gas-oven ten minutes before the men were due home, and frazzle. They ate them with mustard, pickles and brown and tomato sauces, and Mother, for whom bottled sauces were beyond the pale, looked on aghast. She and my aunts ever afterwards blamed their husbands' bad stomachs on Granmer's over-cooked meat and disguising condiments. Years later, though, I was astonished to hear Uncle Fred speak longingly of those dinners, proof that there's never anything like one's mother's cooking.

Certainly Dad, at thirty-one, must have felt he was in clover. He had married the girl he proposed to, still lived at home with his parents, had his every comfort unfailingly supplied by wife and mother, and his brothers to play cards with at night. The blue and silver-papered front room at Number 42 was a scene of merriment when the two younger uncles brought their girlfriends home, and all would group around the piano. 'Play your pieces, George,' Granmer would bid the only son who had taken lessons, and they would all join in with 'If I Should Plant One Tiny Seed of Love in the Garden of Your Heart', or 'Oh by Gee by Gum by Gosh by Jove' or 'Won't You Buy My Pretty Flowers?', Granmer's favourite.

Inevitably, in that tightly-packed household of three generations, there were disagreements. Granmer was an impulsively generous creature who spoiled her sons and grandchildren shamelessly. Her worst riposte in the face of disobedience that I recall was 'I'll be vexed', but of course she was frailer and perhaps less fiery as I remember her. However, her daughters-in-law felt Grampa took second place, and was sometimes teased by his sons to the point of disrespect, although my father discussed problems with him, and valued his opinion.

Grampa was proud of his lads, and Mother said it was a sight to see all five men walking along to the Station Inn for a glass of beer before Sunday dinner, Grampa's head well below the other four. He enjoyed a joke, and would take up cups of morning tea on a shovel, cap on head, a covering he donned as soon as he got up. He had a sea-chest from which he could produce anything one required, like a magician. When he died the family opened the chest expecting great wonders, but there was hardly anything in it.

I think in the early twenties he was working as a 'donkey-man', in charge of a donkey-engine on a tugboat that plied between Hull and Rotterdam. When the tug salvaged a sunken vessel, Grampa was given a crate containing two superb vases, which stood on Granmer's mantelpiece, and which I now own. One is faded, as if by sea-water.

Though a tolerant man, Grampa at times got upset if treated with flippancy and disregard, and once packed his bag and threatened to leave home. It is difficult for me to imagine this mild, loveable old man, who called me his 'little pigeon', standing his ground, and usually Nelly (Granmer) got her way.

She had to give in, though, about the motor bikes. Uncle Jack and my father each had one, while Uncles George and Fred shared another, and when they went off on them, poor Granmer was a bundle of nerves. They would sometimes all drive together to the Yorkshire coast. Hornsea was considered a cut above Withernsea, Filey and Scarborough posher than Bridlington. I feel sure my father must have liked Whitby because he knew Sandsend, and said if ever there was a bonny spot where he would like to live, that was it. But was it on those cliffs above that Uncle Jack started up his machine and nearly went over the edge?

My mother preferred sitting in a side-car to riding pillion, and looked back on those carefree trips with great happiness. She told me how they bought a strange new fruit called a grapefruit and peeled it as they sat by the road, thirstily handing round the segments and expecting them to taste of grapes.

But liberating though these outings were, still Mother had to return to the daily grind of household chores in Granmer's house. Dad was sometimes late home, because when he took the crews' wages on board his company's ships in

Hull docks he might be prevailed upon to stay for a game of cards. I imagine that money must have changed hands, although she never complained of this to me, but altogether she was pretty miserable.

***

THEY HAD BEEN married for about a year when, one night, they went for a walk to talk matters over, and Mother enlarged upon her frustrations to some purpose. In fact, she told my father that unless things changed, she would be leaving.

Quite what my father said in reply I never heard, but he had been unaware of Mother's dissatisfaction, and was astonished and shaken by her revelations. He saw that something must be done, and lost no time in handing in his notice, renting a shop in Porter Street, off Hessle Road, and setting up as a grocer again. Their quick departure from Pendrill Street was achieved with no ill feeling, and from what Granmer always said it seemed clear that to the end of their lives she and Grampa regarded Mother with affection and admiration. My mother, on her part, loved them, especially Grampa's self-effacing personality, although she would smile at the memory of her strong-willed mother-in-law's disarming manner. ('She'd ask you what you thought, agree with you, and then go and do what she liked.')

It must have been so exciting for Mum and Dad, starting off in business together; cleaning and stocking the shop, and awaiting their first customers. Dad went around the neighbourhood knocking on doors and taking orders. Those were the days when sugar and other dry goods had to be weighed out and bagged, butter patted from a large block, hams and bacons strung and sliced, treacle and vinegar decanted from barrels, biscuits displayed in tins with glass lids.

Keeping things cold must have been one great problem, and warding off flies another. One of my strongest childhood impressions is of swarms of flies each summer, circling around every light-fitting, buzzing on every window-pane, congregating in the sugar-bowl, drowning in the milk-jug, alighting annoyingly on bare arms and legs. Sticky flypapers, black with bodies, were part of most people's décor.

Mother was not allowed to help herself to anything in the shop. Dad conducted his business on strict lines so as to keep his books straight. She had to make out a weekly order and pay for it out of her house-keeping, as well as putting money in the till for any incidentals. She was incredulous at first, but that way he knew exactly how things stood.

Dressing a window was a required skill in the grocery trade, and my father was good at it. I have a photograph of their second shop in De Grey Street, with 'Greenwood's' beautifully painted over the impressive length of plate glass (Uncle

Fred's handiwork?) and inside an amazing array of Christmas lines, artistically displayed and labelled. According to Mother, Dad could not bear to see things out of balance, and if a picture was askew he would have to get up and straighten it.

Now they had moved to the bigger and slightly more prestigious premises in De Grey Street, off Beverley Road, they felt happier at being back on familiar ground and nearer their families. Hull was divided into areas defined by the main highways radiating from its centre – Hessle Road, Anlaby Road, Hedon Road, Holderness Road and Beverley Road – and each had its own loyalties. The Beverley Road-ites considered themselves in a different category from the fishing community in Hessle Road, regarding them as people of a somewhat rougher mould.

Business boomed. As well as buying a carrier-bike, Dad invested in a pony and cart for making his deliveries, and Granmer used to tell me how she would be taken for rides. There were two ponies at different times, kept in a nearby stable, and both had gone blind through working and living down coal-mines. How I wished, as I listened to her stories, that I had known the ponies; I would have fed them apples and sugar-lumps, and kissed their sightless eyes. By contrast, the shop cat, Tommy, employed for his ability as a mouser, sounded to have been fierce and semi-wild.

But though all went well with the new shop at first, before long, in the late 1920s, there came the Great Depression, a time of international economic crisis and upheaval which extended its blight to Greenwood's grocery store. Many of my parents' customers were thrown out of work and unable to pay their bills. My father had never been keen on allowing 'tick', with customers running up accounts, but when hard times hit the community he had little choice. Eventually so much money was owed to him that he and my mother had to close down the shop and move to a flat on Beverley Road. They were there for several months, living off their small savings while he tried to find some alternative, and Mother told me he 'wore her out a carpet', pacing up and down.

In the end they managed to return to the grocery trade at 18 Leonard Street, further up Beverley Road. This little shop was a successful venture, and I was born above it in 1933, eleven years after their marriage.

CHAPTER THREE – DOLL

THE SPIRITED GIRL who became my mother was the second of three sisters whose story reads like a Victorian melodrama. Rebecca was the eldest, Dorothy, my mother, arrived four years later, and Annie four years after her. They were known to family and friends as Beck, Doll and Nance, and sometimes my mother got 'Dolly'. Becky and Nancy had Grandad's colouring and were pretty, blonde and blue-eyed, while Mother was 'the dark horse', like the Swifts.

Their parents, John William Nixon and Caroline Swift, were married on January 9th, 1892, when both were twenty-one, and it is only recently that I discovered the ceremony took place in a Register Office in the district of Sculcoates, Hull. The choice of a venue other than a church was unusual for those days, and I think it possible that they wed against the wishes of the bride's family, maybe even without any of her relatives being present. Sometimes I wonder whether Carrie ever regretted marrying Will, but despite his disgraceful treatment of her, she seems to have loved him to the end.

I have separate photographs of my maternal grandparents taken around that time, and they are an appealing pair, each posing near a mock rustic fence. Granma Carrie wears a fitted, fur-trimmed coat and ruched velvet hat, and I think her very beautiful, with her hourglass figure, dark eyes, full mouth and retroussé nose.

Grandad looks younger than she, his open, innocent gaze belying the grown-up formality of his high-buttoned waistcoat, draped with a watch-chain, and the handkerchief folded to a point in the breast pocket of his braided jacket. He carries a high-crowned hat in his left hand, and his right hand rests on the fence, exposing the thumb-nail. He was vain about his beautiful filbert nails, which my mother inherited, and he always pared them with a pen-knife, never cut them with scissors.

Grandad is described on his marriage certificate as a whitesmith, son of William Parkinson Nixon, a cartman, and his address is given as 115 Waterloo Street, Hull. Caroline, of 105 Beverley Road, Hull, is the daughter of William Swift, a tinner, and the witnesses are a G.P. Nixon and G. Read.

I do not know Aunt Becky's birth-date, but my mother was born on November 7th, 1897, at 6 Sydenham Terrace, Seaton Street, Hull, when by this time Grandad was described as a journeyman-whitesmith. Mother was a big baby and the birth was difficult, Granma having trouble passing the head. Whether for this reason, or whether Granma had relinquished her earlier I am not sure, but Aunt Becky went to live with her Swift grandparents and stayed there for the rest of her childhood.

Hers was a vibrant personality, spoilt, precocious, and according to my mother, fascinating. Whenever she popped back for a visit, she would tease and tantalise her younger sisters, and Mother used to recall two particular tricks Becky played on her.

She knew sister Dorothy hated cleaning her own shoes, and offered to do them, buffing the leather of one 'until you could see your face in it.' Then she threw the polish and cloth across, saying, 'Now you'll have to clean the other.'

Mother loved perfume, and one Christmas her sparse stocking contained a small phial of scent, which she put by in her bedroom, too precious to use. When she grew puzzled because the level in the bottle kept going down, Aunt Becky said it must be evaporating. Mother believed her until one day she caught her using it.

There was never much money for presents, but Mother was pleased with another Christmas gift she received, a tiny doll's frying-pan. Stupidly, she walked around with it balanced on her tongue, and swallowed it. She never forgot the terrible feeling of choking, and the pain as the handle of the sharp metal object lodged in her throat. Luckily, as her breathing worsened, a quick-thinking neighbour turned her upside down, thumped her on the back, and the blood-stained pan fell out.

My grandfather, who had five siblings, was a man with a chip on his shoulder. He was born in Brumby, Lincolnshire, and apparently his father had come to Hull to work on the new Botanic Gardens. The story went that after Grandad's mother died, his father married the house-keeper. When he died, followed by the step-mother, it was found that all the family goods had been left to her nephew. This naturally caused much resentment, and Grandad was especially upset about the books he felt should have been his.

If you sat near my Grandad and paid attention, which as children we were usually too bored or nervous to do, he could tell you the most amazing things. His particular interest was geography and it seemed to us, and to his acquaintances at the old men's shelter in Pearson Park, that he knew the whereabouts and characteristics of every place in the world. Books were his passion, and he could mumble on about many other topics, too, if anyone had the time and patience to listen.

Had he lived today, Grandad Nixon might have been able to satisfy his hunger for learning, perhaps gone to university and become a man of letters. As it was, his frustrations showed in most unlovable ways, and his fecklessness, heavy drinking, whiplash tongue, and periods of desertion gave Carrie and their daughters years of humiliation and misery.

Grandad was a skilled worker, and his in-laws, the Swifts, ran a tin factory in Hull, manufacturing, among other things, kitchen utensils such as the loaf and tart-tins they gave my mother as wedding presents, and which I still use. It is hard to remember after all these years, but I think Mother told me they offered Grandad a job. If this is true, I don't know how long he lasted, but I suspect that his conduct sorely tried their patience, for his treatment of Carrie led to much family bitterness and dissension.

***

ON A NUMBER of occasions Grandad rebelled against the daily round of work and family life and, without a word to anyone, set off literally along freedom's highway, abandoning wife, children and employer. Suddenly one day, usually Friday pay day, he would go missing, leaving Carrie and the girls destitute, often for weeks at a time. She would have no idea where he was, and be forced to swallow her pride, admit Will had deserted her yet again, and ask her unmarried brothers, Jim and Billy, for help. They never said no, for they were very fond of their sister, though they could not understand her tolerance of Will's shortcomings, and each time would beg her not to take him back. But she loved him, and she always did.

He would spend days on the road, a book in each pocket, drinking his wages, sleeping in hedgerows and haystacks, communing with nature. Once he had used up the money, he would find work, perhaps at a village smithy. The owner would be impressed by his skill and offer him a permanent job, so Grandad would get in touch with Carrie, and promise to reform.

In this manner, he found work at Stockton-on-Tees, and sent for his wife, who made her way there with my mother and little Nancy. They set up home in the pretty village of Hartburn, where the girls went to school, and Mother had happy memories of this time.

Inevitably, Will lost the job, and Granma and her daughters had to return to Hull and throw themselves upon her family's goodwill. The usual pattern followed: the uncles rented for their sister a little house, bought her 'a few sticks of furniture', and gave her what money they could afford. To supplement this fragile income, and make herself less dependent on her brothers, my grandmother would take in washing, and became an expert laundress. No-one, said Mother, could starch and iron a blouse as she could, and she passed on all sorts of arts, such as the correct way of folding handkerchiefs into a small, tight package to await ironing, and pressing table-cloths so that all the folds ran the same way.

Granma also went out cleaning, and there was one house where the owners were wealthy enough to live with white paint everywhere, instead of the usual brown. They would give her beautiful, fluffy white towels to wash down all this genteel woodwork, and afterwards, as well as paying her, allow her to keep the towels.

Granma Carrie was a good plain cook, and could 'make a meal out of nothing'. She would send Mother to the butcher's at the end of the day, when joints were going cheap, or, if times were especially hard, to ask for a pig's cheek or sheep's head. This would be eked out with big Yorkshire puddings, maybe one with added dried fruit or sliced apple to be eaten as a sweet.

If life without Grandad was hard, it was even harder with him. My mother told me how she grew to dread Fridays, when he would draw his wages and go straight to the pub, coming home late, reeling and abusive. He would snarl and shout, hurling terrible oaths and insults, and although his vicious tongue did not, I think, extend to his fists, he would sometimes turn the family out of the house. Once he drove away Carrie and my mother, locking himself in with the very young Nancy. When they crept to the window and peered fearfully in a short time later, they saw Nancy sitting up happily at the table and Grandad boiling her an egg.

Although Mother would smile as she recalled their relief, these episodes took their toll. As a girl, she suffered severe bouts of migraine almost weekly, and had to lie in a dark room until the blinding headaches, fragmented vision and vomiting wore off. It was some time before she realised that these attacks usually happened on Fridays.

No wonder she joined the Young Templars. This was an organisation attached to a Hull temperance hall, where the evils of alcohol were emphasised. In those days, public houses were open for long hours, and presented temptations that many men, walking home after a day of hard physical grind, found difficult to resist. Some spent all their earnings, and the suffering that this brought on their wives and children has been well chronicled. In this respect, my mother's childhood and adolescence were no different from, and perhaps even less painful than, those of thousands of others.

I used to enjoy it when she sang the Young Templars' rousing anthem:

'Never never drink,
Never never drink,
While there's youth and beauty,
Let us pause to think.
If you take the first glass,
Life may run to waste,
NO, NO, NO, we'll never, never taste.'

But her youth was very far from being all gloom and doom. My mother was an optimist with a quirky sense of humour, and she did not give way easily to depression. She loved mixing with people and having fun, and she was a great one for finding silver linings.

Always there was the support of the Swift family. She was fond of her grandparents, especially Granma Isabella, and there was an interesting network of uncles, aunts and cousins. One major figure in Mother's life was Aunt Jinny, a lively lady only a few years older, who was her mother's youngest sister.

While it is all too easy to portray my grandfather as an unmitigated villain, such wholesale condemnation must necessarily be unfair, for no-one is entirely bad, and indeed, he could be charming, and never gave me the rough side of his tongue. Though he frequently felt trapped, there must have been times when he came home sober, and showed affection for his wife and children, and despite all their differences, Mother accorded him a certain respect, which he on his part returned. I still have a card he sent her for her eighth birthday, addressed in his firm, beautiful script to her maternal grandparents' home, 9 Terry Street, Hull, and posted in Stockton-on-Tees. ('To Dorothy from Your Loving Father'.) He had a good voice and liked to sing popular ballads of the time: 'The Lost Chord', 'Speak To Me, Thora', 'Be Good, Sweet Maid, And Let Who Will Be Clever', and 'Sweet Marie.'

***

MY MOTHER LOOKED back on her schooldays as happy. After Hartburn, I believe the family moved to nearby Norton, and it was possibly at school here that she learned a fragment or two of French ('Le rouge-gorge est un joli oiseau') and to strum on a beribboned mandolin. Eventually they moved back to Hull, and here, with a struggle, and no doubt with help from the uncles, Dolly and Nancy would have new white dresses in which to promenade around the park at Whitsuntide. Empire Day was another important date in the calendar, when red, white and blue ribbons were donned, bunting draped, and Union Jacks proudly waved. On Oak-Apple or Royal Oak Day, the anniversary of Charles II's escape from Cromwell's troops by climbing an oak tree, the Restoration of the Monarchy was commemorated with a special song which began, 'Royal Oak Day, the twenty-ninth of May'.

Mother took her studies seriously. She learned to write in a distinctive hand, with below-the-line loops that turned backwards. I often begged her to show me how she shaped the letters, but try as I would, even with my mouth contorted like hers, I could never remotely copy them.

An enthusiastic music teacher had taught the class certain songs which Mother would sing in her pleasant soprano as I sat on her knee, sometimes joining in.

There was:

'Not a sparrow falleth but its God doth know,
Even as His mandate lays a monarch low.
Not a leaflet waveth but its God doth see.
Think not then, O trembler, God forgetteth thee.'

There was another:

'"Dear mother", said a little fish, "pray is that not a fly?
I'm very hungry and I wish you'd let me go and try."
"Sweet innocence", the mother cried, and darted from her nook.
"That painted fly is put to hide a sharp and barb-ed hook."'

Or I might beg for 'Pippa's Song' by Robert Browning ('The year's at the spring, the day's at the morn'), or Shakespeare's 'I know a bank whereon the wild thyme grows', or the dramatic 'Mariner, mariner lost in the storm.'

In Hull, she joined a concert party attached, I think, to the Young Templars. Concert troupes were popular for both adults and children, and years afterwards Mother and Aunt Nancy still enjoyed singing:

'Once there lived side by side two little maids
Who both dressed just alike, hair down in braids'

or the catchy 'Ching chang ching chang chingalingalingwang.'

She read 'Uncle Tom's Cabin' and 'Swiss Family Robinson', and later bought me copies of some of her favourite books, 'Little Women', 'Good Wives', 'Oliver Twist', and the Gene Stratton Porter tales of American life, 'Girl of the Limberlost', 'Laddie' and 'Freckles'.

Mother taught at Sunday School, and I have three group photographs of her taken about that period, and a studio portrait of her at thirteen, round-faced and with her long, thick hair parted in the middle and tied back in a large bow.

After she returned to live in Hull, she was regarded as one of her day-school's bright pupils, and chosen to sit for a scholarship, which would qualify her for high school. When the day came to sit the exam, knowing what was at stake, her mind seized up. She remembered attempting to spell 'which' during the essay, and trying the word out in the margin in various forms.

When the results were announced, to the school's surprise she had failed. This was something I think she ever afterwards regarded as an opportunity she should not have allowed herself to miss, and although she was offered a chance to take the exam again, she declined. Her confidence had been dented, but on the other hand she was not one to be weighed down for long by disappointment. There were fields she could shine in, and when the time came to look for a job she was presented with two promising possibilities.

CHAPTER FOUR – DOROTHY

AT THIS STAGE of my mother's life, when she was fourteen, Grandad had become more settled. The family rented the little house in Inglemire Lane, which at that time was in a more rural setting than it is today, a short walk beyond the tram terminus at the Haworth Arms on Beverley Road. Grandad must have had a regular job, and he took pride in his cottage garden, producing a miscellany of vegetables and flowers. Mother had memories of scarlet runner beans, nicotiana (tobacco plants), night-scented stocks, and Granma Carrie's special favourites, lilies-of-the-valley.

Aunt Nancy and Mother had been brought up with certain fastidious mores, some of which my cousins and I still observe. Granma Carrie kept a separate bowl for washing pots and vegetables. Table-linen was poshed in the dolly-tub before bed-linen, and to this day my cousins and I would not dream of adding our tea-towels to the general wash. One of Granma's strict rules was never to accept a drink or anything to eat in a house where there was a baby unless she knew the kitchen was run along proper lines. She had once had the horrifying experience, after receiving a cup of tea from a certain young mother, of seeing her ladle water from boiling nappies on to pots in the washing-up bowl.

At school, as well as learning rudimentary household tasks, the older girls did cookery, and Mother had the deft, cool hands of a pastry chef. How lucky I was to be reared on her golden short-crust, faintly singed at the edges to just the right delectable scorched crunchiness. Though not unadventurous, she mostly remained faithful to the delicacies she had been taught – jam or currant slices, custard tarts freckled with nutmeg, steak and kidney pies trimmed with pastry roses and leaves veined with a knife-point, lemon tarts oozing home-made curd.

She was also skilled at crocheting, knitting and especially sewing and making clothes. So she had a great decision to take when she found herself with two choices: either to join Mackman's, a Hull company of bakers and confectioners who were connected to her family, or a small local firm producing corsets and surgical appliances.

Granma Carrie's advice prevailed. She felt it unwise for her daughter to enter the family enterprise, despite a Mackman uncle's enthusiastic offer to show my mother the business 'from A to Z', so Mother took the other job. She joined a work-room of young women in the city, and qualified as a corsetière. More importantly, she learned how to make medical belts, trusses, finger-stalls, and colostomy bags; to pad and line prostheses for amputees, and design individual aids for sufferers of a plethora of dysfunctions, which sometimes required home visits.

The work-room was a happy place, and a certain amount of chatter and laughter was permitted. Mother made four close friends there with whom she never lost touch. They always called her Dorothy, and I think that now she was entering adulthood her full name began to replace the earlier 'Doll' and 'Dolly', although years afterwards Aunt Nancy would address her sometimes as 'You Doll'. She was asked if she would like to move to the firm's Southport branch, and went over to see the premises in Lord Street, but she decided against leaving Hull, and at length took charge of her own familiar work-room.

I still have the cut-glass vinegar-bottle Mother bought with her first week's wage, which Granma Carrie insisted she keep for herself, and soon she was able to afford the instalments on a second-hand treadle sewing-machine. I turned it into a desk, and write on it now.

Always a follower of fashion, my mother could study a garment in an advertisement or shop window and cut it out without need of a pattern. She made clothes for family and friends as well. I, alas, inherited none of these skills, and she was wont to remark at my clumsy attempts, 'Red 'ot needle and bont (burnt) thread. Give it to me, girl', and snatch the thing out of my hands.

Mother was sixteen when the First World War broke out, and as lists of casualties were published, the losses suffered among the young men of Hull impinged deeply on the family, though it was luckier than many. The death which came closest to home was that of Jack Newton, Aunt Jinny's fiancé, killed in France. Thereafter she remained unmarried, and kept house for her bachelor brothers, Uncle Jim and Uncle Billy, following their parents' deaths.

In Mother's autograph album, a G.S.L. Metcalf (late King's Own Yorkshire Light Infantry) has written on August 15th, 1918: 'This is to certify that I was wounded and taken prisoner September 16th 1916, 40 wounds and still kicking.' During her teens and early twenties, Mother knew one or two young men who were 'sweet on her', but she was not easily impressed, and because she was wary of over-familiarity she used to stand on her dignity. She laughed when she relayed to me one neighbour's question to Grandad: 'How's that daughter of yours? Not the plump, pretty one – I mean the tall, haughty one.' In her own words, she was 'very strait-laced', and I think that even to save her life she would have found it impossible to flirt.

But a distant attitude to would-be suitors can lend enchantment, added to which I see tall, haughty Miss Dorothy Nixon as an eye-catcher, for she had a number of good points. The best three were her long, heavy mane of glossy chestnut hair, her even, pearly teeth, which she kept to the end of her life, and beautiful hands, which I always envied. She had a good figure, bound her trim breasts to give her the flat-chested look that went with the fashion of the times, and was as dashingly smart as she could manage to be.

However cool her manner might have seemed to casual acquaintances, she thawed on two notable occasions. First she got engaged to a nice young man called Walter, who lived with his parents in Goole. He joined the Army, but Mother still went to Goole by train on Sundays to visit his parents and sister. Increasingly, however, she realised that the fizz had gone out of the relationship, so she gave him back his ring. Her second fiancé, called Harry, was a policeman, a big man with a strong personality. But that engagement came to an abrupt end when he waxed too ardent, and she fled.

Her autograph album, bought for her at Christmas, 1915, makes fascinating reading. A friend, Florrie Tunnard, wrote then: 'Dolly Nixon is her name, Single is her station, Happy be the little man Who makes the alteration.' Eighteen months later, Walter declared, poignantly as it turned out: 'Hoping to be the happy man to make the alteration.' A man with the initials W.A.R. wrote: 'She's a sweet charming lady Miss Nixon, As charming as man's eyes could fix on, Her large dreamy eyes Would fill with surprise If she saw what we see she sits on.' Mother thought this rather rude, and viewed it with mock horror, as well as the entry by a Chas Wray which said: 'She stoops to conquer – my word, if I catch her bending.'

I knew her as an old-fashioned romantic, who loved the Fred Astaire and Ginger Rogers films, and the sentiment of songs like 'When Love Walked In With You'. She and my father were not the sort to parade their feelings for each other, and flippancy was part of their armour – as when, in childish admiration of what I considered my mother's dark beauty, I likened her to a 'Spanish rose'. 'A Spanish onion, more like', snorted my father, drawing an appreciative grimace from Mum.

They argued, mostly over money. She considered him tight-fisted, and used to urge him to relax and enjoy himself more, speculate to accumulate. He, on the other hand, thought he must rein in a tendency to extravagance in her. I was aware of this divergence in their characters but not unduly worried by it, for I knew how much they both loved me. 'It's all for you and Janet, you know,' he would say.

They made a good team, and though she would have scorned to 'butter him up', she recognised her luck. Thus she was granted an amazing blessing, because, looking back on her emotional life before she met my father as clearly as I can, I wonder that she never developed a cynicism about men and marriage in the wake of her father's back-slidings, and two family disasters. One was a shameful secret, tragically brief. The other was more destructive and lasting, with repercussions that linger still.

***

AUNT BECKY HAD left home to be a waitress. She was in demand, skilled in the etiquette of 'silver service', and enjoyed the camaraderie, and excitement of moving around and working in grand establishments. I imagine her as a head-tossing, pert young woman with a fine line in repartee that tickled her male clientele. She used to come home and talk about life in the dining-rooms and kitchens. Cockroaches were common in the warm areas where the cooking took place, and she said it was nothing to see one of these repellent insects swimming in a pan of soup, and the chef fish it out and carry on serving the soup. The language of cutlery was important, and no waitress worth her salt would remove a plate if the diner had placed his fork prongs-down and his knife with its sharp edge facing inwards.

One day, Aunt Becky came home with a secret. My mother mentioned the matter to me only once, in barest detail. It was a secret that had been closely guarded by a handful of people, and maybe it was intended that the truth should never be told. Suddenly, during one of our quiet discussions while lying in bed, Mother made her startling revelation. Perhaps she was using it as a warning.

Aunt Becky, of course, was pregnant. As she was unmarried, her position was appalling. I do not know how old she was, or whether Grandad was there at the time, but I picture her arriving home out of the blue, her pregnancy well advanced, to announce her shameful condition. Poor Granma Carrie. She was not long in a quandary about what to do, because I gathered from my mother that the baby arrived early, and was born dead. The matter was hushed up, and Becky returned to waitressing, as far as I know. How many of the rest of the family were told about this great trouble, or how many of the neighbours guessed, is a matter for conjecture. I have the feeling that my mother was excluded from the painful details of the situation by my grandmother, who did not wish her to be too closely involved, and after Mother's death I never raised the subject with Aunt Nancy.

Some time later, in 1917, Becky married a man called Fred, who was liked by her family, and they had a son, Jack. I have a studio portrait of her, taken at Scarborough, possibly before her marriage, and she looks slightly quizzical, if very sensible, in a felt hat and tweed coat with a fur draped across her shoulders. She is not beautiful, although I think she has a pleasing face. But her mouth is beautiful, full-lipped, even sensual, though perhaps I am reading too much into it. She faces the camera with assurance, but I wonder what went on in her mind; whether she mourned the child she lost, or whether she felt lucky to have avoided the stigma of bearing a bastard.

Her happiness as a wife and mother was sadly brief, for fate held greater tragedy in store. In the notorious influenza epidemic which cut swathes through the population of Europe in 1919, my aunt fell victim to a severe attack. Although she did not die, she never recovered her old vivacity, and continued to complain of tiredness, gradually declining into what was termed 'sleepy sickness', and eventually developing the uncontrollable shaking of Parkinson's Disease. She entered hospital when her condition became too difficult for Granma Carrie to nurse, but young Jack continued to live with his maternal grandparents. There is a snapshot of him in the garden at Inglemire Lane, aged about four, posed against a bed of lupins, holding Grandad's walking-stick. He died when he was thirteen, of meningitis.

My father, with his strong desire to protect me from communicable diseases, would not allow me to be taken inside the hospital where Aunt Becky was a patient. I do not remember these incidents, but Cousin Margaret tells me that my aunt used to be brought to the top of an outside spiral staircase to wave to me as I stood beneath.

When the war came in 1939, Aunt Becky and the other patients were transferred from the Beverley Road hospital to one on the cliff top at Withernsea. Mother would go over to see her every few months, often taking me with her, and sometimes Annette. Aunt Nancy would make the journey at other times. I used to dread those visits: the bewildering corridors; the strange residents; the odour of disinfectant, boiling sheets, stew, and something else, indefinable but base, like raw potato crunched underfoot – the smell of sickness.

Aunt Becky used to sit in a chair, every muscle in a constant state of agitation. Her arm would fly up, then her leg, and from her trembling lips came warbled words impossible for me to interpret. She had mousy hair cut in a straight bob, parted at the side and caught back with grips like a schoolgirl's, and her sombre frock hung limply on her narrow frame. Suddenly, without warning, she would launch herself out of her chair and set off across the room in her carpet-slippers, shuffling and jerking over the red lake of linoleum with a motion that was shocking in its inhumanness.

It was impossible to imagine this pitiful collection of fitful bones as the golden girl, the superior, tantalising big sister whose precocity had awed my mother, and led her such a merry dance! I was disbelieving, and only superficially stirred by my aunt's plight, and I couldn't wait for my mother's promised sop, a descent to the beach, once it had been restored to public use a few months before the end of the war. Now I find Becky's sufferings deeply moving. Her husband rarely visited, if at all, I think. They had begun to drift apart before her illness, and perhaps he could not bear to see her reduced to such a state. Eventually, he took another partner.

Aunt Becky would send letters to us, dictated to a nurse, and Mother kept one. Dated September 27th, 1945, and headed 'Ward 6, Transfer Hospital, Withernsea', it thanks Mother for a ten-shilling note, adding: 'I was pleased to hear of you winning the sweep, I wish I had been there to have one with you, it seems such ages since I last saw you.' (Mother had undergone a mastectomy the previous March.) 'I was sorry to hear that you had decided to settle in Doncaster, as I shall not see much of you there.' (My mother must have told her that, even though the war had ended, she would not be returning to Hull.) 'I was so glad that Janet liked her parcel. The grapes were out of Matron's garden ... I am just about the same, and pleased to hear of you being much better. And about the coupons, I meant you to send half to Nancy. I knew you would.' (This would have referred to clothing coupons.)

I realise that Aunt Becky was fond of me, most likely because I was my mother's daughter, for she could never have known me properly. One of my earliest memories is of sitting on her knee in front of the fire at Leonard Street when I was about two and she must have been on a visit to us from hospital. At Withernsea she sent staff out shopping for gifts for her family, and one that gave me particular delight was a dolls' tea-set of iridescent green china, the cups and teapot lined with pink. Sometimes she would enclose for me a five-shilling or half-crown postal order.

Did her mind work as intuitively as it once did, even though it was imprisoned in a cruelly disabled body? Her longing to see my mother is heart-breakingly evident in the letter she composed. Fifteen days after sending it, she died, of choking I believe, aged fifty-two. I had already lost weeks of schooling due to Mother's operation for breast cancer, so maybe this is one reason why I did not go to the funeral.

***

AUNT NANCY LEFT school to work in service for two old maids. One of them came to inspect the kitchen where she was washing-up. The pots looked nice and clean – but why hadn't she done the pans? 'Oh', said Nancy, 'Mother always does the pans.' Then she went to work at Reckitt and Colman's factory. She was sweet-natured, strikingly blue-eyed and golden-haired, trusting and malleable. A young man called Mick, with dark good looks, a silver tongue and a reputation as a rake, started to hang around her. He would not leave her alone, and used to waylay her, sometimes coming to wait secretly for her outside the house by the back gate, in the dusk.

My mother and the rest of the family warned her to have nothing to do with Mick, but his powers of persuasion were, according to my mother, almost hypnotic, 'like a snake with a rabbit.' My aunt fell under his spell, and when she found she was pregnant, became his wife at a quiet register-office ceremony. My mother was too upset to attend.

A son was born, Billy, his mother's pride and joy, and Granma Carrie's and my mother's, too. But Billy was not to know much love from his father, who probably blamed him for being trapped in an unwanted marriage. By the time Aunt Nancy was again pregnant, Mick had gone back to his old ways, if indeed he had ever abandoned them. He had girlfriends, it was said, all over town, and he used to make Aunt Nancy iron him a shirt so he should look smart when he went out to meet one.

Auntie told me he hit her in the stomach when she was expecting their second child. My cousin Jack Sykes was a handsome boy, but developed severe epilepsy. In those days, the condition was not easily controlled, and Jack spent years in a special hospital in Liverpool. Although he eventually came back to live at home, he died at the age of thirty-one. His mother always believed his illness had been caused by the blow.

Mick's success as a Lothario was breathtaking, and he took astonishing risks. He courted one young woman, then started seeing her friend, who lived in a street close by. When the first young lady popped round to her friend's she happened to catch a glimpse of Mick, and thought that it must be his brother!

Nancy and Mick's third child was a daughter, Margaret. Because Mick kept my aunt short of money, when Margaret was older she twice called at houses where her father was known to spend some of his time, and was greeted by shocked disbelief when she introduced herself. One householder, convinced that Margaret had got the wrong man, brandished a photograph of her daughter's 'fiancé' – Mick. 'Yes', said Margaret, 'that's my dad.'

My mother was incensed by Mick's treatment of her sister, and hated her brother-in-law with a deep and bitter hatred. She recalled one occasion when she went round to their home with a large bag of potatoes. Aunt Nancy was sitting weeping at the table, with Mick hovering and leering. 'He's taunting me, Dorothy,' she sobbed, whereupon my mother hurled the heavy bag, managing to land some of the contents on him. He responded by flinging a jug of milk at her. Luckily, it missed.

On Tuesday nights, Mother and Aunt Clara, Uncle George's wife, used to go to the pictures, and sometimes they would see Mick out on the town with his current sweetheart. This would drive my mother into such a state of fury and outrage that she would call out, loudly enough for the entire street to hear, that he was a married man. Once as she was leaving a cinema, she spotted him in one of the rows of seats with a girl. She waited outside until the pair appeared, then followed them, shouting, 'Do you know he's got a wife and children at home?'

But although this relieved her feelings somewhat, and accorded with her sense of justice, it did nothing to help Aunt Nancy; the situation demanded an entirely more practical response, and Mother made clothes for her and the children, and provided food and cash when she could. As was to be expected, Granma Carrie and Aunt Jinny were my aunt's equally dedicated, if less vociferous, supporters, while kind neighbours rallied round too. Of course my father knew of my mother's private campaign, and could hardly have been unaware of her often surreptitious contributions towards her sister's meagre resources; counselling caution in her confrontations with Mick, he sometimes co-operated over the matter of supplies, sometimes turned a blind eye.

After Bill, Jack and Margaret, Aunt Nancy and Mick went on to have three more children, Dorothy, Annette, and Michael, who died of diphtheria, aged one. Margaret was six years older than I, Dorothy four, and Annette, at two years younger than I, the recipient of all my clothes. If I turned up in a new dress, Aunt Nancy would say, 'Let's see the hem', and in later years, before she even asked, I would show her how much material remained to be let down.

Crisis-point in my aunt's turbulent existence was reached when Mick was sent to prison for stealing from his employers, and she seized the chance while he was in gaol to leave him. But eventually the hardships and anxieties Aunt Nancy had suffered led to a nervous breakdown, and she became totally withdrawn. She was taken away to a mental hospital, where they removed all her teeth, and wrote on top of her notes in large letters 'Husband Not To Visit'. Mother had told the doctors all about him.

She visited Auntie regularly, sometimes walking with her in the beautiful grounds, and under the healing influence of expert nursing her sister gradually changed back into almost, but not quite, the person she had once known.

Aunt Nancy remained in the hospital for seven-and-a-half months. Young Dorothy took her midday meals with us. Eleven-year-old Margaret walked a total of almost four miles to and from Aunt Jinny's at lunch-time every school day, a marathon we now all find hard to credit. My cousin Jack was away in hospital at Liverpool, but Bill, who, at fifteen, was working as an apprentice engraver, insisted on keeping the family together as far as possible. He paid the rent on the house, and cooked a roast dinner for the two older girls each Sunday.

Poor Annette, at two years old, was sent to a children's home. I expect it was felt that, as she was so young, she would adapt fairly easily to new surroundings. She was not cut off from her dear ones because they called frequently to see her, and she was allowed out on visits, but after two months she developed bronchitis, and was admitted to hospital. From there she was transferred to an orphanage, where the staff would frighten the children by telling them that if they did not go to sleep a mysterious 'Icky' would come to get them. She is still afraid of the dark.

Life grew happier for my little cousin when suddenly her father whisked her away from the orphanage to stay with one of his relatives. Here, fussed over and petted, she settled quite contentedly, too young, of course, to know of her mother's alarm at this turn of events, for Mick's newest move brought my aunt down to earth with a vengeance; she resolved to get her daughter back, and before long became well enough to do so.

Once she had returned home, Auntie took up the threads of life again with great courage. She declined for years to divorce Mick, believing that her solemn vows of life-long faithfulness to him were exactly that. Mick stayed away, took up with another partner, started another family. He was still supposed to pay Auntie maintenance, but often when she went to the Guildhall to collect it, there was no money for her. So she decided to take in lodgers.

Writing now of that terrible period, I realise what an effort it must have cost my aunt to climb out of her dark pit of fear and depression, and face the world again. The peace she found at the mental hospital, and the bodily nourishment and professional guidance she received were important aids to her recovery, but her desperate need to get home to her children was the true motivating force.

She learned to look back on the past with a kind of cheerful irony, and although the black clouds never completely rolled away, this helped her, as did her impish sense of humour, and a daily dose of a nerve tonic called Phospherine, in which she placed enormous faith. Flippancy was another part of her defensive weaponry. I would sometimes squirm under her bantering tongue, but I loved her. Making much of the fact that I was her only niece, she cleared a special space for me in her affections, which expanded as my need of her expanded with the years.

CHAPTER FIVE – DORRIE

WHEN MY MOTHER met my father, she became Dorrie. He always called her that, as did all the Greenwood family, and that is the name I think of her by.

It seemed to everyone such a pity that as the years went by, Harry and Dorrie still had no baby. Not much was said, I think, but while my fecund Aunt Nancy was struggling to bring up her four eldest children, and my mother channelled much of her love and energy towards them, she longed for a 'kiddy' of her own.

In the first year or two of her marriage, Mother had what she assumed were early miscarriages, and Granmer Greenwood told her it was through taking too many hot baths, which were 'weakening'. Then Mother's hopes were effectively blighted when she and my father had a motorcycling accident on his latest, and most powerful, machine, for one dark night they ran into a lorry which my father had not seen because it was parked without lights on the road. The sidecar in which my mother was riding took the brunt of the impact, and she was badly shaken and lost the baby, though how soon afterwards Mother didn't tell me. But she did end by cuddling me and saying, 'So whether it would have been a big brother or a big sister I don't know.'

I, who admired my big cousins and often yearned for an older sibling, used to try to imagine what he or she would have been like. I was enough of a realist to suppose that this hypothetical person would have indulged in a certain amount of criticism, bossiness and teasing, but that didn't matter. What did matter was that there had been a brother or sister in an early stage of existence with the potential for sharing my relationship with my parents. This was a solemn, and at times unwelcome, thought, but mostly the idea that the poor lost soul might have grown into a living, breathing individual filled me with a secret sense of comfort.

My father was so distressed by the accident that he left the bike at the nearest garage and never bought another. Maybe he blamed himself for the crash and its devastating consequences, for the doctor told my mother that now it was unlikely she would ever bear a child. Her recovery was slow, and she felt drained and feeble. She went to visit uncle Jack's wife, Elsie, in a sanatorium, where she was being treated for consumption, and Elsie seemed in amazingly good health, partly because of her glowing red cheeks, which were sometimes symptomatic of tuberculosis.

When the two young women went for a walk, she was strong enough to turn and pull my mother up a hill. 'I wished I was as fit and strong as she was', Mother said, looking back on the incident years later, still guilt-ridden by the memory of her own self-absorption and lack of insight. Soon afterwards, Elsie died. She left two young children, Gladys and Jackie, having lost her first daughter from diphtheria, I think.

It must have been hard for Mother to be the only childless Greenwood daughter-in-law. After Elsie's death, Gladys continued living with her father at Granmer and Grampa's house in Pendrill Street, and Mother used to make her dresses. At first Jackie stayed with his mother's parents in another part of Hull, but one lunch-time Uncle Jack went round and found him still in his nightshirt, a shocking state of affairs to Granmer's way of thinking. She was so upset she sent Uncle Jack back to get him, seizing on the nightshirt incident as an excuse to reunite the children and restore young Jackie to the Greenwood fold. Better by far, of course, for brother and sister to be brought up together; yet the grief and hurt felt by the other grandparents can easily be imagined, and it is small wonder that the link between the two families remained broken beyond repair. In later life, Gladys tried to find her mother's family, who I believe were called Jennings, without success.

Uncle George married Aunt Clara and a boy was born, whom they called Harry after my father, because, my aunt used to tell me, he had been so good to them. The wedding was rushed because she had been pregnant, and my father lent them money to get started. Some years later, when George and Clara had a grocer's shop in Stepney Lane, Hull, they got into financial trouble because Uncle was 'such a soft touch' and would grant 'tick' against any hard luck story. Dad came to their rescue again with a loan to clear their debts, and it was repaid regularly by Auntie, who proved a good businesswoman when she took over the running of the shop. Meanwhile, Uncle went back to work for William Jackson's as a grocery manager.

Auntie always spoke gratefully of my father's generosity, and would never hear a word against him. She used to describe for me, with theatrical gestures and voice rising to a high pitch of excitement, the wonderful party he would throw at the Station Inn every New Year's Eve, when expense was no object.

Dear, brave, life-seizing, unquenchable Aunt Clara, how she loved parties, company, jokes, gin, a night out at a pub, a day at the races, and, as it became popular, bingo (to which she was first 'called' by a promoter at a seaside amusement arcade, responding to his summons like Saul on the road to Damascus, though thankfully with her sight unimpaired). No-one else could generate quite the same amount of jollity and fun, and I used to love being with her, for she had a special way with young people. Even in the aftermath of two appalling catastrophes, the loss of both her sons, her innate cheerfulness could not be extinguished.

Little Harry, as he was always known, succumbed to diphtheria shortly after his first birthday. My cousin Georgie, six months older than I, was fourteen when he died, and for years I treasured a wild bird's egg he gave me the last time I saw him. A few weeks before he became ill, we had been together in the loft above the pigsty behind the shop at Preston, where he kept his display of carefully-blown shells. I had often shared his excitement at finding nests in trees and hedgerows, for in those days if a nest had eggs inside it was permissible to take one, and my cousin was proud of his collection.

Georgie's present to me must have been a spare, and he wrapped the tiny turquoise shell in cotton-wool and placed it in an old ring-box, so I could carry it safely home on the train to Doncaster. His death was unbelievable, and Mother wrote to his parents a moving letter, still in my possession: 'During last night I woke and my thoughts seemed to fly to you both so I just have to write this morning ... Knowing you both so well, I know you will face the future bravely and make the best of things as you always do, and as little Georgie always did, bless him.' (He had been a sickly boy, with the bronchitis kettle steaming in his bedroom every winter.)

Uncle Fred had married Aunt Gwen, and they produced my cousin Brian. Uncle Jack remarried, and he and my new aunt, called Elsie like her predecessor, had Gordon and Dennis. Mother went as Godmother to Dennis's Christening at the end of 1932, and someone asked her, 'Have you come to shake his feathers, then?' (meaning the stork).

My father was awkward with children, seeming not to know what to say to them. Mother's family regarded him as a man of few words, not easy to engage in conversation. He would either disappear, or else sit reading his paper after they arrived, although he would emerge from behind it as they left to observe brightly, 'Oh, are you off then? Cheerio.'

'There's one thing I'll say about Harry, you always get a hearty goodbye', Aunt Jinny liked to jest.

While his stiffness and shyness must have made him an unlikely father figure, he championed Gladys and Jackie at critical times, and my cousin Dorothy remembers a surprising thing happening when she was ill in bed with bronchitis at her home in Folkestone Street. She saw him through the window as he arrived on his grocer's delivery bike to bring her a tin of Palm Toffees and a threepenny bit. 'Aunt Jinny couldn't get over it – Uncle Harry, of all people!'

Mother quietly nursed her disappointment about being childless, and supposed she had kept it hidden. But her own mother guessed, and one day she said to her, 'Doctors don't know everything.' Mother also told me about the fondness and respect Granma Carrie had for my father, sentiments he returned. And if my mother let slip the smallest criticism, Granma always reminded her how fortunate she was to have such a steady, single-minded husband who never gave her any worries about drink or other women.

Despite her concerns about Becky and Nancy, Granma Carrie was finding some aspects of her life easier and more pleasurable. She had a little money coming in now, and Mother made her some new clothes. She even managed the odd day-trip, and came home from an excursion to Otley remarking what a lovely place it was, especially the gardens down by the river. I think of her whenever I go there.

But Granma had her own secret, which she was too afraid to reveal, never telling anyone of the lump she had found in her breast. When Becky's son, Jack, developed meningitis, Granma nursed him at home with the help of a sympathetic young doctor. One day, as he was leaving the house, she asked him to look at her breast, where the cancer was by now painfully advanced. 'Oh, Mrs Nixon, why ever didn't you tell me sooner?' was his despairing cry.

After Jack died, my grandmother's condition worsened, and she took to her bed. My mother and Aunt Nancy looked after her, and it was a time of great ordeal, for she was in such agony. She would fling out her arms and cry, 'O Lamb of God, I come.' She died at Easter, which was early that year, and my mother and aunt shared the task of laying her out. They had seen to all her personal needs, so it seemed the natural thing to do. The young doctor, who had attended Granma Carrie faithfully, never sent his bill.

The following October, my mother was persuaded to go to Hull Fair with some friends, and for a joke to have her fortune told. The gypsy looked into her crystal ball and announced, 'By this time next year I see you dandling a bonny, blue-eyed boy.' My mother smiled disbelievingly.

I don't know how long it was before she realised she was pregnant, or how she broke the news to my father. She could scarcely credit it, and although I am sure she was overjoyed, she wondered aloud to Aunt Jinny about how Harry would be with a baby. 'You'll see,' said Jinny, 'he'll make a doting father'. As indeed he did.

Although having a first baby at thirty-five, my mother's age, was considered somewhat dangerous, my mother was unafraid. She was, however, self-conscious, which seems absurd now, and dressed discreetly so as to disguise her bump. So successful was she that when I arrived, some of the customers at the Leonard Street shop thought I was adopted. She had carried discretion to the length of kneeling well inside the door when she scrubbed the step, stretching her body to reach the far edge, and she thought this must be the reason for the umbilical cord being wrapped around my neck.

The sadness of her mother's death turned to happiness in those waiting days, and she tried to concentrate on calm, pleasant thoughts because she felt a serene attitude would benefit the baby. She recalled sitting one summer's evening by an open window in great contentment, knitting or crocheting for the coming infant, and listening to a song drifting in from someone's wireless which afterwards forever reminded her of that glad state of expectancy: 'All through the night I can hear a brown bird singing.' Physically she had few problems, developing a craving for crystallized ginger, which Aunt Nancy took pleasure in buying for her.

***

THE GYPSY HAD been wrong in at least two respects, for I was not a boy, and my birth date, October 30th, was three weeks after Hull Fair. True, I was some days late, my mother feeling the first twinges while entertaining Granmer and Grampa Greenwood to Sunday tea. The nurse was called, and as the pains grew stronger, Mother told herself 'it will get worse before it gets better.'

Soon after midnight, I was born in the front bedroom, weighing about seven-and-a-half pounds. By this time it was Monday, but Mother, for whom Sunday had represented all but the last minutes of her labour, cheated, and liked to think of me as a Sunday baby, because then I would have all the attributes, and be 'fair and wise and good and gay.'

The nurse joked that if my father intended starting a family (perhaps implying that it was about time, as he was forty-two) he had better go out and buy a bigger teapot. He took her at her word, and returned from a shopping expedition with an enormous brown pot that stood on a shelf at Bentley for years, Dad's humorous salute to fatherhood.

What to call me? A friend with a poetic turn of mind said Greenwood lent itself to a name like Hazel, or April, or Heather. My parents, thankfully, were unimpressed. Dad liked Barbara, but Mother suggested one of her mother's favourites, Janet, or possibly Jeanette. He tried them both out on the back of a letter that came with two handmade bonnets, and Mother kept the torn scrap of paper, along with one of my first pink leather shoes.

In the end, they plumped for Janet, though I wish it had been Caroline. Why not two names, anyway? It seems cheese-paring to give only one. Aunt Nancy, one of my Godmothers, disliked the name Janet intensely, saying it reminded her of a stern old Scotswoman in a stiff white collar and high-button boots. 'Well, we'll just have to buy her a stiff white collar and some boots then,' said my mother unrepentantly. In a last attempt, on the steps of St. John's as they entered the church for the Christening service, Aunt Nancy turned to Mother and begged, 'Don't call her Janet.' But Mother was adamant.

I was a never-was-er, and my father thought me perfect. He refused to have me vaccinated because he could not bear the thought of my being injected with foreign matter. He was afraid something might happen to me, and although a neighbour called Auntie Johnny was allowed to take me out in the high, navy-blue pram, my cousin Margaret, who loved babies, was more restricted because she was only six. She was permitted to push me a few yards down Leonard Street, but told not to go beyond the next kerb, and Dad kept popping his head round the shop door to ensure all was well. Margaret has also told me since that he put a seven-pound weight in the bottom of the pram to stop it tipping over.

Mother, who in the first days had been afraid the midwife would drop me (a fear I scoffed at until I had my own children) was a little more relaxed, but not much. She was reluctant to let me crawl in case I got in a draught, or picked up germs, and Aunt Nancy used to say, 'That child will never walk.' I was eighteen months old before I did, and had words off well before that. Mother had lots of pet names for me, Biddy Maguire, Sugarplum, or Shug for short, Kitten-Nose, and later on, Tinribs, Flossie Flat'at, Trilby, and Miss Flip. She would come into the room and hold out her arms, crying 'Ah! My little chickabiddy', and was taken aback when one day, before she had a chance to say it, I greeted her with my first word,' Biddy'.'

Most Sundays, my father used to push me in the pram to Hull Pier. I think that during one of these excursions I must have been frightened by a big ship, because as a child I had terrifying dreams about being dwarfed by an enormous vessel, and I still cannot bear to see pictures of sinking ships.

By this time, Granmer and Grampa Greenwood were living in a small house in Bethnal Green, Beverley High Road, and Dad would often take me there and shamelessly display my precocious development, which they were eager to admire. He had bought three houses in the Green in 1930, negotiating a mortgage for most of the £750 cost, so as to have two to rent out and one, number 5, for his parents to live in. There, some of my happiest and most spoiled hours were played out.

But of my days in Leonard Street I have only a few faint memories. There are echoes of lullabies ('Ukulele Lady' was one bedtime choice, apparently), and an impression of a toy-box under the stairs, as well as a disturbing recollection of being taken out by a lady (Auntie Johnny?), dirtying a nappy as I sat in the pram, and deciding to keep quiet. I certainly remember biting my pram hood as I knelt facing forwards, the sharp taste of the leather, and crying when I bumped my mouth as we presumably went down a kerb. Less clear is a picture of my father stooping to remove bicycle-clips from his trousers as I stagger towards him, 'K-legged' as my mother used to call it.

The summer after my arrival was hot, and Mother found the weight of her hair was giving her headaches. So she had most of her mane cut off, and what remained shingled into an 'Eton crop', a fashionable style of the time that suited her so well she never afterwards felt inclined to change it. The hairdresser wanted to buy her thick, glossy chestnut plait, but Mother decided to bring it home, tied up with a red ribbon, and keep it in her wardrobe in an old chocolate-box.

I inherited the box, but rarely opened it. Then one day the hair, still springing with life thirty years after her death, seemed too grisly to pass on to my own children, and I threw it away.

CHAPTER SIX – THE STATION INN

WHEN I WAS two, my father heard that the landlord of the Station Inn, a stone's throw from Pendrill Street, was leaving. Dad had admired the pub ever since he started to take a regular Sunday dinner-time drink there with his father and brothers, and he could see himself running it, so he seized his chance, secured the licence, disposed of the Leonard Street business, and we moved in.

The pub was built in mock-Tudor style, with a beamed front gable, leaded windows and stone fireplaces. It stood alongside Stepney Station, where a busy East Coast railway line bisected Beverley Road at one of Hull's many level-crossings. We got used to the trains rattling by at all hours, although visitors were kept awake and wondered how we managed to live there. Only a criss-cross railway fence separated our back yard from the snorting steam-engines, but I was more disturbed by the large concrete bunkers of grit that bordered the rails at intervals, because our live-in girl, Jessie, told me they were graves holding all the cats knocked down by the trains.

The pub had two front doors, one leading straight into the men's tap-room, the other into a long passage which skirted the back of the bar, passing the snug and a small smoke-room to reach a larger smoke-room that had plush benches around the walls, lots of stools and small tables, and a piano. The pub's one wireless was installed there, and this must be why I never remember hearing any of the famous wartime broadcasts. My only recollections are of 'Music While You Work' as Mother and Jessie did their chores, and jolly Radio Luxembourg jingles. One, advertising Andrews' Liver Salts, went:

'If you sing in your bath, and you whistle all day,
It's Andrews that's making you feel that way,
If you feel well and strong and your life is a song,
It's Andrews that's making you feel that way.
If you're fit as a fiddle, slim in the middle,
Light-hearted, happy and gay-hay-hay,
Just a glass in the morning will soon stop you yawning,
For Andrews will brighten you up every day.'

Another rival tune sang the praises of Kruschen Salts, ending with:

'The spring is here, the spring is here, and what gives me the spring?
Enough to cover a sixpence every morning.'

Vera Lynn also came to be frequently on air, but Mother was not a great admirer, disliking the sob that was such a distinctive feature of her voice.

Ah, the scents and sounds of the licensed trade! My whole life between the ages of two and twenty-three, with the exception of eight months in Zetland Road at Doncaster, was lived in and around them. At night, as a child, I fell asleep to the far-off clinking of glasses and the pinging of the till; to voices ebbing like a sea, and rising again on a tide of sudden sharp interjection. I might stir if faint menace seemed to surface in the ribaldry of men and the shrieks of laughing women. Half awake, I memorised distant songs like 'Nellie Dean' and 'Sierra Sue'.

The mustardy tang of smoke-draped air and flowing ashtrays greeted me as I swiftly made my way up the passage and through the big smoke-room during daytime opening hours, for this was in the era when children were not allowed on licensed premises, and I was under orders not to linger, even if hailed by customers. The malty aroma of beer, foaming out of the pumps, glistening in wet rings on the bar and tables, stickily spilled on carpets, pungent on the front of my mother's dress when she came up to kiss me goodnight, pervaded my nostrils. But Mother's own smell was lovely: perfume, face-powder, and warm flesh in silky stockings.

***

THE FIRST INKLING that my home life was not as other children's, and that there might be something shameful in it, came on an evening when I was looking forward with huge excitement to seeing my two cousins, Margaret and Dorothy, take part in a show at Queen's Road Methodist Church, a temperance venue. Before we went, Aunt Nancy suggested that if anyone asked where I lived I should give my address as simply 202 Beverley Road, and not mention the Station Inn. When I asked why, she informed me that drinking was frowned on by the people at the church. I took her advice to heart, and as well as being awe-struck by my cousins' impossible new aura, garbed as sunbeams in yellow butter-muslin, I was terrified that I might forget myself and blurt out my disgraceful secret. More embarrassment was to follow years later when I attended regular morning service at St. Peter's Church, Bentley, during which reference was made in certain readings to publicans and sinners. Knowing what was coming, I would begin to blush well before the dreaded phrase was pronounced.

At Bentley I was sometimes to yearn to live in a 'normal' house like my school friends, but for now, at Hull, especially before the faint shadow of doubt cast by Auntie, I was uncritical of my surroundings, and wrapped all the constituent parts of them around me like a cloak, for they represented (and still do in my deepest consciousness) the comforts of home.

Our living-room was my ideal of cosiness. Drawn up before the cream Yorkist range were my parents' twin arm chairs, of imitation leather known as 'Rexine', with wooden arms and brown velvet seat-cushions. Before the fire, when I was small, I would disport luxuriously in a rectangular wooden bath, which had a bar across one corner to hold 'Soapy Lamb', an amazingly life-like creature standing on a bed of soap grass. Distressingly, he shrank every time I rubbed him with my flannel.

I do not know when I was promoted to bathing upstairs. No older person was expected to take more than a weekly bath (usually on Fridays) although we were all sure that the Queen and the two Princesses would indulge more often, possibly even every day. In the case of people like Aunt Jinny, whose bath stood in the kitchen with its lid doubling as a table for most of the time, ladling hot water from the nearby copper was a big to-do-ment. 'Strip-washes' were popular (one of our enormously fat customers used to quip that she was 'going home to put the egg-pan on') and great attention was paid to children's necks. Mine, for some puzzling reason, was frequently black, according to Mother, who joked as she energetically wielded the flannel that she had found 'enough muck to grow taties in.'

A cupboard alongside the living-room fireplace contained my books, among which I remember a simplified version of Peter Pan, a Mickey Mouse annual (which included early Disney characters like Clarabel Cow and Horace Horse), Aesop's Fables, and one which was to draw many a tear from me, Hans Andersen's Fairy Tales.

Beneath the window stood our dining-table, a draw-leaf square of highly varnished oak the colour of barley-sugar, with legs that appeared to have been cut from one thick log. The side-board had twisted front legs even more like barley-sugar, and its cupboards and drawers were beaded with what appeared to be tiny wooden ball-bearings. Meal times apart, the table was covered with a plush cloth, anchored by a vase of flowers or a bowl of fruit. House-plants were not the popular accessories they are today, and I cannot remember the Station Inn giving room to any, despite our old family saying, 'All done and dusted, and plant-pot on table' (doubtless an aspidistra).

Mother had made fringed window and door-curtains in 'folk-weave', a sort of dark green chenille banded with hunting scenes in fawn, blue and orange. The doors had bronze finger-plates, which fascinated me, because they were embossed with strange human figures and animals. Somewhere around stood the bowl containing Ernie, our goldfish, named by Jessie after one of our customers, who gulped down his beer with just the same mouth actions.

The ladies' lavatory adjoined this room, and its usage was clearly in evidence through the wall. Women customers would come singly, in twos, when they might share the one convenience like giggly schoolgirls, or in a group, which meant a gossipy queue building up outside the door to our private quarters. My evening sessions of reading or being read to would be punctuated by the clicking of shoes on parquet, the shooting of the door-bolt, sighs of relief as urine was discharged, the tumble of water as the chain was pulled; then the feet clicking back into the smoke-room, always, I fancied, with a much lighter tread.

A door in the corner of our living space led upstairs to an odd collection of rooms. First, on the left, our blue-painted bathroom, from which I once fled in hysterics when feathers issued from a hot tap, due, I learned later, to a bird having died in the tank. A wide gallery with windows along one side led to a smaller, darker landing from which there opened my parents' bedroom, the room containing the double bed I shared with Jessie (me up against the wall), a lavatory with wide wooden seat, and our sitting-room. This was furnished with a fawn three-piece suite set out on a carpet geometrically patterned in fawn, brown and green, fawn being a predominant shade in the thirties and forties. A chromium fender girded the hearth, and there was a marvellous window fitted with a seat which overhung the pavement. From this I loved to ogle passers-by, especially when women in long evening dresses and fur coats arrived with their elegant escorts to patronise a nearby ball-room, for sometimes I might catch a glimpse of jewel-coloured satin, or a necklace sparkling in the lamp-light.

Once a funeral drove by as Mother and I were perched on the window-seat. As always, she strove to keep unpleasant things from me, and, not wishing to be drawn into a discussion about death, sought to distract me. But I had caught sight of flowers and the undertakers' top-hats, and protested, 'No, I want to look at those nice, new, shiny men.'

Another time, King George V and Queen Mary passed beneath on their way to an engagement in the city. Mother had a good view inside the Royal car, and was amused to see that the King was seated on what she described as 'some sort of box', maybe to raise him to the level of his tall wife.

The gallery had a cupboard in which my toys were kept, and sometimes a grocer's daughter, whose name I can't remember, came to play. She would bring small bags of rice, in default of sweets, which we shared on 'picnics', gulping down the bullet-hard grains with water. But even if no-one came I was never alone, for in the manner of an only child I had invented a secret companion for myself. Her name was Little Girlie, and she was known also to Mother, Dad and Jessie, who would ask if my invisible friend were there, and even lay a place for her at the table, or hand her a sweet. We had good times together, Little Girlie and I, but then I became shy of acknowledging her, and I think I left her behind when we moved to Doncaster.

Sometimes I would ask my mother, 'Why can't I have a baby sister or brother?'

'You'll have to ask your father', she would reply.

So I would ask him, and he would say, 'You'll have to ask your mother.'

***

I DO NOT know what occasion prompted it, but my father decided to organise a dance at a special venue, and for once my mother bought herself a dress instead of making one. Great was my excitement when she paraded in her long, black taffeta ball-gown, scattered with the silhouettes of pale pink roses, before she and Dad left for the ball. I thought her the most beautiful person in the world.

She dressed up again for a less prestigious but equally rare event, a Sunday afternoon walk with my father, in a richly-patterned frock and a big straw hat. I hated walking, and was usually in trouble with her for 'slodging' my feet. We strolled along an alley off Beverley High Road called Strawberry Walk and came out into fields, and eventually to a farm, where Dad bought me a glass of warm milk from a can I had just seen filled by the farmer from one of his cows. It was too rich and frothy, and I pulled a face and left it. Our milk at home came in churns brought by a man on a horse-drawn cart, but it tasted far less 'cowy'.

The only other Sunday excursion I remember was a family day out by bus to Beverley Westwood. There we all were – Uncle George, Aunt Clara and Georgie, Uncle Fred, Aunt Gwen and Brian, and Mother, Dad and I. We found a clearing in the trees, and the men set up a dart-board. The food included some very large spring-onions, which the grown-ups dipped in a bag of salt, a foolish gambit as it turned out, for the day was hot and we ran out of drinks.

Brian, Georgie and I were sent into the town along a field-path, carrying bottles to fill at the pump in the market-place, which, alas, turned out to be dry. In desperation, we knocked on a house door and asked the lady there to fill our bottles with water, and she kindly complied. But the way back was long, and we were thirsty; we had stiles to climb, and whiled away the journey by jumping over cow-pats. What with one thing and another, by the time we returned to our eager parents, the bottles were empty. Fortunately, they saw the funny side.

Trips to the cinema were red-letter days. My addiction began with 'Snow White' and 'The Thief of Baghdad'. Shirley Temple's 'Bluebird' was not nearly so exciting, but the young star's mop of curls, which she was reputed to encourage with a particular shampoo, inspired Mother to try the same brand on me. In our case the results were less satisfactory, and we had to resort to the tongs again. These were heated in the fire or on the gas-ring, and although Mother wound the ends of my hair for only a second or two around the hot metal there was sometimes a worrying smell of scorching. Theatre trips were rare, as was being taken out by both my parents, for one of them was normally on duty behind the bar. But once Mother and Dad booked three seats for 'Smiling Through' at the New Theatre, and sitting there between them seemed almost as much a wonder as the performance.

I hated Mother to go out with Aunt Clara on a Tuesday night, even though she bribed me with a treat from Mr Hornby, who regularly parked his ice-cream cart nearby. His vanilla cornets were especially delicious with a dash of raspberry syrup, but at times I longed to swap him for the Walls bicycle man, and obey the bidding on the box he carried on his machine. 'Stop Me And Buy One', it urged, and if you did so he would dismount and lift the lid of his box, and hand you a mouth-watering, fruity icicle in a blue and white cardboard wrapper. In order to lick the icicle, the trick was to push it up inside the tube with your finger, but Mother viewed these products as less nourishing, and less hygienic. Nor for years was I allowed the gob-stoppers called bulls' eyes, or chewing or bubble-gum, which I watched my cousins pop with envy, for Mother had heard of a child who choked to death when its wind-pipe was blocked by chewing-gum, and I was on my honour not to try it until I was older. But candy floss and toffee apples seemed harmless enough, and I demanded both when we visited Hull Fair.

***

HULL FAIR! WAS there in Hull a soul so dead who would not be stirred by the thought of it? Every October, dozens of round-abouts and side-shows were set up in Walton Street, bringing together what was reputedly the biggest fair in the country. I am not sure how often I was taken to it before the war, or how many of my memories date from later years, but the glorious confusion of sights and sounds varied little from one visit to the next.

The prospect of being out long past bedtime under the moon and stars, with the brighter lights of perilous enchantments all around, filled us children with quite suffocating excitement. Once the chosen night had come and we found ourselves pushing through the crowds with our anxious guardians, we responded eagerly to the scent of crushed grass and engine oil, the close press of strangers, the torn snatches of music from competing attractions, and the calls of outlandish barkers urging us to roll up and see for ourselves the bearded lady, the two-headed goat and the five-legged lamb. We begged to be allowed to enter the tents where strong men bent bars of iron like liquorice sticks, or where stars of the flea-circus hauled flea-sized chariots around a flea-sized ring.

The huge, steam-driven swing-boats called Shamrocks, netted to prevent their passengers from falling out, seemed the most daring of all amusements, and drew as many screams from their patrons as the most terrifying fairground rides of today. Artificial trumpetings were broadcast periodically from the Pig and Whistle, a fun-house renowned for its distorting mirrors and sudden blasts of skirt-lifting air. The Cake Walk challenged our feats of balance, and the Ghost Train our nerve.

I was not allowed on the Flying Chairs or the Octopus because the seats had been known to break off, flinging their occupants into the crowd. Safer and magically beautiful were the horses of the carousel, rising and dipping genteelly on their twisted rods like the palfreys that bore princesses in the fairy tales. Meanwhile, Gypsy Rose Lee still grappled with the Fates behind the heavy curtains of her gilded caravan.

But there was a price to pay for a trip to the fair. The night was usually cold, and I was padded out in layers of clothing so thick it was hard to move my arms and legs. First a vest, knitted for me by Aunt Nancy from something called 'ab wool', then a liberty bodice, then two pairs of navy-blue school knickers, of the variety designed with a front pocket to take a hanky. A skirt came next, attached to a sleeveless bodice, and above that a jumper and a woollen scarf, crossed over the chest and pinned at the back. All this was topped by a reefer coat, beret and knitted gloves, knee-length socks and Wellington boots. So weighted down was I with garments that I could scarcely bend to sit on my carousel horse.

I had to be careful not to get lost. They had never heard of paedophiles, but still my parents impressed upon me that some nasty man might try to take me away (never a woman). Mother always said that if this man told me that she had sent him for me, and if he promised to take me to her, I was to ask for something belonging to her which she would be sure I would recognise, like a ring or a scarf.

***

SOON AFTER I was five, I started at Park Road School. Mother took me, and I remember it was raining. As we left the Station Inn, I looked down in a puddle to see which of her large collection of shoes she was wearing (she had a weakness for shoes, hats and gloves). She had picked a bar-fronted pair in brown crocodile-skin, probably real, for in those days people had no compunction about dressing in skins and furs, and Mother had, in fact, two fur coats, and a silver fox to drape across her shoulders.

School had a peculiar smell of its own, of chalk, and wooden floors, and children's bodies. I was put into the class of Miss Smith, a kind young woman whom I very soon adored, even though she disapproved of the enthusiastic way I dotted my ' i-s' with big balloons. We sat in pairs at wooden desks, and sometimes when we lifted the lids in a morning we would find that teacher had left us a toffee each inside. We must have squeaked out some of our letters on slates, because I still have a mental picture of a monitor banging clouds of chalk from a big box of rubbers against the school wall. My only other recollections of these early schooldays are of vying for one of three paper parasols which we used to enact the story of the three Billy Goats Gruff, and getting stuck every time on 't-h-e' when learning to read.

I was happy, though, so I was quite surprised when Mother wanted to move me. She had all along wished me to go to St. John's Church of England School, but it was small and already full, and Park Road was the one nearest to where we lived. However, Mother persevered, and went to see the head teacher, and explained our family connections with the church, and the fact that four of my cousins had already been enrolled at St. John's. All this must have swung the balance, for I was accepted, and joined Miss Clayton's class.

I was lucky throughout my schooling to have a succession of good teachers, and Miss Clayton was the second of the line. She was older than Miss Smith, in fact I thought her very old, though she was perhaps in her forties or fifties. She was quiet in dress and manner, but with a definite air of authority, and the skin of her pleasant face hung in folds. She always read to us before the leaving-bell sounded, and when one of the girls brought along Enid Blyton's *The Enchanted Wood*, as each chapter concluded we could not wait for our next adventure at the top of the Faraway Tree.

St. John's was a good walk away, along Beverley Road, and my cousin Dorothy, four years older, was saddled with the unwelcome task of seeing me safely there. First, a friend, Elsie, called for me at the Station Inn. We made our way to the end of Sculcoates Lane, where Dorothy and her friend, Kathy Sewell (one of a family of twenty-one children, not all living) would meet us and conduct us balefully to school. Elsie and I were not allowed to cross the minor side streets on our own, but were instructed to stop at every kerb and wait for the big girls to catch up and give the all-clear, even when there was no hint of so much as a bicycle. This irked us, but we knew we would be in trouble if we disobeyed and our mothers got to know.

As we came home for our dinners, the walk to school had to be completed twice a day, but I was given a penny to cover two rides back on the trolley bus. When my cousin Bill went to St. John's and was asked by a relative what he enjoyed most about school, he replied, 'When the bell goes at home time.' I enjoyed leaving-time too, for a different reason, because the older classes would still be at their lessons, and often they would be singing, and the windows might be open. One summer day, Handel's 'Where'er You Walk' was floating out, and I remember turning my eyes up to the trees surrounding the old school buildings, and seeing with a tightening of the heart that they did indeed crowd into a shade. The school was knocked down and rebuilt long ago, but maybe some of the trees are still there.

Sometimes I might be given an extra ha'penny to call at a shop for a small, triangular bag of my favourite 'goodies', raspberry drops. But 'goodies' was a Hull expression considered 'common', and my mother drew the line at it, and at certain other phrases popular with some of my contemporaries which I tried to adopt, such as 'ta-ra' instead of 'ta-ta', 'gerroff' for 'get off', and 'shurrup' for 'shut up'.

I was always being corrected, it seemed to me. The Victorian ideal of 'children being seen and not heard' was still very much in vogue, and Mother's aim was to be able to 'take me anywhere.' That meant I had to have manners. 'Elbows off the table.' 'Keep your shoulders back.' 'No reading at table.' ' Don't chew with your mouth open.' 'Don't answer back.' How on earth could I remember it all? Possibly I was restless at table because I never felt hungry and had little interest in food, apart from Rice Krispies, steamed lamb chops and tomato, and Mother's pastry.

It was a pain to get me to eat, and when we went on our annual holiday to Bridlington with Aunt Jinny I dreaded the thought of the dinners at Mrs Gill's boarding-house. She served pallid meat and watery mashed potato swimming in pale gravy on Willow-pattern plates. I was totally unable to swallow this fare, and survived the week on bowls of tomato soup and cream-crackers, which Mother anxiously bought for me at a café near the boating-lake.

Those holidays were memorable to me for three other reasons – fun on the beach, sailing around Flamborough Head on the pleasure steamer Boys' Own, and watching dear Aunt Jinny try to dress herself under the bed-clothes in the room we all shared. She was a maiden lady of ultra modesty, and I never quite got over the sting of her undeserved reproof when one tea-time I crawled under her chair, pretending to be a dog. 'Rudey rudey', she said.

I did, however, deserve another admonishment I received for a different kind of rudeness to her. She was regaling us with some anecdote or other when I chipped in with a remark that was often used to interrupt my own rigmaroles, 'What a long tail our cat's got.' Auntie was brought up in mid-flow, and my mother's anger was mingled with astonishment that I could be so disrespectful.

CHAPTER SEVEN – BEVERLEY ROAD

I WAS STRONG-WILLED, and, being an only child, I was spoilt, and had to learn how to share my plethora of toys. I resented lending my beloved Teddy, bought for me by Granmer (who had extracted his eyes on their long, sharp pins and stitched on black buttons instead) and it was equally hard to hand over dolls Sally, Peggy and Mary to the ministrations of others, or allow other hands to operate my two tea-sets, cot, pram and dolls' house, or my desk and easel, or my blue, three-wheeler cycle. I expect I was even loath to share my kaleidoscope or my hollow cardboard policeman, whose head lifted off on a long pink stalk of a neck, and who still smelled of the toffees he had once contained.

I had favourite dresses and protested when the time came to pass them down to Annette because I had grown out of them, even though her need was greater than mine. I had to be taught how not to be mean, and how to control my temper. When I became what Mother called 'an awkward squad', or grew hysterical, as I sometimes did, she would give me a smack on the legs or bottom and lock me on the stairs to cool off. By meting out discipline herself, she was safe-guarding my relationship with my father.

For my father was never drawn into any of this. He was inclined to think me a pretty perfect specimen in every way, although even he must have realised that my first teeth had come through decayed, my 'lazy' left eye drifted outwards when I was tired, and that I sometimes ran round screaming when I felt it stabbing with pain.

It was Mother I ran to when I was hurt, Mother to whom I confided my deepest worries; Mother who with a kiss, a touch, a soothing word could solve every problem, rescue every situation. Mother who knew everything, understood everything, forgave everything. Mother whom I hugged, and hugged, and hugged so tightly that it seemed I might climb inside her, even though I thought I had arrived in the doctor's black bag.

The school doctor sent me to the eye-clinic, where glasses were prescribed. I hated them, for I dreaded being a 'specky four-eyes'. Even worse, Dorothy said that, with my spindly plaits and nose for curiosity, I looked like Keyhole Kate, a character in the Dandy comic. This became her nick-name for me, and I was so mortified I developed an air of studious withdrawal, and began to cultivate a reputation for eccentricity.

Still, it was good for me to have my cousins living only a fifteen-minute walk away, and to have the corners knocked off me by some regular cut-and-thrust.

Dorothy herself was not immune to being teased. One winter, her nose turned as red as a radish, so she became known to the family as 'Rosy Radish', later shortened to 'our Rad'. I saw little of kind Margaret, who had passed a scholarship to Newland High School, and was kitted out with family help. She did not find her passage there easy, for she came from a less privileged background than many of her school-fellows, but she faced any problems with the same serenity and rueful tolerance she still possesses Her spare time was largely spent running errands and cleaning-up for Aunt Jinny and the Uncles.

Dorothy would usually spend the weekends with us, and while she insisted on the deference due to her seniority, we had great times. On Sunday mornings, we would each find a paper bag at the bottom of the bed, containing fruit, sweets, and biscuits, which we called 'lunch', and copies of *The Beano*, *Dandy* or *Film Fun*, and Enid Blyton's *Sunny Stories*. What luxury to lounge around, munching and reading! This, we realised years later, was my parents' crafty way of ensuring a lie-in.

Later, Dorothy would walk me a little way up Beverley Road to Fountain Road, to visit Aunt Jinny and the Uncles, and Margaret would usually be there. The terrace house was filled with the scent of roasting beef, and I would be allowed to grate the loaf of salt Aunt Jinny had waiting on the kitchen-table. But when it became so small that the grater caught my fingertips, Dorothy or Margaret would take over. We were given biscuits, and sweets, and dandelion-and-burdock, and sometimes played 'I spy', while the Uncles lurked in the sitting-room behind the beautiful cut-glass door-knob, and read their papers.

During the week, my mother and Jessie might send me along the road to the nearby shops to buy special treats: ham and egg slices from Thirsk's; maids-of-honour, blackcurrant cream tarts, vanilla slices or Devonshire splits from Jackson's. As I grew older, I was dispatched alone to Ostler's, the barber's, to have my hair bobbed 'to the tips of my ears.' It was quite thick, but Mother sometimes joked as she brushed it that she'd 'seen better hair on bacon.'

Mr and Mrs Dean at the newsagency always gave me a warm welcome, and were willing to spread out every card in the shop when I was looking for one for Mother's birthday. They stocked Du Maurier cigarettes in elegant vermilion and silver boxes, and Mother would send for a packet occasionally, although she smoked very little, and soon gave up. She and Jessie also tried mascara, and came out of the weepy film 'Boys' Town' with black-streaked faces.

***

FURTHER ALONG BEVERLEY Road was Bethnal Green, where Grampa and Granmer lived. Grampa grew snapdragons in the small garden, and I would pick some for a 'wedding bouquet'. Granmer would deck me out in a lace curtain, and I used to sit on the settee with my bridegroom (Grampa) and wave to the crowds from our 'car.' Once, my cousin Brian happened to be there, and to his extreme horror he was pressed into the role of bridegroom instead. The wedding cake was a digestive biscuit, and the sherry, water. Granmer flung handfuls of 'confetti', made from torn-up newspapers, over us. It was my favourite game, but it gave her a lot of work.

If the family congregated for Sunday tea, my father and grand-parents would apparently call upon me to sing or recite. Mother told me later that the Greenwood aunts and uncles were remarkably tolerant and flattering, because I was the only girl, though they surely had private reservations, and my boy cousins must have found it excruciating. Mother herself tried to act as a counter-balance, fearing I might get too big for my boots.

Sometimes I would sleep there, and Granmer would put Grampa in the spare room and have me with her in bed. Much as I loved her, I did not enjoy these nights. She snored, bless her, like a small animal, but worse, she slept between very tickly, thick blankets, no doubt for warmth. She was a scrupulously clean old lady, but I had a distaste for old flesh which I have never quite overcome (not even for my own now), though I would admire her long white hair, and the holes in her ear-lobes which she told me had been made in her youth (by one of her brothers, I think) with a red-hot darning-needle.

Altogether plumper and shinier was her sister, Aunt Hetty, whom I imagined beneath her sober dresses to have a body like a baby's. Her face was as smooth and gleaming as pink satin, her scalp, too, where it glistened through her white curls, which were usually held in place by a fine hair-net. Her eyes were amazingly blue, but one was milky and turned outwards, what we called a 'wall eye'. She wore dark dresses sprigged with tiny spots or flowers, with a piece of white silk or lace let into the neckline, and walked with a stick. On her visits to Granmer, she was normally accompanied by her friend, Miss Lily Taylor, a tall, thin woman with thick glasses, who couldn't sound her 'r's.

Aunt Hetty had married well-off. Her husband, Uncle Joe, was a successful businessman, but eventually his company fell on hard times, and he and Aunt Hetty had to leave their comfortable home, and ended up in an almshouse. I was taken to see them there, and was disturbed to hear it whispered that Uncle had an ulcer which had left a hole in his leg the size of an egg-cup. He died soon afterwards, and I think it was not long before Aunt Hetty and Miss Taylor joined forces. My great-aunt had never had any children, but she always talked understandingly to young people.

Old and middle-aged ladies exercised a peculiar fascination for me, especially those regular customers I got to know, first at the Station Inn and later at the Big Drum. They had such confidence in their ability to run their lives more efficiently than other people's lives were run. They believed theirs was the friendliest street, cleanest house, whitest wash, tenderest Sunday joint, most mountainous Yorkshire pudding. Their children's names were better chosen, their wallpaper more tasteful, their furniture more comfortable, their Christmasses more skilfully planned than anyone else's.

They wore corsets and directoire bloomers, and most likely false teeth, because it had been quite common for people of their generation to have all their own teeth removed once they reached their twenties or thirties. They sat ranged against the wall in double-breasted overcoats and wide-fitting shoes, sometimes with bandaged legs, smears of powder on their noses, brooches from favourite grandchildren pinned on their lapels, hair brought to order by winding it in Dinkie curlers the previous night, or clamping it in metal wavers with teeth like crocodiles. They had capacious handbags, which they rammed down on their knees and clutched with both hands, as if all their worldly treasures were inside.

They knew the best methods of washing-up, and mashing tea, and frying bacon with the trimmed-off rind at the side of the pan to make extra 'dip', and I was in awe of their expertise. I could not imagine that I would ever be so experienced in the ways of the world, and envied them their casual self-assurance.

***

JESSIE OFTEN TOOK me out, and on one occasion, I was licking an ice-cream when a dog jumped up and bit me in the face. She returned home weeping with me, and when Mother saw my badly-swollen top lip she hastened with me to the doctor, who cauterised the wounds. My parents were afraid I might be permanently scarred, but I was only left with two very faint white marks under my nose, which never show. I remember nothing of the incident.

I was very fond of Jessie, who was sixteen years older than I, and regarded her as my big sister. To Mother she was both ally and pupil, eager to absorb everything Mum could teach her, from papering walls to dressmaking. At times I led Jessie quite a dance, but she would not put up with any nonsense; her standard reply to unreasonable requests was, 'I'll dance to you for tuppence', and if I moaned she would say, 'It's a pity your pan runs.'

She was good at making dolls' clothes, and devising treats, and helping at my birthday parties, which followed the usual pattern – potted meat sandwiches, tinned fruit, jelly, blancmange and cakes, and games which included Pinning the Tail on the Donkey, Poor Mary Sits A-Weeping, Postman's Knock and Blind Man's Buff. My cousin Margaret remembers how my father used to stand quietly in the background, watching, but my pleasure was complete if I could persuade him and Mother to work their magic tricks together.

We usually started with 'The Poker Passes'. Mother would remain in the room while Dad went out and closed the door. We children sat in a circle, and as Mother waved a poker slowly above our heads, calling 'The poker passes', Dad's disembodied voice would respond, 'Let it pass'. When Mother said, 'The poker stops', to our astonishment Dad always managed to name the person above whose head it had come to rest, even though he could not possibly see what was going on inside the room. After a time, he and Mum would change places, which only served to increase our bafflement.

Abuzz with unanswered questions, we hoped for better luck at solving the next mystery, the secret of 'The Magic Mirror'. Mother and Dad would take turns to leave the room while someone looked in the mirror over the mantelpiece. Called back inside, they could tell us, by careful scrutiny of the glass, just who that person had been. It was years before Mother revealed the secret of how both pieces of magic were done.

I had a special friend, Eddie, who always came to the parties. He lived nearby in Kottingham Terrace, and was my own age. I was so fond of him I would even lend him my Teddy. He had a tortoise with a section of shell that reminded us both of a trap-door, and we used to pretend we opened it and climbed inside, to a strange green world (brought about by the creature's diet, which consisted mainly of cabbage and lettuce). Eddie's Mum made delicious bread, and one of my happiest memories is of sitting with him on their back doorstep eating warm wedges spread with butter and dark treacle. Aunt Nancy was another fine hand at bread, and Dorothy would come running along Beverley Road with 'hot cakes' for us, straight from the oven.

Uncle George used to help out behind the pub bar at weekends, and he could make any party go with a swing. He was happy to be dressed up by Mother and Jessie, and one memorable night Jessie excelled herself, sending him dancing in among the drinkers as a fairy in a diaphanous short skirt, scattering paper rose-petals from a basket.

Another time, the humour was more barbed. One of our married customers, called Bert, had a lady-love, although he thought he had managed to keep her a secret. He was in our pub with his wife at a late-night party when Jessie answered a knock at the door, and returned with a message that a lady was asking for Bert and would not go away. Apparently Bert's face was a picture when the caller walked in, wearing a fashionable frock, high heels, a fetching hat and a bright slash of lipstick. But of course it was only mischievous Uncle George.

I heard about these episodes, and wished I could have been there. One night the music and laughter downstairs were so compelling that I broke Mum and Dad's strict rule and crept into the smoke-room in my nightie. A customer seized me and stood me on a table, and shouts went up for me to sing. As I obliged with my current party pieces, 'Dancing With My Shadow' and 'Who's Taking You Home Tonight?' I watched Mother with trepidation from my eye-corner. She was gazing at me with what I took to be a mixture of disapproval and pride; afterwards, putting me to bed, she warned me I must never do such a thing again.

**

I WAS QUITE a healthy child, but at times certain remedies were called for. We were not a Scott's Emulsion household, but Mother was a firm believer in Syrup of Figs (to be treated with caution), Glycerine, Lemon and Ipecacuanha for coughs (delicious), Vicks VapoRub (hot and stinging), Fennings Little Healers (tiny pills for chesty colds, no trouble to take), Fennings Fever Mixture (ugh!!), Camphorated Ice (a bit like Vicks), and Virol (a pleasant form of cod-liver oil and malt I called Toffee Medicine, one teaspoonful after each meal).

Bowels were an obsession with most people, and if the question 'Have you been?' drew a reply of 'No, I can't go,' the medicine chest (in our case, a tall glass Smith's Crisps jar from our grocery days) was opened. Mother occasionally dosed herself with a patent containing senna-pods. She might also now and then need warm almond-oil spooning in her ears to soften the wax, and at times swallowed Beecham's Pills and Doan's Backache Pills. Thankfully, none of us needed Sloan's Liniment, the old folks' antidote to swollen joints, for I found its smell depressing when I visited Granmer's friends. Another popular remedy I don't think any of us tried was Dr Williams' Pink Pills for Pale People.

Bad toothache could be eased with Oil of Cloves rubbed on the gum, or an actual clove balanced on the tooth, while barley-water was beneficial for a chill on the kidneys, an ailment I was prone to. Mustard baths were good for colds, and a bread poultice would 'draw' a boil. (Mother and Jessie also used mustard for mending earrings.) Bread was less aggressive in the form of 'pobs' or 'pobbies', soaked in sugary milk, and eaten to aid recovery from illness.

Earache would yield to the power of an onion heated in the oven and wrapped in a sock. A sweaty sock wound around the throat was supposed to be an efficient cure for tonsillitis, but we never tried that. Once, when Jessie had a sore throat, Mother bought sulphur powder and blew it down the back of Jessie's mouth with a straw. The powder was kept in the kitchen cupboard, but after Mother picked up the wrong packet and tried to use white pepper, Jessie pronounced herself cured.

Mother said that when she was young, she cleaned her teeth with salt, or soot from the chimney-back, because they were good whiteners. She would soak camomile flowers in boiling water to make a rinse for my fair hair, whereas a dash of vinegar gave gloss to her own. But she and Jessie had a range of conventional cosmetics too: Pond's Cold Cream, Snowfire Vanishing Cream, Tokalon Face Powder, and scents like Phulnana, Californian Poppy and Evening in Paris.

***

SO PRE-WAR LIFE progressed, busy and eventful, with friends and relatives always dropping in. Saturday was the day for shopping in town, and Mother and I would catch a sixty-three trolley- bus to the city centre and walk past Queen Victoria's statue and across Monument Bridge, where ships clustered almost to the parapet. Then we would pass up Whitefriargate, known to Hullites as 'Whitefra'gate', with perhaps a call into 'Woolies' or 'Marks'. Woolworth's was a Mecca for everything, and stationed behind every one of its brown, oblong counters were two or three assistants and a couple of tills. The counter-tops held compartments separated by strips of glass, where assorted goods were 'filed'.

Turn right into Market Place, and there alongside Holy Trinity, the biggest parish church in the country, the market-stalls were gathered, flanked by a number of red and white-striped canvas booths selling fish and chips. From these alluring little kiosks floated a most distinctive smell of frying, such as no fish and chip shops have ever quite exuded since. But we rarely trod the duck-boards or sat on the benches inside, for Mother preferred to buy our dinner at the wet-fish shop by the bridge, skate knobs, plaice or halibut, perhaps, and cook it herself.

Far less appetising than the aroma from the striped booths was the scent of drying hops, which usually seemed to be wafting across town from the local breweries. I would pinch my nostrils in a vain attempt to block out the sickly brandy snap smell. Even worse was the rank odour sent up by the paper-mills.

Sometimes we would shop a bit nearer home, a little way up Beverley Road, past Dr Twomey's surgery, maybe pausing at Dooks' to buy me a new pair of black patent Kiltie ankle-strap shoes, or at Mallory's hardware store, where I would draw the delightful scent of new pans deep into my lungs. Opposite stood the imposing frontage of Jubb's, a firm of outfitters where the assistants screwed our bills and payments into metal cylinders, and catapulted them along aerial wires to the cashier's high desk.

On Sundays I had to go to Sunday School at St. Mary's Church. Neither of my parents attended church, although they had every excuse to absent themselves on a day when trade was at its briskest. (I have no idea of my father's beliefs, but Mother returned to her religious roots once she left the licensed trade.) The only memory I have of those afternoons is the journey home, straggling in a group along Stepney Lane, and anticipating with no sort of pleasure the dinner that was being kept warm for me on a plate in the oven, usually roast lamb, with peas like ball-bearings, and shrivelled gravy.

But at Christmas we had goose, the apogee of a feast Mother had started to prepare weeks before with the making of cakes and puddings, which entailed washing the fruit and drying it on trays before the fire. On Christmas Eve Dorothy, or later Annette, would sleep with me, and every year we were overwhelmed by the benevolence and perception of Father Christmas. Who can ever forget the heart-thumping excitement of waking in the half-dark, stretching a foot down to the bottom of the bed, feeling the weight of mysterious objects, and hearing the rustle and crackle of parcels? Always we found that the generous old gentleman had left us not only what we had asked for, but things we hadn't even realised we wanted; though we knew that whatever else our bulging stocking contained, there would be sure to be an orange, an apple, a bright new penny and a net of chocolate coins at the toe.

The joy and wonderment of those visits from Father Christmas, so beautifully evoked in the Poem *The Night Before Christmas*, (wherein he is referred to as St. Nicholas) are carried back to me in the memory of my mother's voice. As she read the poem with me on her lap, we shared a sense of anticipation about two particular lines:

'He had a round face, and a little round belly,
That shook when he laughed like a bowlful of jelly.'

Here we would smile at each other and gasp a little, because 'belly' was quite a rude word.

So life went on, happy and secure. Then, when I was five, my dear Grampa Greenwood died.

In their constant desire to protect me, my parents managed to hide from me their anxiety about his illness (stomach cancer) and even their grief at his death, for I do not remember anything of the circumstances. But I must have missed Grampa, and my harmonious visits to Bethnal Green, where he and I had spent such companionable times together, for soon after he died Granmer insisted, against all advice, on leaving their little house. She moved into a one-roomed flat on Beverley Road, a door or two away from where my parents had seen out their fallow months during the General Strike. Dad suggested that he and his brothers should each allow Granmer ten shillings (fifty pence) a month, and after he died my mother continued to honour this unwritten agreement until Granmer's death sixteen years later.

The effect that Grampa's death did have on me was to fill me with a fear of dying. I am sure my parents did their best to explain, but nobody seemed certain about what happened to the person inside a body once it was dead, and the thought of being buried appalled me. I had never been afraid of the dark, but now I would lie in bed at night and will myself not to fall asleep in case my heart stopped beating, and I didn't wake up. My fear of dying was to return in the air raid shelters with the intermittent buzzing of enemy planes overhead, and the whistle of falling bombs, although I was surprised when I was told long afterwards that I had started to drop to my knees and pray.

Since that nightmarish time, much of the face of my old city has changed beyond recognition, ravaged and redrawn by the Blitz and its aftermath, and doubtlessly improved in many ways. But in that year of 1939, in the Hull that was home, no rumblings of the gathering storm reached me, and it was a shock when I learned that our country was at war with Germany, and that strong new disciplines, like being measured for gas masks, would be required of us all.

CHAPTER EIGHT – WARTIME

MY FATHER COULD scarcely believe it when war was declared on September 3rd, 1939. As a result of his experiences in the Great War, and time spent living afterwards among the German people, he had always maintained that our two nations would never repeat the mistakes of the past. Being proved wrong was a great blow to him, and Mother felt it affected his health.

I cannot remember his reactions, being not quite six at the time and only just aware, without being unduly troubled, that changes were afoot. My first wartime memory is of Dad, Mother, Jessie, Dorothy and me trying on gas masks at a distribution centre somewhere. I went last, and laughed uproariously as I watched the others disappear behind the strange visors, because they looked so peculiar goggling through the eye-pieces, and their muffled voices sounded funny too.

But when it came to my turn, amusement turned to fright as an officious stranger manoeuvred my head into the horrid rubber thing, so tight, and smelly, and airless, and growing rapidly wet inside with condensation, and I screamed and screamed. Later, I learned to wear it for short spells during gas mask drills at school, and lost my fear of it, for we all had to carry our gas masks everywhere with us. We wrote our names on the square cardboard containers, which we lugged around by their long string handles, and eventually Mother bought me a brown canvas case to keep mine in. She treated herself to a smart black bag, shaped to her mask's dimensions, with a side-pocket to take her purse.

Someone from the Government came round to issue us all with Identity Cards bearing serial letters and numbers. Dad was JARG: 1, Mother JARG: 2, I was JARG: 3, and Jessie JARG: 4. We were supposed to carry these cards everywhere, and Mother once got into trouble when riding on a bus because she could not produce hers when an official stopped the vehicle to check everyone's credentials.

To screen off any light which might guide enemy planes, complete blackout was ordered at night, and Mother busied herself making curtains out of special blackout material, and brightening them up with coloured borders of rick-rack braid. If the tiniest gleam showed through a chink, an air raid warden would knock on the door or window shouting, 'PUT THAT LIGHT OUT', and the householder felt very guilty.

Street lamps were off, road directions removed, vehicles were driven with masked headlights, and sensible folk carried pin-hole torches to help them fumble through the dark. Mother's was slim and silver, like a propelling pencil. Identity discs in the form of silver chain bracelets became fashionable, though some of the more daring young women fastened them around their ankles. They were the sort who also flouted convention by wearing trousers called 'slacks'.

Where people had gardens, corrugated-roofed Anderson air raid shelters began to appear, camouflaged with grass or earth. Alternatively, there was the Morrison, a sort of cage designed for indoor use. I think my parents found it hard to decide which would be the safest place for us; one of my earliest memories of the Blitz is of crouching under the dining-table with them, and Jessie, and Rap. I remember calling out to Mother because her legs were sticking out, and I was afraid they might get blown off, but she was more concerned about her handbag, which contained all our personal documents.

I remember, too, lying on one of the plush benches in the smoke-room during another air raid, my throbbing brow cooled by a cloth soaked in vinegar, Mother's remedy for headaches. She had baked a batch of the hard scones she called 'bricks', made specifically to see us through long periods of enemy action, and as I struggled to eat one, the vinegar dripped down on its thin smear of margarine.

The cellar must have seemed a more sensible retreat, and we began to use it. It could only be reached by a trap-door in the floor behind the bar, and I enjoyed hearing over and over again the story of how Jessie had hurried after my father down the steep ladder during one alert, and accidentally jammed the heel of her shoe in his eye.

But when we learned that a group of people had taken shelter in the cellar of a pub in town, and been either gassed or drowned when underground pipes were fractured by a bomb, my parents had second thoughts, and decided to patronise the large, brick communal shelter that had been built in Kottingham Terrace, alongside the Station Inn.

On the home front, people tried to run their lives as normally as possible, but being at war was a complex business, even when choosing presents. My cousin Brian was eight in July, 1940, and Mother and I went across the road to buy him a model car at our local toy shop. We picked a good strong one, but when she got the car home and examined it more closely, she was horrified to find that it had been MADE IN GERMANY.

I cannot remember whether we gave it to Brian, although I vaguely recall arriving at his party. He, Aunt Gwen and Uncle Fred lived in a council house up Greenwood Avenue (the road was not named after them) and Aunt Gwen always welcomed us warmly. She possessed a musical voice, an affectionate personality and a romantic turn of mind, and was clever into the bargain, inspiring respect among the Greenwood family for having passed a scholarship for Newland High

School. It was also noted (just imagine Granmer Greenwood's reaction) that she preferred books to housework.

Uncle Fred was artistic, and had painted an enormous swan on their bathroom wall. It was so big and so life-like I was scared to go in, and averted my eyes if I had to. Uncle was a humorous man, very unhurried and easy-going, but when Hull became a target for German bombers he adopted an altogether sharper approach to life, and revealed a new sense of urgency and great courage as a fireman.

Gradually, barrage balloons became a feature of our skies. I could never see the point of them, but they were stately and beautiful objects, floating on their giant strings like huge balls of silver foil. They were given names, usually unflattering ones such as Big Bertha, and I was upset to learn that one was called Janet.

We collected real foil, rolled it into small balls and put these strange new offerings to God in the church collection plate on Sundays. Every scrap was vital for munitions, it seemed, and we even stripped the thin sheets inside cigarette-packets from their paper linings. Housewives were encouraged to give aluminium pans to be turned into aeroplanes, and gracious iron railings were sawn down and carted off, also earmarked for armaments it was said, although there is now some doubt as to whether they were actually made use of. Such a waste if not, for their removal changed the aspect of many old streets and buildings, and compromised the integrity of even the humblest terraces.

But sacrifices were in order, for the famous wartime spirit was everywhere alive, and as shortages began to bite, inventiveness rose above them. Newspapers and magazines carried diagrams on how to turn garments inside-out to give the material fresh usefulness, or how to lengthen dresses by inserting contrasting bands of material. Another suggestion was to cut off frock sleeves and scoop out sweat-stained armpits to make pinafore dresses, while parachute-silk made wonderful undies (cami-knicks or French knickers were quite the thing) and even wedding-dresses.

A father's trousers could be cut down into schoolboy shorts for his son. Knitted items were unravelled and remodelled, and stockings were replaced by a solution of gravy-salt to colour-wash the legs. I know Jessie had trouble trying to hide the network of scorch marks that disfigured her shins, a griddled effect common among quite a few of her sex who had sat too close to the fire. 'Stocking seams' were drawn with eyebrow-pencil, made more convincing by adding lines of tiny 'fully-fashioned' dots. Such pencils were essential because some young women had started to shave off their eyebrows and draw thin, artificial ones instead, which lent them rather a surprised look. Hair was piled up on top in large, loose curls, and the long back section either rolled under in a 'page-boy' or over around a band. Lipstick, gorgeously pillar-box red, doubled as rouge, a trick of my mother's I still copy.

***

MY COUSIN JACK Greenwood, Uncle Jack's son, came to visit us at the Station Inn. He was a young sailor in uniform and brought a friend with him. What fun they were: they could both tear an apple in half simply by twisting it in their hands, a feat I tried in vain to emulate, and Jack became my great hero.

At some juncture, which must have been fairly early in the war, he wrote a letter to my parents from the Royal Naval Barracks in Devonport, describing how he had 'managed to scrape 97 per cent' in recent exams. He goes on: 'Last week we had a series of instructions on torpedoes, mines and electricity. There is more to this sailor business than you would suspect. One minute you are scrubby and the next an office mug.'

His letter says that he has plenty to eat and drink and asks, 'How do you go on for food? Are you rationed or anything like that? I remember you saying what Grandpa thought about me joining this league, and I can tell you honestly that he was wrong. I am just right down here and am going to sign for the twelve years soon. I shouldn't like to think that I had a civilian job. I am where I wanted to be and quite happy about it. You are like Mother, Aunt,' (he means his step-mother) 'the way you worry about things. I tell her that we can swim and that we carry our own life belts (that blow up) about with us but she doesn't seem to get settled. We are as safe in a ship as you are up there, in fact a lot safer when Jerry comes. We have got the stuff to give them but you haven't. So you see it would be me that was worrying if everybody had their rights'.

In the same letter he sent me a message and kisses, and when about a year later we were living in Zetland Road at Doncaster, he came on leave, and he and his equally kind-hearted fiancée, Joan, took me to the pictures. That was the last time I saw him, for Jack was posted missing at sea in September, 1942.

Years after the war, I found his name on the big naval memorial on Plymouth Hoe. Aged twenty-one, he had been a leading-seaman aboard HMS Veteran, one of two destroyers chaperoning a strange convoy of American river-boats and pleasure-craft which had been dispatched across the Atlantic from Nova Scotia to Northern Ireland. It was believed at the time that they were destined to become hospital ships and troop-carriers, should the Allies decide to invade Europe, but more recently it has been suggested that they were meant as a decoy for German U-boats, while the liner Queen Mary, bearing nearly 11,000 American troops, slipped secretly from the United States to England by another route.

Whatever the truth of the matter, the unlikely armada was attacked by seventeen U-boats, and Jack's ship, having picked up survivors from one sunken vessel, was torpedoed and lost with all hands. After the war his father and step-mother tried to find out what had happened to him, but it was only when a Sunday newspaper published a story about the incident a year or two later that they learned how he had died.

Another letter I treasured for years was from Jessie's boyfriend, Arthur. I was devoted to him, and perhaps in reply to a message from me he sent a few lines from Withernsea, where he was doing Army training. There were some lovely flower-beds on the sea-front, he wrote, 'but don't ask me to pick you any, Janet, because I can't.'

My cousin Bill, known in the family as 'Billy Bless Him' because he was such a good lad to his mother, had been in the Territorial Army, so was quickly posted to a gun-battery on Sunk Island in the Humber, where, I was surprised to hear much later, Aunt Nancy and my mother had been able to visit him. Then he was transferred to the Shetlands, from where he mailed us all wonderful Fair Isle knitwear. Eventually he fought in the Greek and Italian campaigns. The troops had their letters censored, but when Aunt Nancy received a message from one of Bill's friends giving news of '.....Bless Him', she knew all was well, though the censor had cut out Bill's name.

***

HULL IS NOW acknowledged to have experienced some of the heaviest bombing of all the English cities, although at the time it was mentioned on the news simply as 'an East Coast town.' We became accustomed to air raid warnings which might turn us out of bed several times a night. Sometimes we would no sooner be back home after the all-clear, and dropping off to sleep, than the dread wailing of the 'buzzer' would start up again, and rouse us for a hurried return to the air raid shelter.

Mother kept a bag packed with necessities in case of a long stay, and we had warm top clothing and our gas masks ready by the bed. Those who were caught unprepared, and left home in a hurry, could turn up looking some very strange sights. Pyjamas and dressing-gowns were commonplace. A few folk copied Churchill, and found his all-in-one, navy-blue siren-suit a practical answer in cold weather.

People furnished the shelters with personal comforts, like their own special chairs, and there were duck-boards to keep your feet dry if rain got in, and a sort of metal dustbin arrangement in a corner cubicle to serve as a chemical toilet. When used, it made an embarrassing rattling noise, so came into action only as a last resort. One old lady, caught short in the Fitzroy Street shelter, appealed to her son, 'Whistle, George!'

We must have made a strangely assorted company, but though we came together in enforced proximity to face unnatural dangers, I do not recall anyone (except me) giving way to gloom or panic. Anger, yes, at Hitler, Mussolini and the rest of the Jerries and Eye-ties, but even such strong emotion was layered with phlegmatic cheerfulness, and a determination to make the best of things. During those nights, pungent with the scent of damp brick, the legendary British bulldog spirit was certainly in splendid vigour.

***

AS THE AEROPLANES were heard approaching in the distance, tongues would be silenced, and ears cocked to detect whether they were ours or Jerry's, for the engines of the enemy bombers sounded different from those of our fighters. It was reassuring to hear shelling from our ground-based ack-ack guns and know they were trying to bring down the raiders. Mines, time-bombs, incendiaries ... devices with differing effects designed for different ends. It might be possible to guess which category a particular one belonged to as the noise of its descent grew louder, but who could tell where it was about to land?

Any faraway thud was greeted with relief, but closer targets could rock the shelter and fill it with dust thick enough to coat the tongue and line the nostrils. This sequence might be followed by the noise of a collapsing structure or a smell of burning, and the shelter's occupants would give their own whistles ('Phew! That was close') and wonder what they might find on stepping outside. Souls of courage or bravado who opened the door during a lull to see what was happening, ignoring pleas for caution from the rest of us, would shout out which buildings appeared to be blazing, or gone altogether. I remember noticing a large red glow on the skyline as we made our way home after one all-clear, and hearing my mother cry that Bladon's (one of Hull's finest department stores) appeared to have been hit.

All these events seemed to go on for a very long time, and although memory can play tricks, and we cannot really have lived our lives as one continuous drama, that is how it appears in retrospect.

Jessie started to stay in bed rather than accompany us to the shelter, which worried us. She refused to give up her sleep, she said, though whether she managed to hold on to it during all the 'fireworks' was debatable. One night we returned to the pub to find most of our doors and windows had been blown in, which, in the context of all the devastation a few hundred yards away, was actually a sign that things could have been very much worse for us. I don't think Jessie had been in bed when it happened, but it was probably the night when poor Rap, left alone in the living-room, shredded a door-curtain and umbrella in his terror.

Cave Street, on the opposite side of Beverley Road, was badly blitzed, and soon after Aunt Nancy moved out of Sculcoates Lane because her home had narrowly escaped being hit by a mine, it was flattened by a bomb which blasted two terraces immediately behind, in Melwood Grove. My cousin Margaret remembers standing in the bedroom window in the Sculcoates Lane house and gazing down at a huge crater which the mine had made. But even the most terrifying ordeals could have a humorous twist. A neighbour's old mother was discovered by rescuers safe and well and upside down inside her wrecked home, protected by her upturned chair. She was drunk at the time, and it was the general opinion that her relaxed condition had helped to save her.

Such quirks of fate only served to underline the tragedies. Two of my mother's close friends, Eva and Harold Woolhouse, who lived in Ash Grove, further along Beverley Road, lost their teenage son, Edgar. They and both their boys had taken refuge in their usual shelter and, during a hiatus in the bombing, Edgar and his father went out to see what was happening, ignoring Eva's pleas for them to stay. Another bomb fell, killing Edgar immediately, and injuring Harold so badly it took him many months to recover.

The landscape kept changing alarmingly as familiar buildings were turned to rubble, then cleared and flattened into bomb-sites, which children in their turn converted into playgrounds. I remember walking out from home one morning to find telephone-poles downed like skittles, their wires snaking across the pavement, threatening to trip unwary pedestrians. Shrapnel sometimes littered the streets, and harvesting the lumps of heavy, silver, pock-marked metal became a childhood hobby, especially among the boys.

Now and again, when in hiding at night, we might hear a plane being shot down, and could recognise its plummeting roar. I recall seeing one German victim, which had been recovered in big enough pieces, on display somewhere, and trying to picture the man who had sat in that cockpit, intending us such harm.

By now I was old enough to make my own way to school, and once I saw a group of men clustered around a large hole in Beverley Road. They were so preoccupied, I managed to squeeze past the barricades without being spotted, and continued uneventfully on my way to St. John's. Only later did Mother learn that the crater had contained an unexploded bomb, but when she told me of the risk I had run I do not think I registered the news with more than a giggle. Another time, we heard that a parachute-mine had caught in the branches of a tree outside our school, and that until it was defused lessons would be held at another school higher up Beverley Road. The crisis was quickly dealt with, and I think we were back in our own classroom within a day or two.

At school we had regular air raid drills, and sometimes the danger was real. A whistle would be blown, or a bell rung, and we would file out briskly to the long, earth-covered shelters, which present knowledge tells me looked like prehistoric barrows. We kicked our heels against the duck-boards in the ill-lit interiors, and sang mocking, defiant songs:

'Whistle while you work,
Hitler is a twerp,
He is barmy,
So's his army,
Whistle while you work.'

Then there was one about Mussolini:

'Oh, what a surprise for the Duce, the Duce,
He can't put it over the Greeks.
Oh, what a surprise for the Duce, the Duce.
He's had no spaghetti for weeks.
His troubadours advance with roars,
Oh viva, Oh viva.
In armoured cars they play guitars,
Wear frilly white skirts ... with black shirts.'

I liked the tune of:

'We're going to hang out the washing on the Siegfried Line,
Have you any dirty washing, Mother dear?
We're going to hang out the washing on the Siegfried Line
Now that washing day is here.
Whether the weather may be wet or fine,
We'll just stroll along without a care,
We're going to hang out the washing on the Siegfried Line
If the Siegfried Line's still there.'

Then Mother told me that the Siegfried Line had proved a disaster for our troops and it would be better if I didn't sing that song again, so I hummed it instead. After all, one had to be public-spirited, like the posters said, and do one's bit for the War Effort, and try not to spread despondency. 'Careless Talk Costs Lives', we were also reminded by ubiquitous billboards, and 'Dig For Victory' (only at the Station Inn we had nowhere to dig). But another order was easier to comply with: 'Coughs And Sneezes Spread Diseases. Trap The Germs By Using Your Handkerchief.'

***

DAY-TIME AIR RAIDS were an ever-present threat, and had us running for cover wherever we happened to be. Dorothy had taken me to Aunt Jinny's one Sunday when the siren suddenly set up its rising wail, and she was filled with a panicky conviction that my parents would want me back home. We set off at a tremendous lick to make the quarter-mile journey up Fountain Road and along Beverley Road. She, being older, was faster than I, and grabbed my arm and kept urging me on. We pelted into the Station Inn, breathless, triumphant and unscathed, for thankfully there had been no enemy action.

Some time later, I asked my father, 'Dad – what's a duck fit?'

'I don't know,' he replied. 'Why?'

'Because it's something Dorothy said you might have if she didn't get me home,' I told him – and wondered why he laughed.

In another incident, Mother, Dad and I were travelling on a trolley-bus intending that I should drop off at Aunt Nancy's stop and walk to her house while they carried on to town to deal with important business. The siren sounded, but I think by this time we were visiting from Doncaster, and the worst of the Blitz was over, so my parents decided to stick to their plan, and trust me to run quickly to Cromer Street.

I arrived at Auntie's as the family were leaving for their usual shelter under the railway bridge in Fitzroy Street. They always had ready the blue pushchair in which to bundle Annette, and my unathletic aunt could bustle along at an amazing rate. I knew most of the people in the Fitzroy shelter, for many of them were Auntie's neighbours, a strange and colourful group.

Any food or drinks that happened to be on the go when the alarm came were snatched up as people left the house. Dorothy still laughs about running with a full jug of cocoa, and finding when she got to the shelter that there was only a mouthful left at the bottom.

In October, 1940 I reached the age of seven, and I remember that birthday morning with special pleasure. It was a schoolday, but instead of meeting Dorothy at the end of Sculcoates Lane, I was told to go to Aunt Nancy's. There I was presented with a beautiful doll, bought for me by Auntie, and decked out by Margaret, a clever knitter, in a white frock, coat, knickers, hat and boots. I named my new doll Jeniffer, and loved her for many years.

***

JESSIE GOT ENGAGED to Arthur, and the wedding was fixed for New Year's Day, 1941. Jessie and Mother flung themselves into preparations. Although new clothes were less easy to obtain now we were at war, and clothing-coupons had been introduced in 1940, Jessie was able to buy a long bridal gown of white taffeta, with a 'stand-up' collar like Snow White's, and chevrons of silver tinsel on the bodice (very scratchy when I came to use it for dressing-up later).

Jessie made the bridesmaids' dresses. The older two wore gold satin, while the two smaller attendants, of whom I was one, were in dark blue satin, with collars of écru lace, 'Juliet caps' of gold mesh, gold sandals, and ruched satin muffs. Jessie wore a blue garter over one of her 'flesh-coloured' stockings, her veil was held in place by imitation camellias, and she carried a bouquet of pink-tinted white chrysanthemums. I was acquainted with these details well before the wedding, and enjoyed rolling them secretly off my tongue.

Much culinary activity had gone on beforehand, as the reception was to be held at the Station Inn in the big smoke-room. Extra food was hard to obtain, but somehow a tasty spread was assembled, possibly with help from Aunt Clara, who was struggling with allocating rations at her Stepney Lane grocery shop, and Uncle George, who was working for William Jackson's. Mother made one of her sherry trifles in her biggest glass bowl. An elderly aunt (not from 'our side') kept helping herself, and demolished practically all of it, to everyone's disgust. From then on, the lady was always referred to as 'Auntie Trifle'.

Jessie had seemed a bit nervous at the thought of my father giving her away, said Mother, but afterwards she disclosed that he had been very kind and reassuring as they rode in the bridal car to St. Mary's Church. He must have concealed the fact that he was suffering particularly bad stomach-pain that day, perhaps because he was nervous, too. The photographs show him looking quite lined and grim, which is a shame, because those two wedding groups are the only pictures I have of my parents and me together. I look peaky myself, because I had just got over German measles, and to my great chagrin, Mother made me wear a shawl until we got to church; yet I had been well enough to run to the bridegroom's home with Cousin Dorothy on the wedding morning on some urgent errand or other, the purpose of which now escapes me.

The only other things I remember about Jessie's wedding are that Arthur had a sticking-plaster on the back of his neck, and that at the party that night my mother was prevailed upon to sing 'The Bells of St. Mary's', which, considering the choice of church, was very appropriate.

***

READING AFTERWARDS ABOUT the Hull air raids, and trying to sort out my jumbled impressions, it is clear that their effects were far more serious than I gathered at the time.

The first alarm sounded in Hull the day after war broke out, September 4th, 1939, although it was a false one, and the first bombs fell on the city some months later. After one or two lighter raids between August, 1940 and February, 1941, during which nineteen people were killed, the serious bombing of Hull began in March, and here the statistics are mind-shattering. Marked out one spring night by the Luftwaffe as a primary target, the city endured an assault lasting from 8.40 p.m. to 4 a.m., during which it was blasted by 316 tonnes of high explosives and 77,016 incendiaries.

The raids continued intermittently, and in April a direct hit from a parachute-mine killed sixty people in a public shelter off Holderness Road. I have since read that on the first night of two of the heaviest attacks, May 7th–8th and May 8th–9th, 1941, seventy-two German bombers unleashed 110 tonnes of high explosives and 9,648 incendiaries, starting at least thirty major and over 100 smaller fires, most of the bombs falling on the city centre. On the second night, 120 aircraft dropped 167 tonnes of high explosives and 19,467 incendiaries. A total of 450 people died on those two nights, 350 were seriously injured, and several hundred slightly injured. More than 32,000 houses were destroyed or damaged, and more than 10,000 people were made homeless. Half the shops in the city centre, docks, factories and public buildings were left in ruins, Paragon Railway Station was put out of action, and the city's gas supply was cut off.

Hull's fiftieth air raid occurred on the night of June 2nd, 1941, but after a heavy raid in July the attacks became more sporadic, although alerts were still sounded fairly constantly. The last air assault of all took place in March 1945; by this time, the city had been subjected to a total of 824 alerts and eighty-two actual raids, in which 1,258 civilians had been killed. From a total of 92,660 houses, no fewer than 86,722 had been destroyed or damaged, and 152,000 people had been made homeless.

When my parents took the decision to leave the Station Inn in 1941, at first they had the idea of moving into the countryside near Hull, and my father went to look at one or two village pubs. I have a dim memory of being taken with him in a friend's car on an investigative tour. But in the end they decided that it would be more sensible to put an even greater distance between us and the air raids, and although Doncaster, where Uncle Jack, Aunt Elsie and my cousins Gordon and Dennis lived, was only about forty miles away, and a centre of industry, only one or two bombs had fallen there, and it seemed altogether a much safer place.

By this time, Aunt Gwen had left Uncle Fred. Aunt Clara took Brian under her wing, and sent him and Georgie to stay in Withernsea, also considered a less dangerous spot, although not far along the coast. She commuted there herself by train. Evacuation seemed the answer to many people, but Aunt Nancy said she would never part with her children again, and invited Grandad Nixon to stay. After Granma Carrie's death, he had lost his home in Inglemire Lane, and most of the furniture, when he got behind with the rent. He was living a rackety life in rooms, so Auntie took pity on him, thinking, too, that it would be some comfort to have him around, as she was nervous during the raids.

It must have been a blow to my aunt when Mother and Dad announced that they were moving miles away, and Mother felt badly about leaving her sister. But the die was cast, and a Mr and Mrs Ablett were eager to take over the Station Inn. Jessie, pregnant, although I did not know it, went to live with Arthur's parents while Arthur was away in the Army. Aunt Nancy said she would have Rap. I knew he would not be as contained in the Cromer Street household, and feared for him on the roads, crying bitterly at our parting; not without cause, because soon after we left he did get knocked down and killed.

The removal men came and chalked all our furniture with either H (for home) or S (for store). We took the H-marked pieces to the two rented rooms Aunt Elsie had found for us at 71 Zetland Road, Doncaster, and, for the eight months we were there, lived a quieter and very different life in the uncertainties of limbo-land.

POST SCRIPTUM.

Jessie, now aged eighty-six, came to my seventieth birthday party in Hull on October 30th, 2003. I had not seen her for more than thirty years, apart from one brief meeting at a family funeral, so it was wonderful to sit down to a meal with her, and talk about old times. Her memories were clear, and she was as brisk, alert and sensible as ever.

I had already sent her the chapters about the Station Inn to read, so now I asked if there was anything she thought was inaccurate. 'Yes,' she said immediately, 'that part where I fell down the cellar-steps on to your dad.' My father, she said, would have been upset by the suggestion that during an air raid he had entered the cellar before everyone else was already there. (The implication of this had never crossed my mind.) He was always the last one down. First he made sure no-one had been left behind, then he went round locking all the doors and windows. (She was so insistent about this that I felt chastened, for it brought home to me the responsibility of recording childhood memories.)

The truth was that, while Jessie did indeed fall down the cellar-steps on top of my father, cutting his face with her shoe, it happened not during a bombing alert, but while she was serving behind the bar. He had descended without giving her the usual warning that he was leaving the trap-door open, and she reversed into the hole as he was climbing back up.

Was my father difficult to know? No, she said, she always got on well with him. This was interesting, because my mother had conveyed the impression that Jessie had been rather nervous about Dad giving her away. A long-standing puzzle was also solved for me. I could not remember why Cousin Dorothy and I had been sent round to see Arthur at his parents' home on his wedding-day. Apparently there had been some doubt as to whether he would arrive in time for the ceremony (he was serving with the Army in Ireland). It must have been a huge relief when Dorothy and I returned with the news that we had found him stretched out on his mother's settee (far too relaxed for a bridegroom, in my opinion).

I reminded Jessie how she and Arthur had brought their new baby, Jimmy, to the Drum, thinking this must have been after my father died. No, said Jessie, my dad had been there, looking just as usual. This meant the visit must have taken place very soon after we moved to Bentley.

Trying to gauge the reliability of my memories through talking to Jessie was intriguing. No doubt if we had been able to spend longer in each other's company, she would have put me right about a few other things, but these were the main points she made. I add them as an indication.

CHAPTER NINE – CROMER STREET

THE FRONT DOOR at Number 1 Cromer Street, Aunt Nancy's rented home, had a personality of its own. It was wider than those in the rest of the street, an impression strengthened by the opaque glass panels on either side. There was a small oval plaque above the letter box that proclaimed 'No Hawkers, No Circulars'. From this snooty warning alone it was possible to deduce that the house, the only double-fronted one in the terrace, and the only one to have been built with a bathroom, had seen grander times.

Unless Aunt Nancy was out, or in bed, the door was never locked, but open to all who felt like popping in. Twist the knob, and it moved easily in a mere half-turn. Thus encouraged, the door would snatch itself out of the caller's hands and swing inwards with a 'whumph' and a rattle of its glass pane, as if of its own volition. As we sat in the living-room we would gather from these sounds that someone was arriving. A gust of air would rush down the hallway and penetrate the room, catching us coldly across the back of our necks. There would be a cry of 'Hello Mrs Sykes, it's only me,' and we children knew from the voice whether we were in for a long talking session (much dismayed face-pulling at the thought), or whether there was a chance of merciful brevity.

Life in Cromer Street was eventful and warmly spontaneous. Everyone knew everybody else's business, more or less, though in certain cases there were hints of a secret past that kept us pleasurably guessing.

One reason why Number 1 sometimes became like Piccadilly Circus was because Aunt Nancy was the unofficial collector for a 'club', whereby items were chosen from a catalogue and paid for at so much a week. The Cromer Street club members would leave their subscription-cards and cash instalments with my aunt to ease the task of the agent, Mrs Rudd, who called on Auntie every Friday, and used a corner of the living-room table, sometimes with a meal spread on it, to enter up her books.

Mrs Rudd was as smartly-dressed as befitted her position, and she wore striking spectacles and dangly earrings, and had a ready laugh. She had been coming for so many years she was almost one of the family, and she would be pressed to a cup of strong Rington's tea, and perhaps a slice of cake or pie purchased from Needley's exceptional bakery.

For a bit of fun, Auntie would sometimes 'read our fortunes' from the tea dregs in our cups. Any remaining liquid would be swirled around three times, then emptied carefully into our saucers. Among the leaves left stuck on the sides and bottom of the cups Auntie would pretend to see tall, dark strangers, and other surprises that were coming to us. Leaf-dust floating on the surface of full cups was a sign of money.

One of my aunt's oldest friends was Mrs Wood, a widow who lived around the corner. Her voice rarely rose above a soft mumble, and her fine-pored, creamy complexion always reminded me of the skin on ground-rice pudding. Tragedy had befallen her when one of her sons died after swimming in Barmston Drain. As far as I could grasp, the cause seemed a mystery, but I overheard my aunt say that before he died the lad had coughed up something that looked like a small frog or tadpole.

The most eccentric of all Auntie's acquaintances was Miss de Lacey (known to the irreverent Sykeses as 'Fanny de Flop'). She gave us many a laugh, despite her kind heart, for she was a true Mrs Malaprop, though she never realised it.

Complaining about the number of cats in the vicinity, she declared, 'It's just like a cats' colliery round here.' (She meant colony.) She had seen some poor invalid being conveyed in a 'spaniel carriage' (spinal carriage), and witnessed a speeding motorist almost knock over the 'pedestals' (pedestrians) on a crossing. She would refer to alcoves as 'alcohols', and if she got on her high horse would ask, 'What do they think I am – a non-de-plume?' (nonentity). It was hard to keep a straight face if she said of anyone that they 'looked like the wreck of the Hebrides', but perhaps her most hilarious gaffe was when she went to the chemist's and ordered 'tincture of mirth' (instead of myrrh).

Once, when she and Auntie were running for a bus, she cried, 'Hurry up, Mrs Sykes, the bus is commencing to go.' She used the same phrase on another occasion to describe a table-cloth with a hole in it. Cousin Margaret believed she had found the word 'commence' in knitting-patterns, and considered it more upper-class than 'start' or 'begin'. Her demeanour hinted (especially with a name like de Lacey) that her ancestry was more privileged than most, and although the term 'well-spoken' might seem inappropriate in her case, her intonation laid claim to a certain gentility.

The funniest thing about Miss de Lacey was that she used to correct my aunt and cousins about their English, and take pride in her own facility for it, which could be irritating. She recognised (though for the wrong reasons) that people found her conversation humorous, and enjoyed their reactions when she expressed her opinions. After one such confrontation with strangers, when she had set the room rocking, she reported to Auntie: 'They looked at me, and they simply howled.'

This surely had nothing to do with her appearance, for Miss de Lacey's lively, triangular face was not very unusual, her attire, which mainly consisted of good old tweeds, was conformist, and although her legs were like thin little sticks, and looked scarcely able to support even her bird-like body, she moved well on them, scurrying off for long walks with her beloved terrier, Bruce. Bless her, she was a faithful friend to all the family for many a year, although I am afraid we impatient children tended to view her as long-winded, and a fuss-pot. But later, when Margaret and Dorothy had their own children, they were grateful for Miss de Lacey's indefatigable energy as she took the toddlers off their hands, trudging for miles with the pushchair.

Next-door-but-one to Auntie lived Mr and Mrs Drummond. Their son Alan was in the Army, and their daughter Eva was in the A.T.S. (Auxiliary Territorial Service). Tiny Mrs Drummond had a foreign look; her face was yellow, and her soft frizz of hair surmounted it in a halo. She had a high voice, like the squeak of a mouse. I was fascinated, and thought her quite exotic. An air of gloom hung about Mrs Brandon, she of the rolling brown eyes. Auntie referred to her behind her back as 'Agony Wagon', because she was so fond of a good moan. Mrs Whitlock, another nearby resident, was Belgian. Her English was heavily accented, so she seemed a bit wild, and she brought us an intriguing whiff of a Europe we could never imagine visiting.

***

CROMER STREET WAS one of those terraces that were, and still are, typical of Hull, cul-de-sacs at the end of wider streets. Two short rows of bay-windowed houses with minuscule gardens faced each other across what was little more than a footpath. They were a cut above some of the other properties around (for example, the 'sham fours', presumably so called because they consisted of two rooms upstairs and two down). The Cromer Street homes had front doors set back in porches, and from each of their thin halls, known as 'passages', opened a separate 'front room' and 'living-room.' The kitchen, normally referred to as the 'scullery', protruded into the back yard, with coal-house and outside lavatory adjacent. Upstairs were three bedrooms, the smallest one, in some fortunate cases, converted to a bathroom.

Aunt Nancy's more imposing residence had reputedly been built for the landlord's mother. When Auntie and the family moved in after being bombed out of their previous home, the low garden walls had been topped by iron railings, and there was a pillared gate, but these appurtenances were soon cut down and carted off for the War Effort. Inside, however, Number 1 retained some of its distinguishing features. It had, for instance, delft- racks, and handsome black marble fireplaces in both main rooms, the kind that after the war we couldn't wait to get rid of, but which nowadays are much sought after and copied. There was an extra front window to light the stairs, which bent at right-angles instead of curving upwards like the rest of the staircases along the street. There was a large, bay-windowed kitchen with black and white floor tiles, a range for cooking and heating the water (not always lit, because there was also a gas oven), a deep sink, and a walk-in pantry.

But although these refinements told of a more impressive history, Number 1 still had to contend with the problems faced by the occupants of other, smaller, rented houses that had succumbed to harsh wartime conditions. Naturally, private landlords could not be expected to maintain properties when there was so much devastation going on, even had labour and materials been available, and Auntie had a constant struggle to keep her surroundings ship-shape, though she did her best, making a point of leathering her windows regularly, and donkey-stoning the front step, which, like the hall, took continuous punishment from tramping feet. (Her household tasks were carried out with much indrawn hissing of breath, especially when cleaning pans. She still lacked confidence when it came to pans, an inhibition possibly reaching back to childhood, and I remember her holding one out for inspection when washing-up at Bentley, and asking me, 'Is this pan clean enough for your mother?')

Damp was a nuisance at Number 1, and the sweet foist of it was perceptible in the room on the left of the hall, and in the kitchen. Worse, bombs had the habit of churning up foundations and sending cockroaches scudding to safer quarters, and these repellent insects had taken up residence behind the big range in Auntie's kitchen, resisting all attempts to dislodge them. Their presence was a blight that, whenever I slept at Number 1 in those days, turned my nocturnal excursions to the outside lavatory into a nightmare. In Auntie's own words, they were 'as big as chotches' (churches).

I would lie beside Annette in the double bed, willing myself to forget that I urgently needed to 'go'. Awareness of what lay ahead if I gave in to the demands of my bladder chavelled at my resolve, until, in the end, I knew I must summon my courage and face the beetles. Annette, if she were awake, would whisper with some relish of the ordeal before me, adding on a kinder note that the creatures were harmless. Then she would turn over and fall back to sleep; she was case-hardened, after all.

Case-hardened ... A subconscious choice of phrase, perhaps, because it was the hard, shiny cases, or shells, of the cockroaches (or black-clocks as we called them) that I found so impossible to come to terms with. Hammered half-heartedly with a shoe-heel, the horrid things would scutter off uninjured through the cracks in the skirting-boards. It took a determined person to smash such a shell and splatter its contents across the chequered floor, and the quietly-sobbing being inside me was not capable of delivering even a sketchy blow.

Down I would go and steel myself to switch on the kitchen light. This sudden burst of brightness would reveal dozens of dark shapes flitting across the tiles, and though I tried not to look, I dared not shut my eyes in case they ran over my feet. As they moved, they made a rustling noise.

Once the floor was clear, I would continue outside to the lavatory, taking care to leave the kitchen light on. Moisture rose up through the concrete lavatory floor, but its painted brick walls housed nothing worse than the occasional spider, and it was well-ventilated, due to the gap at the top of the door.

We conformed to working-class mythology by wiping our bottoms on newspaper, Auntie's sources being *The Daily Mirror*, *The Hull Daily Mail*, *The People*, and *Thompson's Weekly News*. The task of cutting them into squares, puncturing one corner, and slotting them together with string sometimes fell to Annette and me, and we regarded it as part of our War Effort.

There would be no sign of the black-clocks in the kitchen on my return, unless one or more had happened to climb into the sink. In such a case, I would shelve any plan to wash my hands there, especially if a pool of water had collected, setting their legs awave.

I was less squeamish about the fleas with which we were sometimes beset. People en masse were less clean than they are today, and it was quite easy for fleas to jump on you in school, on public transport, and in buildings like air raid shelters, and quite common to see folk walking around with red bites on their skin. We never had fleas at the Station Inn, and Aunt Nancy was convinced that some of those that ended up in Number 1 came from the chickens on a nearby allotment. They were a nuisance because their bites itched and made us scratch. But Annette and I, impressed by the trained performers we had seen at Hull Fair, caught some of ours, and raced them on the bedroom mantelpiece.

And then there was Lecky, a major foe in the eternal battle for cleanliness, yet so familiar, and so huge that we would often forget it was there. Lecky was the electricity power station that loomed close up behind the wall at the end of Cromer Street, its huge chimneys (known locally as the 'Five Woodbines') and cooling-towers producing a gassy smell all of their own, and shedding a fine, sooty drizzle over the neighbourhood. Eventually they were knocked down, and the sky opened up as a strange, empty back-cloth, but they were a worry while they remained as a target for enemy planes.

***

TO LOOK AT my mother and my aunt, you would never have taken them for sisters. Auntie was shorter and bonnily plump, with a smooth, round, pink face, Granma Carrie's retroussé nose, long, pale brown hair, which she wound up round a band, and a jaunty walk. Unlike Mother, who was a Liberal turned Conservative, Auntie was a Socialist, which is why she took *The Daily Mirror*. I used to enjoy reading it when I stayed with her, especially the Cassandra column, the Old Codgers' replies to readers' letters, and the strip-cartoons.

Both sisters were Monarchists, strongly patriotic, with a great admiration for the King (George VI) and Queen Elizabeth. They said if everybody did their job as well as the King and Queen did theirs, the country would be a lot better off. They were a bit critical, however, about the Queen's choice of clothes. ('She will have her frills and feathers.') Like most of the populace, they despised Edward VIII, who they felt had let the nation and Empire down, and they hadn't a good word to say for Mrs Simpson. Naturally, they viewed Churchill as a colossus, and were roused to jingoism by his speeches.

One of my earliest memories of Aunt Nancy is of watching her stir a spoonful of condensed milk (which she called 'conny-enny') into tea in a violet-patterned cup, as I sit on her knee with my mother opposite. Auntie's fingers continuously stroke back the hair behind my right ear as she talks. When she gets to a juicy bit of her story, which she regards as unsuitable for me to hear, she covers my ears, and whispers to Mother across the top of my head with much emphatic face-pulling. Preservation of innocence mattered to them, but I found censorship frustrating.

Mother and Auntie were sentimental, especially about children; in fact Mother used to embarrass me by shedding tears whenever she heard young voices singing. As the years wore on, Auntie was blessed with thirteen grandchildren, all living nearby, some even as close as next door, for Margaret had moved there after her marriage, so her five, though strung out in age, seemed to always be running in. Auntie would waste no time in taking the little ones on her knee, and kissing them, and crooning to them in baby language, and singing old songs. ('As Tommy was walking one fine summer's day-ay/ Some cherry-cheeked apples he saw on his way ...')

Family resemblances would be sought, found and argued over, particularly where the new-born were concerned. She claimed to have a particularly soft spot for the boys ('Give me lads any day') because she said they were more loving and less temperamental, and perhaps also because she sensed in them a specific vulnerability. But once all the children had reached a certain stage, that would be the end of the kissing, for sloppiness was frowned on among the grown inhabitants of Number 1.

Auntie was not a religious person as such, but she insisted on the Churching of new mothers. No-one who had had a baby was allowed into the house unless she had visited church first. Christenings, of course, were a 'must', for what kind of parent would deprive a child of such a prop, resource and insurance policy?

The naming of infants was a responsibility that constantly exercised the minds of the Sykes household, and preferences and hates were tossed around in conversation, leading to much pleasurable debate. Some names would be consigned mockingly to the roll-call of undesirables. 'Peter' was out after Margaret once heard a mother call to her son, 'Do you want to pee, Peter?' 'Philip' was hooted down because Auntie would immediately quip when she heard it, 'Philip my glass.'

Names that were reminders of disagreeable people were automatically black-listed, and trendy choices were an anathema. Occasionally one of us might bravely put forward a new suggestion for general consideration. ('What – you can't like that, it's horrible! Fancy saddling a kiddy with a name like that!')

Nicknames stuck forever, and comic phrases and verbal blunders would enter clan coinage, and be mentally filed for future reference. Years afterwards, they still popped up in family dialogue. Some small child, unable to pronounce my name, had once called me 'Jaye-at', and Auntie often addressed me thus, much as I disliked it.

It would do no harm to prick my posh little ego, of course, but in truth I was not singled out for special treatment, because all the family enjoyed poking fun at each other. As in any close group, personalities would sometimes clash, and tempers flare; but a tendency on the part of the protagonists to laugh at themselves as well as at others usually saved the day.

Anyone arriving at Number 1 who was acknowledged to be part of this privileged inner circle might be greeted by 'Hello, look what the wind's blown in' (or, in the case of true intimates, 'Look what the cat's dragged in.') While I was in a growth spurt, and so skinny that Auntie was afraid I would snap off at the waist, she would hail me with a cheerful 'Here she comes, that great long streak of bad luck.' Consequently, Margaret's husband, Norman, always called me 'Streak'.

Opening salutations were usually followed by, 'It's nice to see you – when are you going back?' If, on leaving, the visitor said, 'See you again soon', the fast answer would be, 'Is that a threat or a promise?'

Auntie and Mother shared the same expressions, some no doubt in fairly general use at the time. If you were foolish enough to ask 'How do I look?' they would assure you that 'A blind man on a galloping horse wouldn't notice you.' Any instance of wishful thinking would produce the wise saw, 'If ifs and ands were pots and pans there'd be no work for tinkers.' Protracted stories would be cut short by '... I see, as the blind man said to his deaf and dumb daughter as she waved her wooden leg in the air ...' Slack jaws and unstifled yawns merited the warning, 'Shut your mouth, there's a bus coming.'

Auntie used pithy phrases I never heard from my mother. She would liken an exceptionally ugly face to 'a diseased grid-iron', and a ruddy one to 'a well-slapped arse' (though when I was around she changed this to 'bottom'). If she felt a man was hen-pecked, she would declare his wife 'led him a life like a toad on a harrow.' My cousins also tell me that if any of them misbehaved when young, Auntie would threaten to 'twank your backside till your nose bleeds buttermilk.'

She was more superstitious than Mother, although she claimed to have fined down her list of bad-luck portents to only one or two. At one time we had to be careful of crossed knives, passing on the stairs, opening an umbrella in the house, putting new shoes on the table, and spilling salt. (Pinch it up in the fingers of the right hand and throw it over the left shoulder to counteract the ill-fortune. Spilled sugar, however, signified joy.)

It was vital to leave the house by the same door we had come in by, unless we had sat down first, and if we accidentally put on a garment inside-out, our luck would change if we changed it back. It was also tempting fate to say 'rat' instead of 'long-tail' and 'pig' instead of 'grunter', or wear opals unless they were your birth-stone. If an ornament or walking-stick fell over, it was a sign of death, and nobody would ever dream of sending a greetings card to Number 1 that had a bird on it.

My Mother's one big fear was of a bird flying in the house, for, as well as being terrified of the fluttering, she regarded this as an omen of death (something that had happened when my father died). But my aunt had a greater dread of pearls, even imitation ones, coming into her home. Her superstition about them sprang from her grief at losing her baby, Michael. At the time she had been looking after a pearl necklace for someone, and for ever after, to her pearls meant tears. None of her daughters ever wore them, and when her son Jack bought her a necklace of them, she put it in the coal-house.

***

WHILE MOTHER AND I were at Bentley, she and my aunt exchanged weekly letters. Both wrote unselfconsciously, just as they spoke (which is the best way) and Auntie's letter always arrived rolled up in a Hull weekly newspaper and the *Chicks' Own* comic for me. Her handwriting was not like Mother's, but had a flowing distinction of its own.

After one particularly bad air raid on Hull, there was quite a long gap when no news came from Auntie, and Mother grew very worried. Sending a telegram was out of the question, because if Auntie was in a fit state to receive it, she would fear it contained bad news. The only method of finding out if anything had happened was to go and see for ourselves.

The train ride from Doncaster to Hull Paragon took an hour and twenty minutes, after which we made the short trip on the sixty-three trolley to the end of Sculcoates Lane. Mother must have spent the journey anxiously picturing Cromer Street as a smoking ruin, whereas, despite my prayers for the family's safety, I could not stifle a secret sense of excitement at the prospect of high drama.

We rounded the corner to see the side wall of Number 1 rearing as solidly skywards as ever, still flying its contrasting band of yellow bricks. The roof was on, the door and windows were intact, there were no gaping holes, no rubble, no signs of damage anywhere. The house, along with all its neighbours, looked just the same as usual.

'Why, it's still there!' I gasped, and I must have sounded extremely disappointed. 'Of course it's still there – did you hope it wouldn't be?' said Mother crossly, giving me an angry little shake in her relief.

***

TO SAY SHE had led such an unhappy married life, Aunt Nancy was surprisingly unembittered about men, maybe because she had boys of her own. She was critical of the ability of the male sex to draw curtains properly, but she said that a man with a beautiful voice could wrap it around you like silk. (Sadly, there weren't many beautiful voices in Hull.)

Knowing her father as she did, Auntie must have had some idea of what she was letting herself in for when she invited him to share her home during the war. Grandad Nixon was still in thrall to the demon drink, and although at one time he had set himself up in a small white-smithy off Beverley Road, and moved first into one lodging, then another, his drinking always led to his getting behind with the rent, and being evicted.

Auntie was nervous of the air raids, and thought his presence would be a comfort, but above all she had a kind heart, and would not have seen the old man destitute. She might even have hoped he would mend his ways, and from his two small pensions contribute a little to the household needs. As it turned out, he became her Old Man of the Sea.

He was a fixture at Number 1 for years, until he died at the age of eighty-one in 1951, and my cousins grew up learning to cope with his drunken rages, when he would stagger in from the pub boiling with resentment, taunting them and flinging insults. Perhaps deep down he knew he had lost his way in life. But the troubles that had led him to his finishing point were largely of his own making, and the family's sympathies quite naturally lay with themselves. The bad old days were back, and he was a hard man to live with, especially as he was reluctant to bathe, or to change his under-clothes, forcing Auntie to sneak them off the end of his bed when he was asleep. His ablutions normally consisted of a light anointing of hands and face with what she called 'holy water', then a rub with a clean towel.

Grandad's drinking occurred on Friday nights, after he had drawn his money, and, if he happened to have any left, on Saturday nights as well. In addition to his pensions, he earned a small sum stoking the boiler at a Methodist Church on Beverley Road, and matters grew worse when he was asked to fire-watch there. The premises provided a convenient bolt-hole for sleeping off his excesses, and if he had wet himself he could dry his trousers on the boiler. On one occasion he left them too long on the hot metal, scorching them so badly they were unwearable. Luckily, he found someone willing to go to Auntie's and collect another pair so he could walk home.

An even more unedifying story that has come down to us concerns the time when Grandad, having wet himself after yet another alcoholic spree, put his underpants to wash in the boiler. The congregation used the water to make tea before the ploy was discovered, Christian charity found its limit, and he was fired.

There were quieter times, of course. By day, Grandad would set off for Pearson Park, where he met his cronies at the old men's shelter. Pearson Park was one of my loved childhood haunts, within walking distance of the Station Inn, and its name still triggers in my nostrils the cucumber scent of mown grass. In those days, park grass commonly bore 'Keep Off' signs, and was sometimes scalloped round the edges with metal hoops, or protected by posts and heavy chains, handy for swinging on. We knew the patrolling keeper was on constant alert for naughty children. ('Look out, Parky's coming!')

Nevertheless, it was the place for flexing our limbs, especially for the hundreds of us without gardens. Here we were allowed to run across certain open sections of grass, and play hide-and-seek down secret pathways. In the playground we could ride the bucking iron horse, dizzy ourselves on the roundabout, rise and dip on the swings, before crossing the bridge over the duck-pond to the island where Jack the caged jackdaw might, if we were lucky, engage us in stilted conversation.

But if we saw Grandad sitting by the shelter near the bowling-greens with the other old men, we would hide, or move quickly away. Old men did not figure amiably in our scheme of things, and we were far less anxious to speak to them, or to be singled out and identified by our unpredictable grandfather, than we were to chatter to Jack the Jackdaw.

Grandad was always circumspect when he knew Mother was coming to Hull, and she never saw him at his worst. If pleased with his dinner, he would push away his plate with the comment, 'I've enjoyed that, Nance', and move to his armchair by the fire. He might fall to reminiscing, recalling between pulls on his pipe some incident from his youth, faded blue eyes staring into the middle distance. Or he might try to interest me in some aspect of his pet subject, geography. But it was not an interest of mine, and in any case, though he had forfeited some respect from us all, I was in awe of him. I dared not ask him about the past, because I knew it was delicate ground, and there was usually so much bustle going on around us that my conversations with him flagged almost as soon as they had started.

On occasion, after a particularly bad example of his drunken conduct, Aunt Nancy would say it was time we had him to stay at Bentley. ('Wouldn't you like to have your Grandad for a few months?') I knew, or at least I hoped, that she was joking, for the idea of Grandad living on licensed premises, with alcohol on tap, was inconceivable; had he run true to form, Mother might have lost her job, and our home with it.

Besides, Grandad had no wish to budge. His wandering days were over, and he had settled into a comfortable groove at Cromer Street, doing pretty much as he wanted. He probably realised that my mother was not as tolerant as Aunt Nancy, and would have tried to make him behave. For her part, Mother was grateful to Auntie for shouldering all the burden of caring for their father, though she did put out a feeler by inviting Grandad to take a holiday with us. As I remember, he came only once, by train with my cousin Jack, who was by now discharged from the Liverpool hospital and also living at Number 1. I was afraid that poor Jack might have one of his epileptic fits, when he was liable to fall down and foam at the mouth. All went well, however, though they only stayed for the day.

When Grandad died and was laid out, Aunt Nancy learned something I found oddly haunting: the skin beneath his clothing was amazingly clean, white and baby-soft. It would have been dishonest for any of us to pretend regret at his passing, though we hoped his unquiet soul had at last found peace. After we buried him, whenever the sideboard door creaked open, as it sometimes did for no apparent reason, Auntie would turn to it and say sharply, 'Get back in, John Willie Nixon.'

***

CONSTANT CROSS-CURRENTS and undertows of arrivals, departures, contingencies, wise-cracks, laughter, jealousies, joys, rows, sarcasm, gossip, generosity, criticism, loyalty, banter, detachment, unity, grief, irony, disappointment, triumph, self-deprecation, pig-headedness, flippancy, fatalism, hurt and healing, pride and love ... on such a rich flood-tide of events and emotions, the Sykeses, like many large and volatile families, kept a remarkably even keel.

As the drama and comedy were played out, a rival contender in all the flux was Auntie's treasured wireless. It stood in a corner of the living-room, issuing over the dear old Home and Light programmes the encouraging noises we had come to expect from the BBC in wartime Britain.

With calm correctitude and perfect King's English, broadcasters like Freddie Grisewood, Alvar Liddell, Frank Phillips and Wynford Vaughan-Thomas charmed the air. Their voices were so reassuring, we felt we could not possibly lose the war. Vera Lynn would come on, singing 'The White Cliffs of Dover' or 'We'll Meet Again', and some evenings Tommy Handley (not my idea of a funny man) would discharge his repartee like pistol-shots.

Auntie had a marked taste for light classical music, especially as rendered by Max Jaffa, Josef Locke, Anne Ziegler and Webster Booth, Richard Tauber, and Sandy MacPherson, and if her favourite bit of opera, 'Softly Awakes My Heart' from 'Samson and Delilah', happened to be sung, she was transported. During the evenings, Number 1 was a bit less populous, and she could put up her feet and hear the concerts, though it was a rare night when there were no comings and goings.

They move at random in sharp relief across my mind's eye, those people who passed at one time or another through that warmly welcoming room. First my Cousin Bill, who had emerged from his war service with his nervous tensions at first well concealed, though they were to overtake him later. He married his childhood sweetheart, Ann, and they lived with her parents a few streets away. Bill used to cycle home from his work at City Engraving, and almost daily made the short detour to call on his mother, often at dinner-time (midday). ' How's tricks, Toots?', he would ask her, stealing a carrot from the pan, and savouring the steam from the meat. Then, after briefly satisfying himself that all was well, it would be leg over frame, and off he would pedal. Not for nothing had he been dubbed by one of his young nieces 'Billy Bikes'.

When Ann was expecting her second child, she asked Aunt Nancy if she could give birth at Number 1, so the front room became a maternity ward. Tragically, the baby was rushed to hospital with an intestinal blockage, and did not survive. Although I felt sorry, and listened sympathetically to Auntie's descriptions of what a beautiful baby he had been, the full import of his loss did not really strike me until years later, with my own first pregnancy. Afterwards, Bill and Ann, who already had a daughter, had another son.

If she knew I was coming to Hull in later years, Auntie would make either steak pie or roast beef and Yorkshire puddings. Servings were brought ready-plated from the kitchen, piled lavishly high, and small appetites were frowned on, although she knew I was faddy, and ribbed me about it. Even so, before the landlord finally got around to creating an indoor lavatory where the pantry once had been, she would ensure that the outside one was de-spidered and (if it needed it, and I brought a boyfriend) given a fresh coat of paint. As for the cockroaches, they had long since been defeated.

Bill would roll in to see me. ('Hello, Cousin.') If, later, I had my children with me, he would, in his casual way, produce a half-crown for each of them. Yet it seemed no time at all since, looking just the same, he used to greet me as a schoolgirl, and demand to know whether I had had the cane yet, or got myself a paper-round.

Cousin Jack, after years of being institutionalised, struggled in his slow, trembling, painstaking way to lead a normal life, and even got himself a girl-friend (another worry for Auntie). But his epileptic fits worsened, and in the end my aunt reluctantly bowed to medical opinion and let him go into hospital in Hull. Her horror was unbounded when she discovered he had been given electric-shock treatment, and she blamed this for the pitiable state she found him in. He died soon afterwards, but the memory of his last days continued to haunt her.

Two of Auntie's lodgers were charming Irish brothers from a big family, Paddy and Tommy Mohan. Number 1 quickly became their home-from-home, and Auntie a mother figure. The months they spent in Cromer Street were times of merriment, and their status as very nearly family members was endorsed when Auntie brought them to stay at the Big Drum. She said they must have had a wonderful mother, because they always showed such politeness, respect and gratitude. Everyone missed them when their work in Hull ended and they had to leave town.

By being who they were, Paddy and Tommy diluted the strong prejudice against Roman Catholics which Grandad Nixon had instilled in his daughters. To Mother and Auntie, the Catholics were a group who paid far too much attention to the Virgin Mary, and who, once they had made their confession, felt free to sin again. Mind you, they felt compelled to agree that 'a good Catholic was a good person'.

Grandad, a self-acknowledged 'Lincolnshire yellow-belly', had also passed on something of his distrust of Welshmen and Norfolkmen, and Mother believed that as a race the Welsh were two-faced. She prided herself on being a good judge of character, and was wary of people with eyes set close together, or ears with no lobes.

**

WHEN MARGARET, DOROTHY and Annette married, all three chose to have their wedding receptions at home, so the house's rarely-used spare front room proved useful.

Margaret married Norman when I was twelve, moved into Number 3 next door, and had three babies quite quickly, followed by two more ten years or so later. Dorothy and Walt had started their own family of four girls by the time I was working, and the infants added a new and anxious dimension to my Hull visits. Later Annette married, and she and her husband, Terry, had two sons.

Like my father, I had always been nervous of babies. It was not that I didn't want children myself, I did. But I never knew how to hold them, and had to be shown how to support their spines and heads, or, if they turned red in the face and started to yell (which they nearly always did when they were given to me), how to shoulder them to get up their wind, and be ready to dodge an up-rush of curdled milk. I never knew what to say to them, and perhaps my fumblings made them feel insecure, or maybe they smelt my adrenalin. Their own smells were not always pleasant, either. Nevertheless, it was expected that I should nurse the latest addition, and admire it. A clean nappy or apron would be spread on my knee, and one or two family members would sit by to give advice, and gauge reactions. 'Who do you think he's/she's like, then?' 'Oh look, he's/she's smiling for Auntie Janet.'

The distaff side at Number 1 were up to their eyebrows in baby-lore. They all knew about bottle-mixing, feeding solids, how to interpret the contents of nappies, and how many blankets to put in the pram on a cold day. All shared a disapproval of dummies, which were unhygienic, distorted mouth and teeth, and took some giving up in later life. They were undismayed by orificial discharges, hiccups, screams, rashes, sore bottoms, or the sharp drawing up of knees, which I was told signified wind. Because looking after babies came to them as second nature, it followed that they found my awkwardness and reluctance entertaining.

I recall arriving in a new, blue hopsack suit, being given a baby to hold, and assuring myself, as usual, that it was wearing waterproof knickers, only to sense shortly afterwards that liquid was penetrating my skirt and warming my thighs. I relinquished my charge in disgust, and dashed to the kitchen, where my spongings were the source of quiet amusement. I had always been given to the vapours, and here I was, over-dramatising again.

As babies, the newcomers were unknown quantities, but as personalities I grew to like them. Margaret's eldest daughter, Argie, came to stay at the Drum for the first time with Annette when she was only two, and together we mothered her. Madeleine, the second child, not to be left out, started to visit us at an early age too, and every summer for quite a few years one or other of them would spend a fortnight's holiday with us. Argie called my mother 'Auntie Granma', an apt title that stuck.

Aunt Nancy's last lodger was Bob Jackson, a divorced father of a grown family. Bob was a carpenter who worked for Hull Corporation. He made himself useful, not only around the house, but in dealing with Grandad and Jack as well. He was dogmatic and a bit masterful, but wonderful with children, and bolstered my aunt enormously, and eventually they married. My mother liked Bob, though I know that initially she feared for her sister's hard-won independence; but he was a strong support to Auntie, and to Mum once she moved back to Hull, helping her in many practical ways.

It was only to be expected that his elevation from lodger (when he was inevitably caught up in family affairs) to husband and step-father would lead to some problems and dissensions, but I can speak of Uncle Bob only as I found him, and I remember him with affection. He was a man generous with his time and efforts for others, and he delighted in producing special treasures, such as books or bits of old brass, for the recipients he had been bearing in mind as he rooted through the Corporation tip.

Auntie thrived under his hovering care, sure of a husband's steady income for the first time in her life. They took regular holidays, she sporting a range of new 'rig-outs', and explored London together, something she had always longed to do. He championed her in all matters, seemed to know as much about the Swift and Nixon families as we did ourselves, and went to great pains to make visits to Number 1 as welcoming as they had ever been for Mother and me.

My mother died nine months before our elder child, Thea, was born, and knowing I had years of accumulated experience in pregnancy and child-rearing to draw on at Cromer Street, I was grateful. When she was three months old, my husband Malcolm and I took her to stay at Auntie's on the anniversary of Mother's death, and Margaret and Dorothy, her Godmothers, came to supervise the bath before the fire. I was still something of a greenhorn, and they were unsurprised that my procedures took about an hour.

Auntie and Uncle Bob became substitute grandparents to her and our son, and there was soon a rapport between Uncle Bob and Patrick, who burgeoned under the Cromer Street brand of teasing. They would arrive at our home in Harrogate laden with gifts, and Auntie would take the children on her lap and sing to them all the old family songs, seeking in Thea a resemblance to her dead sister that was not really there.

Once, Uncle George and Aunt Clara came to stay at the same time, and so the children were exposed to a particularly intensive round of fuss and spoiling from people of my parents' generation who had known and loved them. Although the children were already blessed with loving paternal grandparents, this was important to me.

Patrick relishes a memory of Uncle Bob and Uncle George, who were in their seventies, and gravely out of condition, puffing together across a playing-field, both grasping the string of a kite, which trailed on the ground behind them, refusing to fly. Following with an equally determined burst of speed came the two aunts, yelling encouragement. I don't think, for all their efforts, they managed to raise the kite more than a foot or two, but they had a lot of fun trying.

CHAPTER TEN – MOTHER TONGUE

MY MOTHER'S OLD treadle sewing-machine stood on the wide, sunlit landing at the Station Inn, and to the accompaniment of its busy needle I learned a new language. Mother made most of my clothes and hers, and although I was never any good at sewing, I was fascinated by the vocabulary.

Mother bought many of her materials at Andrews' on Beverley Road, and sometimes she took me with her to choose the gingham or print (printed cotton) for my 'washing-frocks', which could be had, if memory serves me correctly, for as little as 'one-and-eleven a yard' (one shilling and eleven old pennies, equivalent nowadays to less than ten pence a metre). Indeed, many commodities seemed to sell at 'something-and-eleven', just as ninety-nine pence today sounds considerably more of a bargain price than a pound does.

I liked having new clothes, but was irked by the preliminaries, and submitted to the fittings with ill grace. Mother, deeply concentrating, manoeuvred me like a jointed doll, and insisted on several try-ons as the roughly-tacked garment took shape. Finally, I would grow bored, and droop. 'Straighten up and put your shoulders back. Frame, girl, frame', she would order, turning me round and round to check the hem. But if she was pleased with me, I might be her 'owd two o'rum and a crusher'. (I think this dated from a notice in the Haworth Arms advertising hot toddies, each consisting of two-pennyworth of rum and a sugar-lump, complete with crusher.)

My new dress would usually have *puffed* sleeves, a *gathered* waist and a '*Peter Pan*' collar, and it might also have a *yoke*, or a *smocked* or *pin-tucked* bodice, which could also be *darted*. If mother were tailoring me a coat, it could have either *raglan* or *set-in* sleeves, would probably have *revers* with *facings*, and any matching hat would be stiffened with a *petersham* band. If making a skirt for herself, some *goring* might be called for, unless it had pleats, which might be *inverted*, *unpressed* or *box*. Alternatively, it could be '*cut on the cross*'. It would be sure to have a *placket*, unlike an *edge-to-edge* coat, which did not even have buttons. Jackets might be '*frogged*', and equipped with *slit* or *patch* pockets, perhaps finished with *bias*-binding. Little girls' party dresses sometimes had matching drawstring *Dorothy* bags and *Alice* hair-bands.

Basting was another term Mother used, but I was never quite sure what this meant. Any item fashioned from material liable to fray might require *French* or *whipped* seams. *Jimping* was another option, although this was unnecessary on a *selvage* edge. One had to be careful to cut certain textiles *with the weave*, and coat linings were very often 'shot'.

The colours then in vogue had a language of their own. The stylish combination of dusky pink and nigger brown carried no hint of political incorrectness. Marina green (named after Princess Marina of Greece, who had married the Duke of Kent) was close on the spectrum to ice or duck-egg blue, and rust and burnt orange were other popular shades.

Clashing colours were a sign of appalling taste, and the family were fond of repeating to each other the reassuring comment someone had once made to my great-aunt: 'You all too-an (tone), Jinny.' No outfit was properly complete without hat and gloves, and during the war old hats could be revived by steaming them into a new shape on a basin, and giving them fresh trimmings.

***

GRANMER GREENWOOD HAD an old-fashioned way of talking, and some of her words were strange to me. She called a vest a 'singlet', and would say 'sneck the door.' She referred to currants as 'kerrens', and to the lavatory as 'the double-yew' (short for W.C.). If she told us she would do something 'presently', that meant it would not be done immediately, but if she announced her intention to do something 'directly', that was much more promising. And she had a wonderful word to describe a miserably grey day, or a feeling of melancholy: 'dowly'.

Granmer taught me, simply by having me by her, how to knit, make beds, set and 'side' (clear) a table, and sew. We would sit together, darning Dad's socks: that is to say, she darned, while I drew the sides of the holes together with big stitches that resulted in their becoming 'all cottered up'. Once I stitched the tops up by mistake, and long afterwards she would grow weak with laughter at the memory of Dad trying to get his feet inside.

It was Granmer who presented me with my first riddle, and she did the actions, with Mother repeating them in the background:

'Four stiff standers,
Four dilly-danders,
Two lookers,
Two crookers,
And a wig-wag.
What is it?'

Answer: A cow.
Then there were the posers, 'Why did the chicken cross the road?' and 'Why

does a stork always stand on one leg?' The answers ('To get to the other side', and 'Because if it lifted the other one up, it would fall over') left me puzzled; but I was very young.

Mother had her own favourite jokes, and two of them contained donkeys. The first concerned a poor farmer who had just got his beast down to eating one oat a day when it unfortunately died. The second was about another farmer who, on being told he could not take his donkey on the train, tied it to the back of the guard's-van. As the train gathered speed, the farmer remarked to his fellow passengers, 'Neddy'll be legging it now.'

I could not see the funny side of these, and indeed felt more like crying. But one of her jokes I always laughed at. It was a verse supposedly carved on a gravestone:

'Beneath this pile of rugged stones,
There lies the body of poor old Jones.
His name was Brown, it wasn't Jones,
But Jones was put to rhyme with stones.'

She used the phrase 'Hunch up, icicle' if she was trying to find room for herself near someone, and this sprang from another joke, about a tramp who broke into a mortuary, thinking it was a hostel. In the dark, he made out a figure on what he took to be a bed, pulled back the sheet and climbed in. But the person felt so cold, and there was so little space, that the tramp pleaded, 'Hunch up, icicle.'

Mother looked impish when she told the joke about the little girl who was given a bell and a bottle of scent for Christmas, and shyly said to a visitor, 'If you hear anything and smell anything, it's me.'

**

GRANMA CARRIE ALWAYS called people she was fond of 'honey' or 'oney', and if asked what was for dinner, she would say 'Chums and buttered 'aycocks'. (Although a 'chum' can be a dog-salmon, Granma's meaning is no clearer, even if one assumes she was referring to 'haycocks'.) I regard it as a far cleverer reply than the customary 'Run round the table and kick the cat', and it sounds much more appetising than Jessie's usual response to me, which was 'Sausages and tapioca pudding' (my two pet hates). Aunt Nancy used to tell inquirers to expect 'Pigeon's milk and nanny goat's liver', or else 'Stewed niffnaffs.'

Mother had a long catalogue of amusing sayings, some in general use at the time among the Northern working-classes, others more idiosyncratic. I think she must have got the quainter ones from her own mother, because Aunt Nancy knew a lot of them, too. As I grew older, especially in my teens, I grew irritated by these expressions, and would sigh, and shrug them off. Now, recalling as many as I can, I find the list impressive.

Critical (but said with great good humour):

'The sun's burning your eyes out' (to a lie-abed).

'You've the cheek of the miller's 'oss (horse), that ate its own corn and then the miller's.'

'Pussy had another sardine' (of someone helping themself to more).

'She's caught her voice on a nail' (of a squawky singer).

'She sounds as though she's got her head fast (ditto).'

'She should be a good singer, she's got legs like a lark.'

'If she was hung for beauty, she'd die innocent.'

'It's a face only a mother could love.'

'Looks like you've lost your appetite and found a donkey's.'

'It smells like broken glass' (of cheap perfume).

'A brave soldier never looks behind' (of a hastily-cleaned pair of shoes).

Certain folk were 'only as big as two penn'orth o' copper', 'squinted like a basket of pups', or 'smoked like Sheffield.' A fussy body was 'Fanny Fernackerpan', and weak tea was 'blashy'. If imperiously asked to perform a favour, Mother's reply would be 'Oh, yes, twice nightly.' Sniffles would be greeted with 'Blow your nose and slide home', and a child's stubbornness challenged with ' No to me, and your father in work'ouse?'

Describing someone who had been unusually ingratiating, Mother would say they were 'all smiles and backair'. Years after her death, it dawned on me that she meant 'back hair', and this was her version of 'bowing and scraping'. If she liked someone's open countenance, she would say they had 'a face you could borrow money off', and if she were admiring a person's new clothes, she would comment, 'Fit and style guaranteed'. She enjoyed quoting a description she had once read of a baby's bottom: 'Two eggs in a silk handkerchief'.

After a large meal, if she felt mischievous, she played to the gallery by puffing out her cheeks and saying 'Please wheel me from the table', or 'I can still chew if I can't swallow' (though not, of course, in polite company). When asked where we were going as we set off for a walk, she was likely to answer 'There and back to see how far it is', and, when asked her age, or indeed any measurement, her reply might be 'As much again as half'. Making a faux-pas she called 'letting a fox pass', and if she felt unwell she was 'a bit wowwy'. A bad pain or a difficult person could be 'mustard', which was also one of my father's words. People who got angry 'raised Cain', 'played the deuce' or 'played Hamlet'. Anything sticky, like mud, was 'clarty', and if Mother, to use her own mother's phrase, got 'conflustrigated' (flustered), she announced that she didn't know whether she was 'on this earth, or Fuller's'. Child-like, I often wanted to know when a certain event was going to happen, but I could never make out what she meant by 'When Nelson gets his eye back.'

Some of mother's maxims had a philosophical twist:

'Large as life and twice as natural.'

'I might as well as wish I had.'

'I would if I could, but I can't, so I won't.'

'The darkest hour comes before the dawn.'

'It's looking black over our Bill's mother's.'

'It's a long road that has no turning.'

'Constant dripping wears away a stone' (if I kept asking for something).

'Good night, sweep repose, half the bed and all the clothes.'

'Man proposes, God disposes.'

'A cat may look at a king.'

I have never known anyone except my mother use the phrase 'as black as the Devil's nutting-bag'. For years I thought she said 'knitting-bag', and tried to imagine the Devil knitting. She employed comparatives with relish, and I recall:

'As lazy as Ludlum's dog' (that leaned its head against the wall to bark).

'As long as Dick's hatband' (that went nine times round and still wouldn't tie).

'As slow as wood.'

'As sweet as a little nut.'

'As miserable as sin.'

'As light as love' (especially said of dumplings).

'As right as ninepence.'

'As mischievous as a barrow-load of monkeys.'

'As fussy as a dog with two tails.'

'As happy as Larry.'

Of all her sayings, I have my favourite. She used it apologetically when dishing up a scratch meal. It has a Biblical origin and it goes: 'Better a dinner of herbs where love is, than a stalled ox and hatred therewith.'

CHAPTER ELEVEN – INTERLUDE

I LOOK BACK on the time we spent at Zetland Road, Doncaster, as an interlude in the normal business of living. One of the dictionary definitions of 'interlude' is 'any period of time or any happening different in character from what comes before or after', and those eight months certainly were that.

Aunt Elsie, Uncle Jack's wife, had inquired around the area where they lived in Doncaster and found us two rooms in the semi-detached home of Mrs Warne, whose husband was away. Mrs Warne had a daughter, Maureen, a little younger than me, and she occupied the box-room, so my single bed went into my parents' double room. It must have been hard for Mum and Dad, suddenly squeezed with a minimum of possessions into such a straitened space, and having to share kitchen and bathroom. It must have been difficult for Mrs Warne, too, but we got on surprisingly well, although Mother was peeved when sometimes Mrs Warne took the cream off both bottles of milk for Maureen's cereal. Still, for the sake of peace she made no claim on my entitlement.

Afterwards, Mother said that Dad, although he was very worried about the outflow of money with no business to back it, seemed determined to be a bit more relaxed about spending. Our great weekly treat was a Friday night visit to the Gaumont Cinema in town. There would be two big pictures, and, on Fridays, 'Con Docherty at the Organ', for this was Community Night, and when the instrument rose out of the floor like a huge rainbow blancmange, there was the maestro already at the keyboard, inciting us with a flourish of chords to a session of hearty singing.

Up on screen the words would flash with a dancing ping-pong ball as a pointer, so we had no excuse for attacking them with anything but gusto. We threw off our inhibitions for nonsensical songs that I can no longer spell, but which sounded like 'Hutson Rawson on the rillera and de brawla brawla suet', and 'Mersey doats and dozey doats and little lamsitivy'. We grew a bit tearful during poignant renditions of 'When they sound the last all-clear', which became my father's favourite:

'When they sound the last all-clear,
How happy my darling will be,
When they turn on the lights, and the dark lonely nights
Are only a memory,
Never more we'll be apart,
Always together, sweetheart,

For the peace bells will ring, and the whole world will sing
When they sound the last all-clear.'

How I looked forward to those Friday nights! Mum and Dad would meet me outside Intake Junior School, and we would catch the bus to the cinema. There, sitting between them in the warm, velvet darkness, I would eat the jam sandwiches and drink from the little screw-top bottle of milk which he had for me in his raincoat pocket. Such homely treats became synonymous with musical extravaganzas like 'Moon Over Miami', starring Betty Grable.

Once the film was Orson Welles' 'Citizen Kane', of which my parents had heard a great deal. But they could not understand it, and the 'Rosebud' ending foxed them completely. Now ranked as a masterpiece, even claimed to be the best film ever made, it was decidedly too far ahead of its time for them. I myself did not expect to follow the plot, and found the whole thing bleak and troubling. But mostly we slipped easily inside Hollywood's latest Technicolor dream. I needed those Friday nights, though for a while the happiness they brought me was tinged with a dread of the morrow.

When I started my new school I had been given a health check, and it was found my teeth needed attention, for in Hull such niceties had been interrupted by the bombing. So every Saturday morning Mother took me to the school clinic in Wood Street, a forbidding Victorian building. We would climb the echoing stone staircase, I moaning at the thought of the brutal grip and grind of the dentist's extraction tools, and the spongy, blood-filled wells they would leave in my gums. It was a routine that seemed to go on for weeks, so my relief once the treatment came to an end could best be described as ecstatic. From now on, every Friday I could give myself over to Con and Betty with no white-coated torturer hovering in the wings.

My teeth could and should be fixed, but Mother was upset about the school nurse's verdict on my legs. When, during my check-up, I was asked to stand up straight, I did my usual trick of pressing my knees back as far as I could.

This must have given a bowed effect, because the nurse said, 'Look, she's bandy-legged.'

'She is NOT', said my mother indignantly, but it did little to bolster my morale.

I was already a glasses-wearer, and Intake Juniors was a school where 'Specky Four-Eyes' was a popular term among the pupils for people like me. Another burden I arrived with from Hull was my accent. Along the North-East coast, until one gets up as far as the attractive sing-song of Tees and Tyne, vowels have a peculiar flatness. I do not remember my father's voice, only his words; my mother's never seemed particularly 'Hull' to me until its inflections were magnified by the telephone, although in speaking fast she might miss off some aitches. I, however, seemed to have brought undesirable tendencies with me. My teacher, Miss Tune, was not unkind, but she was anxious to set me straight, and corrected me in front of the class. 'It's not boook, Janet, it's buck. It's not coook, Janet, it's cuck.' I bent my head in shame.

At St. John's I had already begun trying to master copper-plate script, but my new form-mates were just learning to join up basic letters. One might have thought I would have found myself at an advantage, but not so, for I still had terrible trouble, especially with looping my f's, and I always seemed to make a lot of smears and blots. At the start of handwriting lessons, everyone in class would rush over to the box where the wooden-handled pens were kept, hoping to grab one with a decent nib. More often than not, the nibs were crossed, and very wayward. I can see one of my efforts before me now, disfigured with the usual splutterings:

'Good, better, best,
Never let it rest
Till your good is better,
And your better best.'

I made a few kind friends, some of whose names and faces I remember gratefully. Ruth Park learned ballet, and when the time came for the girls in the class to put on a show and dress as fairies, she mesmerised the rest of us by appearing in a real tutu with a big red satin heart on the bodice. Suddenly, the turquoise frock Mother had made for my seventh birthday party, of which I had been so proud, seemed entirely inappropriate for the affair in hand. Even the act of waggling my wand (a tinsel bow pinned to a painted stick) had completely lost its charm. We stood around Ruth admiringly, and hoped some of her stardust might rub off on us as, without any seeming desire to impress, she quietly criss-crossed the straps of her ballet-shoes. But I never told Mother how I had felt, because I knew she might be hurt.

Maybe it was a desire to emulate Ruth that prompted another girl in the class to invite me to the air raid shelter in her garden, which she assured me was equipped with a stage and lots of beautiful dressing-up clothes. I could hardly wait to get there after hearing her describe everything, but alas, the stage turned out to be just a table, and there were no costumes at all. I hid my disappointment well, I thought, but I was puzzled as to why the girl had told such a story when she must have known she would be found out. It has only just struck me as I write of it that maybe she, on her part, was disappointed with me for being so hopeless at make-believe.

A few of us walked to school together past a sweet shop where they made their own ice lollipops, frozen fruit juice on sticks. These would be waiting for us at peak times, lined up in a tray on the counter. They cost a penny each, and one day, when the shop was crowded and I was in a hurry, I put my penny down on the counter, took a lollipop and started to leave. I was called back by the angry owner, who was only partially mollified by my explanation. In future, she told me, I must hand her the money and she would serve me.

I have never forgotten this lesson, nor the tide of hot blood that rose to stain my face. The worst part was wondering whether my parents would be told. They were not, but I dared not go back for any more lollipops.

**

HAPPY EVENTS ... SAD events ... painful events ... those months we three spent marking time in Zetland Road have an air of unreality now, as though we had exchanged our lives for those of other people. But these strange new lives bestowed on us a boon even greater than escaping the air raids, for we had much more time to spend together.

Instead of having to go on duty behind the bar, Mother and Dad would both be there in the evenings, on either side of the fire, keeping me and each other company. Dad and I played endless games of Ludo and Snakes and Ladders, and usually he let me win, because otherwise I cried and protested so much. At tea-time the embers would be stirred to redness in the grate and the wire toasting-fork brought into action. He and I spread margarine on our toast before the jam, because the taste of it did not worry us as it did Mother, and we let her have our butter rations.

Some days Mother combed Doncaster Market for material, or treadled away on her sewing-machine. Dad walked. The neighbourhood was different from the one he had been used to in Hull, for here were smart suburban houses, some detached, with trees, hedges, lawns and flower-gardens. The most popular colour scheme for paintwork was green and cream, like ours at Number 71, but a few were red and cream, or grained.

At weekends he would sometimes take me with him along the footpath across Town Moor to Elmfield Park, or round to the Cattle Market, where I had my first glimpse of animal husbandry. One abiding memory is of a bull with a ring through his nose, which I thought immensely cruel, for his nostrils were oozing blood. The

Pet Market was equally distressing, with boxes of puppies, and kittens, and chicks, and ducklings for sale, along with caged birds and rabbits. Who could tell what sort of people would buy them? Maureen kept a lonely rabbit in a hutch in the back garden, which was really just a stretch of worn grass. The creature smelled terribly, and seemed to fulfil no purpose at all in being there.

My father was desperate to secure the tenancy of another public house, and spent many hours contacting breweries, visiting likely premises across a wide area, and generally keeping his ear to the ground. He would call into locals like the Lonsdale at the bottom of Zetland Road, or the Wheatley Hotel further up Thorne Road, for a glass of bitter. I imagine him comparing notes with the landlord, and seeking news of any pubs that might be coming vacant.

Sometimes Mother would make a trip back to Hull alone, sometimes we would all go. We used to stay with Aunt Clara, Uncle George and Cousin Georgie at their rented semi-detached in Anlaby Park Road, and it was a squeeze, because Uncle Fred, his son, Brian, and Granmer Greenwood were all living there, too. I slept between Mother and Dad in a double bed, and after he died I shared the same bed with Mother and Auntie, who used to whisper loudly to each other as they gulped their morning tea. Auntie's teeth were in a mug beside her, so her whispers were hard to interpret.

While Auntie and Uncle were at work in their different grocery shops, and Uncle Fred was at the Fire Station, Granmer was in charge of the house. Auntie had a woman in for the heavy work, so all Granmer had to do was a bit of cooking and dusting. She was quite frail by this time, and when we got boisterous she found us children something of a handful. To calm us down, she played dominoes and did jigsaws with us.

Mother, Dad and I spent Christmas 1941, at Zetland Road. I remember walking with my parents along Sandringham Road towards the house in Bruce Crescent where Uncle Jack, Aunt Elsie and my cousins Gordon and Dennis lived. We were on our way to tea, and I remember feeling very excited, for I always approached my rascally boy cousins with the expectations of a hero-worshipper, and Christmas Night in their company promised to be even merrier than usual. We gathered round as Aunt Elsie sat at the piano, and called out our favourite tunes. Auntie herself was particularly keen on 'The Barcarole' from 'Tales of Hoffman', but I think it was that Christmas she was prevailed upon to give us a new song, 'I Don't Want To Set The World On Fire'. Uncle Jack's party-piece was 'Hello Susie Green'. Gordon, three years older than I, liked 'I've Got Sixpence', because when we reached the line, 'No pretty little maids to deceive me', he changed it to 'No naughty little girls', and gave me a maddening grin.

***

DURING OUR STAY in Zetland Road, we heard from Hull that Uncle George had been called up at the age of forty. He had the delicate Greenwood digestion, so everyone was amazed that he had been found fit enough to join the Army. However, not long after being drafted for training, he collapsed whilst drilling on the parade -ground and was rushed to hospital at Sheffield with a perforated ulcer. This was the same condition that was to kill my Father just over a year later, but Uncle was luckier, and came through the operation, even though his life had at first been despaired of.

He was in hospital for some time, and Aunt Clara used to visit him at weekends, travelling to Doncaster by train from Hull on a Friday evening after she had closed the Stepney Lane grocery shop. She spent two nights in Doncaster, made train trips to Sheffield on Saturday and Sunday, and was back in Hull ready to open her shop on Monday morning. At first she stayed for the weekend with Aunt Elsie and Uncle Jack, then, when that arrangement had to change, she would come to us in Zetland Road. She slept with Mother, and Dad used the settee downstairs. He must have found this very uncomfortable, because its arms and back were as hard as nails, and it was only a two-seater.

Another time, Granmer Greenwood came to see us at Zetland Road. I don't know how long she intended to stay, but the decision was taken out of her hands when, one night while Dad was outside filling the coal-bucket, she fell and broke her ankle. I saw it happen, and remember him rushing into the room when he heard her cries. The ankle had to be put in plaster, and she was unable to walk on it for a considerable time, so my single bed was brought down from upstairs and placed in the bay window, and Granmer slept on that.

It was unfortunate that while all this was happening, another crisis developed. True, the new one was less serious, but it carried a terrible stigma. The nurse came to school to examine us all, passed a pencil through my hair, and declared I had head-lice. Even though everyone knew they could be caught from other people, lice in those days were associated with dirty families, and the nit-nurse's bombshell made Mother desperately ashamed.

She and I were sent home immediately, and advised to call at a chemist's on the way to buy some Derbac Soap (which would kill the lice) and a 'scurf-comb' to dislodge both them and the nits, or eggs, which clung stubbornly along the hairs close to the roots. From then on, it seemed that Mother was continually holding my head down in bowls of hot water, lathering it with the evil-smelling soap, and running the fine comb across my scalp until she drew blood. After some days, she was satisfied that no lice were clambering among the hairs, and the eggs seemed to have disappeared, too, so she took me back to school. The nurse examined me, said, 'Sorry, she can't come back yet, I can still see one or two nits', and home again we had to go for more scalp-raking. Mother was so upset and mortified, she cried as she stood over me that night. This sort of thing had never happened to us in Hull.

One day, Granmer, sitting up in the single bed in the bay window, and scratching and scratching her head, asked Mother to pass the scurf-comb. Oh no, surely not – not Granmer too! But when she spread a newspaper on the coverlet and started to comb, small black insect bodies pattered on to it out of her long white hair, audible even when mingled with Granmer's cries of incredulity, and Mother's horrified spate of apologies.

Eventually, the lice and nits succumbed. Mother and Dad escaped the infestation, and I still wonder how, especially as I had been sleeping between them. I went reluctantly back to school; Granmer's ankle healed, and she went home to Hull.

While I was banished from school for being nitty, I received through the post a necklace of delicate blue and pink crystals from my old teacher at St. John's, Miss Clayton. I cannot remember what she said in the accompanying letter, and I still do not know why she sent the necklace to me, but I still treasure it. Dear St. John's! Where we had sat quietly together singing 'Jesus bids us shine with a clear, pure light, Like a little candle burning in the night' as we watched teacher tidy up the classroom. At Intake, we learned a hymn I found frightening:

'Matthew, Mark and Luke and John,
Bless the bed that I lie on,
Four angels round my bed,
Two to bottom, two to head,
Two to hear me when I pray,
Two to bear my soul away.'

A strange dirge to teach children, I think. It brought back the fear of dying in my sleep which had troubled me after Grampa Greenwood's death. But perhaps if I had settled more happily at the school, I would not have been so worried.

So it was with no reservations and a great deal of excitement that I welcomed the move to Bentley, especially after Mother and Dad had described the Big Drum, for it sounded like the Land of Heart's Delight. I was not disappointed in what I found there; and although my father died less than a month after our arrival, and there were many problems to be faced, Mother and I grew accustomed to our place in the Drum's scheme of things, and looked on it as home.

Chapter Twelve – The Big Drum

IN MY MIND'S confusion about our first weeks at the Big Drum after Dad died, one impression is clear and comforting: Mother and I were not alone.

We were in a place humming with liveliness, constantly surrounded by people. While it must have been hard for Mother to go behind the bar and face the customers, their sympathy helped to carry her through. The staff had their set routine, which made it possible for her to spend time in Hull for the funeral, and to see our solicitors, Gale and Easton, who had offices in the city's famous Land of Green Ginger; and while the brewery's dealings with her were brisk, we were not turned out as she had feared. In addition, we had visits from the family to bolster us.

I remember Aunt Nancy coming to stay, bringing Annette, and taking us both to the Don Cinema, three trackless stops up Bentley Road. Once again, the 'pictures' came into their own as a solace in time of trouble, even though we walked there and back, which did not suit Annette and me, and sat in the cheapest seats on the very front row, craning our necks to see the screen. The film was about a group of pith-helmeted Americans lost in a jungle full of wild creatures, and when a huge snake slid towards the heroine down a tree-trunk it actually seemed to be slithering down on us.

Two wonderful new people came into our lives around this time. Mother was sitting in the office behind the lounge bar very soon after Dad's death when there was a knock on the door and a stranger stood there, a woman of about Mother's own age, who introduced herself as Laura Dunn. She knew how my mother felt, she said, because she had lost two husbands herself. At first Mother was taken aback by such forthrightness, but Mrs Dunn was undeterred. In the many years we grew to appreciate her sterling qualities, we were often chagrined or amused by her straight speaking (as, for instance, when she asked 'How long is it since you dusted those chair-legs, Dorrie?'). But never was there a more loyal friend.

Mother had arranged for me to be taken to St. Peter's Church Sunday School, across the railway bridge, by a customer's daughter, and there I had met a girl in a white frock with big red buttons down the front who was very friendly, and smiled a lot. By a stroke of good fortune she lived in one of the houses opposite the Drum, and, perhaps because she knew my father had died, she rang our side doorbell and asked if I would like to play.

Her name was Brenda Newland, and she was nearly three years older than I, but about the same size. Eagerly I invited her in, little realising then what a marvellous ally she would prove to be, for her cheerful companionship was just what I needed to help me through the difficult months after my father's death. Based on such a firm foundation, it is hardly surprising that our friendship has lasted for sixty-five years, even though we have seen less of each other since our youth due to the changing patterns of our lives.

***

THE DRUM, POSH name the Bentley Hotel, had an intriguing cross-section of customers. The tap-room, home to thudding darts and clicking dominoes, drew in miners from Bentley Colliery, with their deep thirsts, and blue-scarred hands and faces where the coal-dust had lodged beneath the skin. They were a jovial crowd, who bared their chests and were known to wear their wives' bloomers for the sweaty toil below ground. In this sense, they were literally the salt of the earth, although once substantial sick benefits came in, some of them spun out their ailments in order to wheedle notes from the doctor for extended time off. Mother used to get silently indignant when she overheard them admitting to such ruses, but theirs was such a dreadful and dangerous job it is hard to condemn them too roundly.

They had their own terminology: they carried their sandwiches to work in 'snap tins', wore 'Davy lamps' on the front of their helmets, liked 'spice' (sweets) to suck, and if they felt chilly, they were 'nesh'. They called daft folk 'fond' and bad-tempered ones 'mardy'. Another phrase I learned around this time was even odder: if I asked the whereabouts of anything, it could often be located 'at back o' Brough's on bacon side'.

Of course, the miners did not stick exclusively to the tap-room, but used the lounge more in the evenings, sometimes with their wives. Certain customers had tacit claims on sections of the bar, and 'Doctors' Corner' was one of these areas. A few of the local doctors congregated there, always standing, never sitting (there being no bar stools). They were often joined by Mac, a Scottish dentist, who could not help but regard Georgina's two front teeth with a professional eye when she smiled as she handed over the drinks. The teeth had come through brown and ridged at the ends, and Mac offered to cap them for her, an improvement which, in due course, he effected to general acclaim.

A foot or two beyond the doctors stood the butchers, mingling on the fringe. Butchers, because they had such responsible decisions to make during wartime meat rationing, were very important people whom we all treated with respect. To my embarrassment, two of the teachers at my school were also among Mother's customers, and I knew at times my progress was discussed. Businessmen, too, dropped in, and on Monday evenings members of a Home Guard battalion based at the Drum would relax in the billiards-room, which contained two full-sized tables.

The Home Guard did their drilling in the garden, and at some stage cadets joined them, lads who provided Cousin Dorothy with vast entertainment during her visits. She and I would watch from the upstairs kitchen window as they practised their grenade-throwing on the rough stretch of grass beneath us. A high wooden bar had been suspended between a couple of poles, which stuck up like rugby posts, and the would-be soldiers took turns to run towards it carrying a dummy grenade. As they ran, they pulled out the pin, hurled the 'grenade' over the bar (if they were lucky) and flattened themselves on the ground. More than once during these manoeuvres Dorothy flung up the sash and yelled, 'England's last hope!'. The poor lads must have been mortified, although some of the bolder ones rewarded her with cheeky grins.

That window was regularly thrown open so we could empty out the teapot dregs, and a sizeable pile of old tea leaves gradually built up beneath it, beside the grate where frogs and toads lurked. However, Mother drew the line at the disposal of other rubbish by this means, apart from shaking the table-cloth. The window was also useful for mushroom-spotting, and often their white blobs were discernible in the tall grass, inviting a trek outdoors to pick them.

One of our living-room windows was above the side door, and we raised the sash when the bell went so we could lean out and see who was ringing it. If it was someone we knew, we would drop the key and they let themself in. There were two reasons why I had no need to look out to know that Brenda was the caller: I could hear her doing a little tap-dance on the concrete as she waited, and Paddy would let out a strangled growl that sounded like 'B-w-e-n-w-a-h', eyes glinting green with jealousy. Brenda used to laugh at him, which only made him angrier.

One of the reasons I think Brenda danced was to take her mind off the caterpillars. At a certain time of the year, hundreds of green and yellow-striped, furry caterpillars crawled from nearby allotments and climbed the green-glazed walls of the Drum, lodging themselves in the mortar between the cracks like a Plague of Egypt, and spinning their cocoons. Perhaps it was a miracle of nature, and they had been aiming for what they thought was a giant cabbage, but Brenda and I found them repulsive, especially as they sometimes dropped on us as we waited to be let in at the side door.

Mind you, if she had a few minutes to spare Brenda would break into a dance routine for no particular reason. Tap-dancing was her passion, and she yearned to have lessons, but they cost sixpence a time at Zena Morris's dancing school in Bentley, and her mother wondered how on earth she could be expected to find sixpence for something so unnecessary. So Brenda used to stand outside the Catholic School Hall and stare in through the window as 'The Bentleyites' went through their paces, trying to memorise their actions, which she intended to pass on to me. At first Miss Morris tolerated the eager face pressed against the glass, but in the end she told Brenda to go away. Only temporarily dashed, Brenda persuaded one of her friends in the troupe to keep her-up-to-date with the latest steps.

Our living-room had four windows, two at each end, and from the inner pair we looked down over a roofed area open to the sky, for, to let as much illumination as possible into this vast building, the Drum had been designed with a central well to accommodate extra windows above ground-floor level. Cousin Dorothy recalls being in the living-room with my father, who was resting in his armchair in the throes of his last illness. He was worried, apparently, about my Greenwood cousins, Gordon and Dennis, who were also visiting us. They had shown their dare-devil streak by climbing out of one of the inner windows and dropping down inside the well in an effort to catch pigeons, alarming my father with their cheerful disregard of danger, for the grey, leaded roof looked suspiciously thin, and he was afraid they might fall through it. I don't know how they managed to climb back up, but they never worried about such matters. (Cousin Dorothy, mistress of irony, referred to them behind their backs as 'The Little Darlings'.)

Another challenge to the boys' spirit of adventure were the attics, which Mother had told us not to enter because there were no lights up there and she feared the floorboards were unsafe. How could we resist such a lure? I secretly pictured skeletons falling out of cobwebby cupboards, chests holding coded documents, secret panels, ghosts walking. Gordon and Dennis probably had less lurid reasons for wanting to explore, but were still very keen. Mouthing a weak warning that Mother wouldn't like it, I followed them up the stairs.

Those floorboards certainly creaked alarmingly, even though the Drum had been built only thirty years before, a fact we were unaware of. To us, everything seemed incredibly old and spooky. First a long corridor, from which opened several large rooms with bare sash windows. Cobwebs there were aplenty, and cupboards, too, along the far walls, with drawers beneath. The paintwork, doubtless original, was a faded bluey-green, the distempered walls were peeling, and dust lay everywhere. There were no carpets, no furniture, no chests, no phantoms that we could sense, and no secret panels, apart from a food-lift. But when we opened one of the cupboards, a strange sight met our eyes. The shelves were stuffed with empty medicine-bottles and cardboard pill-boxes. How they came to be there, or who had placed them there, was an enigma we never solved.

From time to time a group of us would secretly return to the attics, perhaps when Brian and Georgie came to stay in the summer holidays; and although the urgency to explore had evaporated, it still seemed deliciously daring to ascend with our torches in the dark, especially if the wind was moaning around the chimney-pots and rattling the panes.

If Annette went up with us, her fear was real, for she was a nervous child, and would widen her blue eyes dramatically and cling to me at the slightest sound. She believed in ghosts, which I did not, and her suspicions about the Drum were confirmed one night when she and I were both in our bed with the door ajar, permitting the landing-light to shed a band of brightness on the dark wall.

Suddenly she clutched my arm and pointed. Silhouetted against the strip of brightness, we could see a woman's head with a long, curving nose and sharp chin, and what appeared to be an arm stretched across the door-frame. The head remained motionless, although I think we called out to it; but by the time we had turned to each other and back again, Annette squawking with fear, it had disappeared.

I said that Mother, or Aunt Nancy, or Georgina, or someone must have peeped in to make sure we were all right, and that the shadow cast by the landing-light must have played a trick on us. But the silhouette's witch-like profile was too convincing for Annette; and although I got up and peered out on the empty landing, and scoffed at any idea of ghosts and witches, I could suggest no object that might have cast such a shadow, and she took some settling down. We could not blame Brian and Georgie, for they were not staying at the Drum at the time, and when we asked the grown-ups next morning whether they had looked in on us, and nobody had, she became even more certain that something supernatural had occurred.

While I did not believe in such things, I was still a bit apprehensive about going to the lavatory at the end of the landing in the dark. There was a stretch of narrow corridor before we reached the door, and the lavatory itself had been overlooked when electric lights were installed. We managed by fumbling, or took a torch, or left the door partly open. Then someone tried the tap on the gas-jet in the lavatory and discovered that it still worked, so during the winter a tiny, bare flame was kept burning to stop the cistern freezing.

It was quite a long walk along the landing and down the corridor, and once inside the lavatory, the flickering flame cast eerie shadows on the cream and brown-painted walls. When the toilet was flushed the water rushed out with unnatural loudness, and this was the nervous person's cue to run. Annette, Brenda and I developed the knack of opening the door, pulling the chain and bolting down the passage almost in one movement. Then came further unbearable delay while we paused to wrench open the heavy, self-closing landing door. I might not believe in witches, but it was a witch whose clutches I planned to evade as I fled back to the welcome glow of the living-room. My companions appeared to feel as I did; but it would have taken far weaker imaginations than ours to ignore the menace implicit in those night-time excursions.

The bathroom, situated at the opposite corner of the landing, was forbidding in a different way, not ghostly, just large, cold and gloomy. Apart from the landing, which had two radiators linked to the cellar boiler, the bathroom was the only part of our quarters meant to be centrally-heated, having been intended for guests when the building was an hotel. But now its radiator refused to work, the big, frosted-glass window leaked draughts, and the marble floor and dado struck icy even in summer, for the window overlooked the sunless inner well.

We had little trouble with the wash-basin, which received both hot and cold water through an inflow shaped like a shell. But cold water trickled so feebly into the claw-footed bath that we had to leave the tap turned on for about ten minutes before running in any hot. There was a lavatory, but we tried not to use it, as no water reached the cistern. Under such spartan conditions, teeth might sometimes chatter as we observed our rituals. Until, years later, John Smith's sent workmen to unblock the water-pipes, resuscitate the radiator and paint the dark green walls peach, we shivered our way phlegmatically through our ablutions; for while the bathroom's peculiarities made it a bit like conducting personal hygiene in a mortuary, it truly was a great place for singing.

Another of the Drum's odd features was the food-lift, a small cupboard which could be let up and down a shaft by means of a rope. Access to the lift was gained by a series of hatches from attic to cellar, one opening on to our living-room, with the end of the rope anchored to the wall there. My cousins and I had fun unwinding the rope and dispatching secret messages to each other. Mother was afraid we might try to climb into the lift ourselves, and warned us that it was not designed to carry anything but food, and that the rope was probably rotten. If it snapped whilst one of us was inside, and we were pitched down the shaft, we could be killed or terribly injured. She made us promise not to try anything so foolish, so as a compromise Gordon proposed putting Paddy in and lowering him down. Whether this actually happened, or whether it was just an idea, I cannot remember, but, either way, Mother was not amused. Afterwards the lift was used occasionally for hauling coal and coke-hods up from the cellar, but only if there was a strong man around.

***

APART FROM THE coal-fired range in our living-room, which was black-leaded every Friday morning, there was a gas-ring balanced on a tin tray on a stool in the kitchen. This was the only alternative means of cooking, or boiling the kettle. Mother concocted meals with the most basic equipment, all her measurements being done with a spoon, or by guesswork. She used a table-spoon to whip her Yorkshire-pudding batter, mashed potatoes with a fork, and minced cold meat for her delicious sage rissoles with a sharp knife. (Raw minced beef was never bought.) She possessed no whisk, no sieve, no scales, no chip-pan. Her chips were thick slices of potato cooked in a thin layer of dripping in the frying-pan, and normally eaten only with fried fish.

When the laundry-woman left soon after we moved to the Drum, Mother deserted the garden wash-house and accommodated her big, free-standing mangle, galvanised dolly-tub, copper posher and ridged glass scrubbing board up in the kitchen. She and Georgina shared the weekly wash-day, and if I was at home I occasionally tried thwacking the long-handled posher down on the clothes in the tub. A deal of strength was needed to make water spurt out through its holes.

The sink was used for rinsing, blueing and starching, and then everything was put through the mangle before being piled into the heavy wicker basket and borne down through the pub to the clothes-line in the garden. Once I grew strong enough to carry the basket, I would often be greeted when I returned home from school with a request to get the washing in. Sometimes I did it willingly, sometimes under duress. It seemed a long, long trail down the stairs, through the bar, along the corridor that led to the outside lavatories, then down the flight of steps into the garden, and back again.

Mangling was another of my chores when Mother was satisfied I was unlikely to trap my fingers in the thick wooden rollers. Once the dry table-cloths, bedding and two dozen red-bordered glass-cloths had been folded into oblongs, they had to be put through the mangle a second time before being ironed.

Ironing was a marathon conducted on one end of the long kitchen table, which we padded with old sheets. Mother had kept her flat-iron for emergencies. I remember seeing her heat it on the gas-ring before testing its temperature, first on a bit of old cloth, then by holding it near her cheek, but mostly she employed it as a weight for pressing ox-tongue. I never used a flat-iron, because normally we had the electric one in action, plugged into the ceiling light-fitting the same as the vacuum cleaner had to be, for the Drum had no wall-sockets.

On Sundays it became my task to prepare the vegetables for dinner, make the mint sauce (which had to be very finely chopped) if it was lamb, and set the table. In season I had to go and beard old Jack Grain on his allotment, and ask what he might have for sale, an expedition I dreaded, for he spoke in monosyllabic grunts, and I did not know what to make of him (nor he of me, I suppose). If he proffered runner or kidney beans, I was resigned to long, painstaking chopping, for Mother liked them sliced paper-thin with an old fruit-knife.

At about half-past one she would dash up from the bar to check the roast and put the Yorkshire puddings in. She would have mixed them earlier with powdered egg, and left the batter to stand, and it was vital I keep my eye on it, for Pussy Willow, our cat, who adored egg, had been known to jump on the table and take swigs at intervals, leaving tell-tale rings inside the basin.

As I grew older, I whiled away the time until dinner by reading the papers. John Smith's generously footed a weekly newspaper bill which included deliveries of *The Daily Express, Yorkshire Evening Post, Doncaster Gazette*, and magazines like *Everybody's, John Bull, Woman's Own* and *Picture Post*, with *The People* and *News of the World* on Sundays. This last carried dense columns of court reports about divorces and sexual misdemeanours, and, though couched in less explicit language than today's, made matters plain enough. As well as having my eyes thus opened, I also learned the whereabouts of most English towns, for they nearly all featured in the scandal- sheets at one time or another, complete with county.

***

IT REALLY WAS amazing that Doncaster, on the main road and rail network, ringed by coal mines, and home to a major railway engine plant, brass-foundry, rope-works, tractor and nylon manufacturing centres and other industries, escaped German air raids. Apart from one or two bombs, possibly rogue ones released by Luftwaffe planes as they made their way home after onslaughts on Sheffield, the town and district remained unscathed. Before we moved into the Drum, one of these bombs had landed between Royston and West End Avenues on the opposite side of Watch House Lane, wiping out some houses and the post office, which reopened in Bentley Road.

Brenda and her parents and brother, Colin, used to flee to the small brick air raid shelter in their back yard when the sirens went, and there they would sit by the light of a candle with gas-masks at the ready. She remembers hearing a loud bang and glass breaking on the night the bomb fell, and later going to see the devastation and learning that a boy from her class, who had lived in one of the houses, had been killed.

Although we were never afterwards subjected to air raids at Bentley, the sirens would wail at night sometimes, and Georgina, Mother and I would rouse ourselves and go downstairs. There seemed safety and comfort in numbers, so Georgina began to sleep in the single bed in the same bedroom as Mother and I.

I have no idea where the nearest public air raid shelter was, for we never attempted to leave the Drum, but stood trembling in the open doorway in our pyjamas and overcoats, and peering up at the night sky as enemy aircraft sometimes passed overhead. Mother hoped that because the pub was so large, it might look like a hospital from above, inclining the Germans to be merciful and not bomb us. But this period of anxiety did not last long, I think. My father had been right to bring us there.

Chapter Thirteen – Brenda

MONDAY WAS MOTHER'S hardest day. It was the time when she drew all the threads of the preceding week together, made a call at the Westminster Bank in Doncaster with the weekend takings, and reported to John Smith's district office in Wood Street.

After breakfast, she would spread out her papers on the long living-room table, and begin her book-keeping 'in triplicate'. The big accounts book showed my father's calculations for the first two or three weeks after our arrival; then Mother's hand replaced his. The takings were recorded by two ornate brass tills, one in each bar. When their keys were pressed, price labels shot up behind their glass windows and their drawers sprang open. Push the drawers to close them, and they snapped shut so viciously it was easy to trap one's fingertips and raise blood-blisters under the nails.

Readings were taken from both tills every night, and balancing the cash-in-hand against these figures, after staff had been paid and other outgoings subtracted, was a nerve-wracking business on Mondays, especially as Mother was expected to make good any loss from her wages. Now and again a worker might prove dishonest, and money or cigarettes go missing, but mostly the staff were, in Mother's words, 'as straight as a die'. Even so, figures did not always tally, and many a time I watched helplessly as she went over her sums again and again, head in hand and close to tears. She was quick at arithmetic, but had to teach herself book-keeping because Dad had never shown her how.

Counting money was something I had learned at the Station Inn with him, and occasionally Brenda and I would be set to work by Mother sorting silver half-crowns, florins, shillings, sixpences and tiny threepenny-bits into fawn paper bags, ready to be weighed at the bank, and copper pennies, ha'pennies, farthings and larger threepenny-bits into blue ones. Most coins were heavier in those days, and Mother used to be weighted down when she caught the trackless for her journey to the bank on Saturdays and Mondays.

She herself smoothed and counted the pound and ten-shilling notes. Now and again there was a big white fiver from an unusually wealthy customer, and we would all examine it with interest before she folded it to fit in the wallet with the rest of the notes, admiring its fine paper, and the elegant restraint of its black copperplate script.

The delivery wagon would come from the brewery at Tadcaster on Monday mornings, laden with wooden hogsheads and barrels; crates of bottled beer, lemonade and cordials; cartons of cigarettes; and a small selection of spirits, port and sherry, if available. The driver and his mate, both well-muscled chaps in strong boots and aprons, would fling open the outside trap-door leading to the cellar, and haul any empty barrels up the concrete ramp before letting down full ones containing three different sorts of beer then in vogue: mild, dark and bitter.

The barrels were rolled on to gantries, ready to be 'tapped' and connected to copper pipes which reached the bar pumps through the cellar ceiling. It was a skilled task, keeping the beer at the correct temperature; hammering hard, soft or 'sparkler' wooden pegs into holes in the barrels to condition their contents; 'chocking up' barrels with wedges as they emptied, to keep the beer flowing; flushing out the pipes once a week with hot water laced with soda-crystals, then rinsing them thoroughly to ensure no soda lingered. These rituals were our cellarman's job, too physically hard for a woman, but Mother was well acquainted with the mysteries involved. Wartime shortages meant that beer sometimes ran out, and the Drum had to close for a few days, spreading despondency amongst the regulars, who were never slow to voice their grumbles.

Once a month, also on a Monday, the stock-taker came. His name was Mr Smith, and he was tall and gentlemanly, and struck Mother as being far cleverer than the post demanded. She would have a fire lighted in our downstairs sitting-room for him, and lay out the books on our oak dining-table. It was always a relief when he pronounced that all was well.

At lunch-time she would set off for town, dreading her visit to John Smith's in case the District Manager wanted to see her. He was a rubicund, white-haired figure, a bit like Father Christmas in appearance, but Mother found him terse and unsympathetic. She had the feeling she was at the Drum under sufferance, and needed to justify herself because she was a woman, when I think all the other managers were men. Consequently, if the office staff told her Mr. Hubbard wanted a word with her, her heart sank.

His criticisms were usually about not keeping costs down. I suppose it was his role to rein back any perceived extravagance, but Mother considered she ran the Drum sensibly, and his suspicions depressed her. During one carpeting, she was incensed when 'Santa' complained about her electricity bill, and asked, 'Do you read in bed?'

'Believe me, Mr. Hubbard, I'm too tired to read when I get to bed', she replied with some heat, and was still boiling with indignation when she came home later that evening from her weekly trip to the cinema with Mrs Dunn.

Afterwards, the funny side of the interview struck her, and she took to laughing at it. But from then on, she privately referred to her bête-noire as 'Owd buggerlugs'.

Now, as I recall the incident, I can't help wondering whether his question had merely been meant as a joke.

***

AS A WIDOW, Mother found herself the target of unwanted attentions from men. She was still a shapely, dark-haired woman in her mid-forties, brisk and smart and intelligent, and some of the male customers seemed to think their overtures would be welcome. They soon learned differently, though, for she would stand no nonsense. Rude language or undue familiarity were received coldly, or with a sharp reprimand if she felt matters were getting too serious to be laughed off.

When we lived in Hull, a certain man had become a friend of both my parents. On the first occasion I met him, I confused him with another customer I'd heard mention of, and asked him, 'Are you Mr Chesterfield?' He was tickled by this, and replied, 'Yes, if you want me to be'; so from then on, although it was not his real name, I called him Mr Chesterfield.

He always made a fuss of me. He had a son and daughter of his own, but was separated from his wife, and did not see his children, I think. He was a failed businessman, public-school educated, well-read and cultured, with a charming voice and manners, and he regarded my mother with an open admiration which led to her being teased a little, even by Dad, I think, in his own dry way.

Learning that Mother lacked one of life's great staples, *Pears Cyclopaedia*, Mr Chesterfield bought her a copy. It became an oft-thumbed reference book in our household, and I grew to consult it on many fronts, including how to employ the right form of address for people of differing social strata, write and respond to invitations, check on worrying bodily symptoms, recognise national flags, and care for pets. The volume, inscribed on its battered front cover 'Dorothy Greenwood', with the initials 'JC' below, still stands among my books.

After Dad died, a number of people came to stay at the Drum to support Mother, bringing their rations or ration-books, as one did during the war. Because we had six bedrooms, there was space enough, though I recall the tedious business of airing mattresses and bedding by the landing radiators. I am not sure how it came about, but Mr Chesterfield was one of our visitors for a short time. I have the feeling that he just turned up, and was allowed to remain, as he had nowhere else to sleep, though I do remember Mother had reservations about his being there.

His brief stay was brought to an end after Aunt Nancy, also one of the house-party, became flustered at encountering him in his pyjamas. I cannot say whether he was wearing a dressing-gown, too, although his gentlemanly background would make this seem likely. If I am not mistaken, he took her early morning tea to bed, and she was quite put out by it. Both she and Mother had already begun to look obliquely at the many signs of his attentiveness, which they found embarrassing, and although I was not taken into their confidence, I heard them agree that he was too 'tutti-frutti' (fussed around them too much), and seemed too ready to make himself at home.

Perhaps she scented danger, perhaps he revealed his feelings, or perhaps it was simply that his courtliness was too much to take. Whatever the reason, Mother prevailed upon Mr Chesterfield to leave. But if she thought that was the end of the matter she was wrong, for the poor man was besotted, and would not be dismissed from her life so easily.

It was whilst Mr Chesterfield was still with us that we discovered Cusworth. Someone local must have suggested it as a fine place for a Sunday afternoon walk, and so, after closing time, we followed directions and strolled to the end of Watch House Lane, crossed over the Great North Road, and wended our way up Cusworth Lane. At first the lane was disappointing, because there were houses on both sides, but then it gave way to open countryside. Soon we were dipping down to the left towards a field, and there, in the golden haze of a perfect summer's day, we spread out our food. It is a memory that has stayed with me as potent as first love, for that is what Cusworth came to be to me, a geographic love affair.

'Let's go into the country' was a phrase we town-dwellers, young and old, used in those days to express a peculiar longing that seized us now and then. We would experience an ache around the heart that could only be soothed by the elemental balm of farms, fields, bluebell-woods, playful streams and reedy rivers, violets in hedgerows, birds never seen or heard in city streets, roses splayed against cottage walls, vast houses set in parkland, the musk of hay, even the doubtful effluvia of pigs and cows. Tiny Cusworth, with its ancient, grey-walled, narrow streets and picturesque hall, fulfilled most of these requirements, set as it was in one of the prettiest corners of that disregarded territory which has since come to consider itself South Yorkshire.

The preserves of my enchanted land were invaded, the spell almost broken, when during my absence upstart houses sprang into being. Though this appals the dreamer in me, other folk have different dreams, of new homes in pleasant places, and Cusworth is not the only English village to have suffered fringe development. In its old streets, too, existing cottages have been improved, and indeed made very attractive. But the bones of Cusworth are intact, and still dear to me, and some old mysteries are secrets no longer, for the hall has become a museum.

***

IT MIGHT HAVE been on the day of the picnic, certainly it was while Mother and Mr. Chesterfield were still on friendly terms, that he broached the subject of Alice. *Alice's Adventures In Wonderland* and *Through the Looking-Glass* – had I not heard of her, nor read the books? Did I not have my own copies? No? Then this was a state of affairs that must quickly be put right. He would buy them for me.

Mr Chesterfield was a man of his word, and very soon afterwards he presented me with both books in one volume, which he inscribed. They proved a source of delight to which I have returned again and again. Now, as I set down the story of Mr Chesterfield's unrequited affection for my mother, the pathos of his situation finally dawns on me, and I see the lonely course he set himself as immensely moving. I wish I had thanked him properly for his kindness, and let him know how much his gift enriched me.

But re-examining events through the soft focus of lapsed time can make the act of forgiveness all too easy. I must not forget the frustration and anxiety that Mr Chesterfield's obsession caused my mother, for although she told him she could never regard him as more than a friend, he simply would not believe her.

In pursuit of higher hopes, he came to live in Doncaster, and put up at the Waverley Hotel in St. George Gate. He used to cause Mother embarrassment by calling in at the Drum as a customer and making a jealous nuisance of himself. In the end, he was asked to leave by Big Sid, our waiter, and Mother invoked her prerogative and banned him from the premises. If he failed to comply, she told him, she would call the police. Then Mr Chesterfield started to hang around outside the Drum, lurking in doorways, and following Mother to town. When she and Mrs Dunn went to the pictures on Monday nights, he would sometimes be there, watching and waiting, keeping an eye on them. They joked to each other when they passed his lovelorn shadow in the street, but it was very wearing, and must have been particularly nerve-wracking in the blackout.

There was no suggestion that Mr Chesterfield posed any serious threat, and as far as I was concerned he was still a benevolent presence, for once he stopped me and Brenda when we were out together, and tried to give us sixpence each. I cannot believe it was meant as a bribe, for I think he was fond of me, and perhaps I reminded him of his own daughter, but it seemed to Mother that he was attempting to worm his way into my confidence and gain access to her through me. Although we treated the poor man's hoverings with wry amusement, I knew that they troubled her, so I told him I could not talk to him, handed back my sixpence, and made Brenda do the same. Loyalty demanded no demur, even though she had already earmarked the unexpected windfall for a possible dancing lesson.

Later we heard that Mr Chesterfield had got a job at Briggs' Motor Bodies in Doncaster and moved into digs, and if we saw him it was by accident. When, some eighteen months later, I won a County Minor Scholarship to the Grammar School, I got a postcard from him bearing a lucky black cat and white heather. I still have the card, but I do not need to consult it to remember what it says: 'So you have won a scholarship all by yourself. That is the best news I have heard for a long, long time. Congratulations dear, and love from "Mr. Chesterfield"'.

I do not know how long afterwards it was that we heard he was ill and had been in hospital, then that he had died. His tall, rounded frame had shrunk so much that he was almost unrecognisable, somebody said. He had been a Freemason, and at an early stage of their friendship had asked Mother to look after some regalia for him, but never reclaimed the mysterious items. Mother had no idea what to do with them, feeling uneasy about having in her possession things she associated with dark, secret rituals. In the end, she discovered that one of our customers had Masonic connections, and passed them on to him. But I still have Mr Chesterfield's 'Alice', and his postcard, and in a box somewhere a photograph of him with his wife and children, to substantiate my memories of that time so long ago.

When I started to think about these events again after so many years, my feelings were confused. Of course it was despicable of him to plague my mother and restrict her sense of freedom, so that for months she felt unable to leave the Drum without first peering nervously through the window. The only explanation for this seeming change in personality is that something, maybe his past troubles, had conspired with loneliness to unbalance him, and he was therefore to be pitied. Now, at the end of my reappraisal of his pursuit of my mother, it is his patent unhappiness that leaves the most lasting impression. Devotion, if taken too far, becomes an alarming burden, and who can know his thoughts during those cold, dark vigils? My pity is real, and more than sixty years on, his sad ghost and I bear each other no malice.

***

ONE OF THE regulars in 'Doctors' Corner', a good-natured, unmarried physician named Gerry, probably in his late thirties, was intent on taking Mother and me for a trip in his car. Perhaps he felt sorry for us, perhaps he was simply proffering the hand of friendship, although at the back of my mind ever since has lodged the (maybe unworthy) notion that his interest in Mother verged on the personal.

I have no idea how long Mother prevaricated, I only know that one Sunday afternoon he called for us after the Drum closed at two o'clock, and whisked us into the country. To bowl along in a car was a rare and wonderful treat, and kind Gerry was great company, chatting happily as he drove. We came to the village of Marr, not many miles up the Barnsley road, and there we called upon Gerry's friend, the local G.P. That is to say, we went to his house, but he was not at home, though whether out on a call I cannot say. His wife gave us tea, but I remember it as an uncomfortable occasion. I cannot vouch for the truth of my impressions, but she seemed somewhat sharp and flustered, as though she had been wrong-footed. She had a young child or children, and perhaps this was why I recall a querulous pitch to her voice. Or possibly she felt it inappropriate for a doctor to be out for a spin with the landlady of his local pub.

When you are a child, there are two types of grown-ups: those who talk to you (even sometimes at your own level) and those who ignore you. Gerry was in the first category. Either our hostess was in the second, or my perceptions were blurred by shyness and the business of balancing my cup and saucer as I perched on the edge of my chair. I am certain that Mother felt a wrong note had been struck, and maybe Gerry felt so, too. She resumed her distance, and there were no more excursions with him, although he remained on good terms with her as a customer.

***

I BECAME NINE four-and-a-half months after my father died, and I must have had a party, because Mother considered it an automatic requirement until I reached fourteen. Among my gifts was an inspired choice from Georgina, a volume of Hugh Walpole's *Jeremy Stories*, still one of my best-loved books.

I do not remember anything of that particular party, but I expect it set the precedents for all those that followed. As a great treat, the eggshell porcelain tea-set that Dad had ordered from China when he worked for the shipping-line would be set out in our downstairs sitting-room There would be another special concession, a fire in the grate, and we would observe the family rubric of 'Jelly and Postman's Knock', which was how a very young Cousin Margaret once described high jinks at a party she had been to. We had no wireless to call upon at the Drum in those days, but music there was, of the very grandest order, for Sharley would entertain us: Mother's gramophone.

I think he had been bought in the Twenties and he was still an enviable possession. He consisted of a square oak box on legs, with a lid which could be propped open by an expanding rod to reveal a dark blue velvet turntable, operated by a switch. Sunk into the base on which the turntable rested were two metal cups. New needles (at the time no longer available, I think, but once purchased in small flat tins) had to be inserted, and tightened with a screw, at surprisingly frequent intervals, because they soon wore out, and acquired no end of fluff. Fortunately, Mother had a small stockpile. New needles were kept in the left-hand cup, old needles in the right. It was important to remember which were which, and sometimes we got confused, and used old needles again.

Before anything could happen, Sharley's spring had to be wound by a starting-handle sticking out from the side of his box. Then we would position a record, quite thick and heavy, on the turntable. But to ensure the music would emerge loud and clear, a double door on the front of the box had to be opened so the sounds coming through the loudspeaker had unobstructed passage. Regular rewinding of the handle was essential, otherwise the music would slow to a deathly pace, until it stopped altogether

Sharley's title arose from another of the infant Margaret's attempts at communication. Aunt Jinny had owned a similar gramophone on which she was fond of playing a hit song of the time, 'Oh Charley, Take It Away!' One day, Margaret wanting to hear the record, but, unable to make herself understood, tugged Auntie by the skirt and pleaded, 'Sharley, Sharley'. The name stuck, as it was bound to in our family.

We did not have that particular recording, but Mother had quite a selection of others. Oh, those lovely old seventy-eights! I wish I had not thrown them away after she died. There was a gem which had 'Bye Bye Blackbird' on one side and 'When The Red Red Robin Comes Bob-Bob-Bobbing Along' on the other. To recreate the sound convincingly, one must pinch one's nose. 'Empty Saddles in the Old Corral' and 'Ol' Faithful' were tear-jerkers supposedly sung by cowboys, which I recall with special fondness. 'There's a Blue Ridge Round My Heart, Virginia' was almost as melancholy, but 'Roll Along Covered Wagon' and 'Rio Rita' struck a happier note. 'When You and I were Seventeen' captured a time when 'love was all', and we simpered as we waltzed to it. I may deride the sentimentality of these old songs now, but I wish I could remember more about them.

I taught 'Red Red Robin' to my daughter Thea and her two young children when they came on a visit to England from Australia. They were charmed, so much so that it became their theme song, and they sang it as they flew home. Thirty-five years after I threw Sharley on the scrap-heap, it was oddly satisfying to think of them jetting to their far hemisphere with him still calling the tune.

***

WITH BRENDA AROUND, I had more freedom. She was older, knew the way into Doncaster on the trackless and the whereabouts of Woolworth's, was sensible and responsible, and trusted by Mother, who was often too busy to keep an eye on me. Brenda taught me all she knew about dancing, and we would make a stage at the end of the long living-room and tap away on the lino. Her favourite song to dance to was 'Save A Little Sunshine For a Rainy Day', and although her ear for music was less reliable than her twinkling feet, and she always sang off-key, she was quite unabashed, and laughed if we smiled at her efforts, knowing we did not mean to be unkind.

Set into the landing floor was a skylight designed to shed light into the office below. It consisted of a five-foot square of reinforced glass bricks, and one night Brenda and I discovered that tap-dancing on it produced a sensational effect. Up rushed Mother, who had been sitting beneath, to investigate the fearsome clattering, convinced the office roof was falling in. Not only was it noisy, it was dangerous, she said.

Occasionally, too, our energetic footwork on the living-room lino brought her flying upstairs because customers were complaining. But to smooth our ruffled feathers she would often bring with her a tray of lemonade and crisps. As we grew older, she sometimes turned the lemonade a beautiful shade of pale pink with the addition of a few drops of port. Port-and-lemon was a proper ladies' drink, and we felt very grown-up as we sipped it.

Mostly men came into the Drum without their wives, but sometimes on a Saturday night they would be brought in for a treat, and wonder what to have. A port or a port-and-lemon might fit the bill, although some of them professed not to drink. In this event, to Mother's quiet amusement, they might be pressed to a whisky or brandy, which they regarded as medicine. But others of their sex who were seasoned pub patrons enjoyed beer and stout in the ladies' tap-room, and when in the lounge called frequently for 'shorts': perhaps gin-and-French or gin-and-It (Italian vermouth, as opposed to the French variety), gin-and-orange, gin-and-lime, rum-and-orange, or rum-and-pep (peppermint).

One memorable night, when preparing the pink lemonade for Brenda and me, Mother was in a hurry, and her hand slipped with the port. She came up later to find us both overtaken by a fit of the rolling giggles, and Brenda went home even happier than usual. What would Brenda's parents think? Mother was much more careful after that.

***

THERE WAS A cinema on Bentley High Street called the Coliseum, known also as the 'Laugh and Scratch'. It cost fourpence to sit in the front seats, and Brenda introduced me to collecting empty jam jars to take back to one of the corner shops. We were paid a small sum for them, which we put towards tickets for the 'bug-pit'.

We also joined the Young Citizens' Matinee Club run on Saturdays by the Gaumont Cinema in town, where we were treated to Westerns, usually starring Gene Autry or Roy Rogers, or comedies featuring Abbott and Costello, The Marx Brothers, Will Hay, Old Mother Riley and George Formby. I thought them too daft to laugh at, but could appreciate Laurel and Hardy, finding in Stan Laurel a strong resemblance to Uncle George, though Stan was undoubtedly funnier.

Before the performance, the cinema-manager used to come on stage and encourage us to sing the Young Citizens' theme song:

'We come along on Saturday mornings,
Greeting everybody with a smile.
We come along on Saturday mornings,
Knowing it's well worth while.
As members of the G.B. (Gaumont British) Club
We all intend to be
Good citizens when we grow up,
And champions of the free.
We come along on Saturday mornings,
Greeting everybody with a smile, *smile*, SMILE,
Greeting everybody with a smile.'

Brenda took me into town to buy Christmas presents. We invaded Woolworth's, and the choice was satisfying. One of the counters displayed songbooks with sentimental old lyrics, and golden thoughts framed to hang on the wall, like 'God Gave Us Memories That We Might Have Roses In December'. Another went: 'I shall pass through this world but once; any good thing therefore that I can do, or any kindness that I can show to any fellow-creature, let me do it now; let me not defer or neglect it, for I shall not pass this way again.'

I always made for the stationery counter, taking stock of its shiny exercise books, cloth-bound volumes holding promise in blank pages, wads of pastel blotting paper textured like sugared almonds. Back at the Drum, the day would come when we wrapped our Christmas presents. Brenda would bring hers across so we could work together, she demonstrating how to cut out the requisite amount of paper, and how to fold the ends into neat 'Vs'. I had not inherited my father's talent for parcel-wrapping, which had been a byword due to his grocery training, and Brenda usually had to smooth out my efforts and start again.

That first Christmas after Dad died, through a wonderful gift I entered a world of knights and dragons, captive damsels, hideous monsters, trees that bled when you cut off their branches, and foul witches who took on the appearance of beautiful maidens to achieve their evil ends. It was a simplified, illustrated version of Spenser's *Faerie Queen*, given to me by Wyn, our barman, and still a treasure. Wyn and his wife and young married daughter, Joyce, whose husband was away at war, felt sorry for me, I think, because I was alone so much, and had me to sleep at their house once or twice, and gave me special treats. I would have preferred to be at home, especially as I slept with Joyce, who, no doubt missing her husband, cuddled me at night as she might her own child. Still, they were so kind I knew I could not refuse.

But oh, it was such happiness to get back to the Drum! Nothing can match the comforting arms of home after even a very short spell away. I wandered around all the rooms to detect signs of how life had moved on despite my absence: a vase of fresh flowers, a letter from Aunt Nancy, a new cake of soap in the bathroom, a bone on Paddy's dish, Mother's slippers kicked off under a chair, the remains of her egg-and-milk, which was all she sometimes had for lunch, still clouding a glass. Everything was bigger than I remembered, more colourful, slightly unnatural, like coming downstairs after being ill in bed. Everything was familiar, yet demanding reappraisal, re-acquaintance, repossession. Changed, yet unchanging. Home, home, home.

***

THE MONTHS SLID on. Brenda took me to the roller-skating rink but while she sailed around adeptly, I retreated in bruised disorder. On Sundays we went to morning service at St. Peter's, decked in green coats with brown velvet collars and brown felt hats, outfits which, though not identical, were near enough to ensure we looked like sisters. Once Mother, with a bit of time to spare, made us both similar summer dresses, of which we were inordinately proud. We sat together through the boring, drawn-out Communion services, close to Miss Connors, one of the Sunday School teachers, who drowned us out in the hymns, especially if it happened to be 'As Pants the Hart for Cooling Streams'. We shifted restlessly through the Reverend Norman R. Campbell's sermons.

I remember only one of his tales from the pulpit. It concerned a missionary who went to Africa, taking with him his piano. The heathens he had been sent to convert were mystified when he called them together around the instrument, threw open the lid, and began to play hymns. They thought the piano must be some sort of animal, and that by pressing on its teeth he was making 'the poor beast howl'. The laughter this fragment of pale humour engendered among the congregation was disproportionately loud, for its merit lay in its rarity. Brenda and I stuffed our hankies in our mouths.

After church we might walk to Pipering Wood, returning in season with armfuls of bluebells, then home for a scratch lunch (Brenda's Mother used to dip bread deliciously in the juices of the roasting meat for her) and off to Sunday School, hoping to be given another religious bookmark to add to our collections.

Mr Campbell was an earnest vicar, and took his duties seriously. He once called on my mother while she was out, and left his card among the empty milk-bottles on the doorstep, setting her a-fluster, for if he should return she would not know how to treat him. Could she possibly invite a parson to step inside licensed premises? (As it happened, he never came back.)

We had a curate at church, Mr Sutton, a tall, handsome fellow, with shining black hair, who thrilled us with his lovely baritone during the concerts that were a feature of social life at St. Peter's. But alas, one night the uplifting effect of his performance was nullified by a comic turn that followed him on stage. The stranger who confronted us besmirched the proceedings with jokes quite unfitting for a church hall, though very mild by today's standards. They provoked the odd titter from the audience, but soon heads began bobbing uneasily. The climax was unforgettable.

It concerned a story about a lavatory seat, which the funny-man produced and hung around his neck. Hardly was he into his stride when the Vicar, who had been sitting on the front row with his wife and two adolescent daughters, got up and marched his family out. A gasp went up from the rest of us, and the jokester must have realised his blunder, for he soon quit the stage. How could such an unsuitable act have come to be on the bill? Questions would obviously be asked the next morning, but I never heard the outcome.

If Brenda and I got wind of a marriage at St. Peter's, we would either go and stand outside the porch to see the wedding party leave after the service, or, if we knew the bride's address and she lived fairly close, join the group of neighbours gathered around her front door to watch her leave for the church. Though we often had a long, cold wait, anticipation ran high as we listened to those who had perhaps had a preview of the dresses, or could tell us anything about the happy couple and their families. Suddenly, the front door would open and, to admiring gasps, the bride's mother, aunts and grandma would issue forth in their finery and take their seats in the first cars. Next came the bridesmaids, moving far too quickly for us to grasp the details of their dresses and accessories. ('Were those carnations in their bouquets?'

'Did you see their shoes?') Lastly, after another long wait, the bride herself appeared, dazzling in white, a vision apart; distinguishable, too, by that puzzling glow which makes even the plainest girl look beautiful on her wedding day.

***

THROUGHOUT THIS TIME at Bentley, often a very happy time, I occasionally showed signs of 'nerves'. I would be convinced I had dropped something, and kept looking back over my shoulder when out walking. I continued to bite my nails, a habit I have never lost, and would have days when I continuously cleared my throat. I compounded my reputation for eccentricity by standing on my head (either propped up against a wall, or in an armchair) to stimulate my brain. I day-dreamed, or lost myself in books until my tired eyes became, in Mother's words, 'like a pair of currants'.

If my mother caught a chill, or showed the slightest indisposition, I worried she might die. When she developed one of her sick headaches and lay in bed beside me with her eyes closed, I held my hands alternately on the cold iron frame beneath the mattress and placed them on her brow to cool it. When she recovered, I had to keep reminding myself to stop worrying. I fretted about my own health as well, especially about getting lockjaw, or catching scarlet fever. Having overheard someone describe how scarlet fever began with a rash between the fingers, I would spread out mine and examine the webs of skin between them for tiny red spots. If I found any, which I regularly did, I would await further developments with a sick heart, convinced I would soon be whisked off to an isolation hospital.

But for a long time, my fears of us being seriously ill were unfounded, and Mother and I remained quite healthy, though one day word came that poor Wyn, who had been off work suffering from asthma, had died. He had been a good friend and we missed him, and not just because Mother had to find someone else to take charge of the tap-room bar. Mrs Dunn's daughter, Ena, a bright young woman, was eager to exchange her milk-round for a new, indoor situation, and trained up magnificently, while her husband, Charley, took over the cellar duties.

He was very kind and patient with me, having a young daughter of his own, and I used to enjoy his easy company, and keep my ear cocked for his arrival so I could descend to join him. He would ask me about school, and what mischief I had been up to, and sometimes we would sing, raising splendid strains in the echoing vaults. ' Everybody's Doing It' was one of our favourites. Once I asked Charley what it was they were doing. 'Picking their nose and chewing it', he said surprisingly, sending us both into fits of laughter.

THE FAMILY TREE

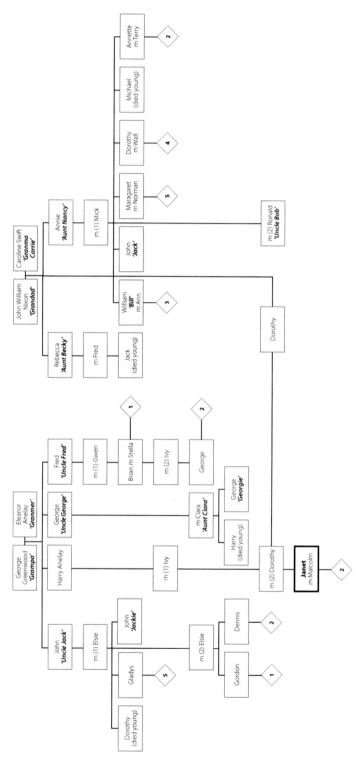

Grampa Greenwood.

Granmer Greenwood.

Grandma Carrie aged 21 (Nixon).

Grandad Nixon, aged 21.

My father in his army greatcoat
and driving goggles.

My father after the 1914-1918 war.

My father at the wheel of the army Rolls Royce.

One of my father's Duty Orders, dated 1919.

Margaret and Dorothy, 1931.

Mother aged 19.

My mother aged 23, 1n 1920.

Aunt Becky as a young woman.

Aunt Bel when young.

Great-aunt Jinny holding me.

Aunt Nancy and Annette, aged nine. January 1945.

Mother and Granmer outside 42 Pendrill Street, 1922.

Mother and Dad.

Me aged 6 months, held by Mother.

Above: My parents' grocery shop in De Grey Street, Hull.

Left: Aunt Nancy dressed for a wedding.

The Station Inn.

The Big Drum.

Mother in the backyard of The Station Inn.

My cousin Bill in desert uniform.

Sicily, November, 1943.

Jessie with me in the yard at The Station Inn, with the railway line alongside.

The family on the beach. Back row, l-r: Aunt Jinny, mother with me, Aunt Nancy with Michael. Front row, l-r: Jack, Dorothy, ?, Margaret.

Annette, me, and Eddie Guest (holding my teddy) in the yard of The Station Inn.

CORONATION YEAR 1937

Georgie and I.

Myself in the garden of the Big Drum, wearing the Girl Guide uniform made for me by my mother.

Jessie and Arthur's wedding, 1941. (Dad, Mother and I on the right.)

Paddy and I in the garden
at the Big Drum.

Brenda (right) and I in our
dancing costumes, 1945.

Me, aged 13.

Joy, aged 13.

Joy as a sixth-former at Percy
Jackson's Grammar School.

Me, George Henry and Mother at Blackpool, 1949.

Mother and I in Düsseldorf July 1951.

Uncle George's car, with a proud Aunt Clara.

Above: Uncle Bob, Aunt Nancy, Uncle George and Aunt Clara with my son Patrick at Bolton Abbey.

Left: Aunt Nancy with my daughter Thea, 1965.

CHAPTER FOURTEEN – SCHOLARSHIP

THE GIFTED TEACHER in charge of Standard Five, the Scholarship Class at Kirkby Avenue Juniors, was Miss Martin. I still do not know her first name, nor much about her, except that she appeared to be aged around forty, cycled to school from her home in Finkle Street, Bentley, often wore a green tweed suit, clamped our noses hard to the grindstone, and did everything morally possible to get us through the 'County Minor'.

In Standard Three the County Minor Scholarship had loomed a distant inquisition, a test of self to be faced eventually, but not, thank heavens, yet. At the end of our time with Miss Finney, certain pupils were granted an extra year's grace, passing into Standard Four. But that September of 1943, when I was two months short of my tenth birthday, quite a lot of us were considered ready for immediate coaching by Miss Martin. If we passed the spring exam we would win free places at the Percy Jackson Grammar School. If we failed, it was off to the Secondary Modern. (One could be 'paid for' at the Grammar School, but I knew nothing about this, and would not have been affected by it anyway.)

Miss Martin was talked of as a strong disciplinarian who countenanced no slacking, and our worst fears were confirmed when we filed into her classroom on that first morning and learned that total concentration on the five aspects of the County Minor would be expected of us for the next six months. There was no time to be wasted. Throughout that autumn and winter, urgency seeped like an odour through the glazed partition between us and the hall, where the fourth-years kept to a less pressing schedule, and a piano sometimes tinkled. This happened when Miss Davis, black hair rolled to meet in two horns at the front of her head, taught singing. I was glad the dividing wall was so thin, for I welcomed the English folk music favoured by Miss Davis as a soothing antidote to brain-fag.

Our five-pronged attack on the County Minor required constant practice-runs through old scholarship papers. The syllabus consisted of an Intelligence Test; Comprehension and Composition (to prove ability in English); Mental Arithmetic; and Problems (a greater maths ordeal, posing questions along the lines of: 'If it takes three men two hours to dig a hole five feet deep, how long would it take four men to dig one twice the depth?' Or sums about filling baths with water, or calculating how long cars or trains would take to travel at different speeds over varying distances. Such enigmas presented very definite problems to me).

It did not help matters that on the first day Miss Martin had engineered unpopular seating arrangements. 'When you take the County Minor' was the trumpet-call frequently on her lips, still more the yardstick against which all else was measured. She varied the phrase with references to 'March the First', the date of the exam. If we wished to pass the scholarship, and she assumed we all did, nothing should distract us. So (horror of horrors!) girls and boys must sit paired together, and she would do the pairing. Without giving us the chance to do more than groan an agonised 'Oh MISS!' she waved us into the old double desks, boy-girl, boy-girl, promising to relax this rule 'after March the First', when we would be able to sit wherever we liked.

After The County Minor ... a state of grace too wonderful to imagine. It was embarrassing to have found ourselves pitched up so unnaturally close to the opposite sex, near whom, with few exceptions, we girls were wont to experience prickles of discomfort (or at least I was). But, as far as I remember, the lads, though equally dismayed, caused us little actual bother.

Thus, we resigned ourselves. Then we began to notice the gleam in Miss Martin's eye, and how humorously she handled us, and dared to think that life in Standard Five might have some savour after all, for her strictness had a cheerful buzz to it. Although she might criticise, she was not unkind. She brimmed with enthusiasm, had perfected ways of stimulating and holding our interest, and, being well-versed in the requirements of the County Minor, strove to disentangle them for us. She was unquestionably our ally. I cannot speak for the rest of the class, but my own scant hopes of passing the scholarship sprang from a desire to please her (and Mother, of course). Mind you, I thought it far more likely I would end up at Bentley High Street Secondary Modern; in fact this school held special appeal for me, because Brenda was already happily ensconced there.

The fact that Mother had failed a scholarship was another reason why I was fairly sanguine about failing one myself. There would be no shame in being like her. I knew she felt I was capable of passing the County Minor, but her only real expectation was that I should try my hardest.

Miss Martin pursued a stick-and-carrot policy. The stick could be a real one, for at school in those days the cane was a permanent threat. Although I appear to have blanked out the memories, I am assured that she sometimes fetched late-comers a sting across the hand in front of the class, though possibly only the boys. She regularly warned us that she would abandon us to our fate if we did not behave. A timetable hung on the wall, containing subjects like history and geography, and when we displeased her she would gesture towards it, and threaten to move on to this syllabus instead of helping us to pass the County Minor. Such a threat always brought us to heel; she was, among other things, a brilliant psychologist.

But the carrot she proffered was even more inspirational. After a draining day, she would read to us before home time, a treat we begged for, and which, in her cleverness, she knew could lead to exploratory forays of our own. She would engage our pin-drop interest with the first chapter or two of a book; then, having set the drama in motion, leave us panting to know more. Sometimes she would oblige us by reading on.

She introduced us to three of Robert Louis Stevenson's best-loved works, *Treasure Island*, *The Black Arrow*, and *Kidnapped*. Who can ever forget the first sight of tarry-pigtailed Billy Bones arriving with his sea-chest at the Admiral Benbow Inn, or Blind Pugh's tap-tapping menace as purveyor of the Black Spot? Or the chill induced by the leper's bell in *The Black Arrow*; or the terrifying reception of David Balfour by Uncle Ebenezer at the House of Shaws? She dipped into the works of other authors, too. I remember how skilfully she exploited the humour of the ice-skating episode in Dickens's *Pickwick Papers*, and how her interpretation of the opening chapters of Sir Arthur Conan Doyle's *Sir Nigel* persuaded me to choose it as a school prize some time later.

When we had finished our work, she encouraged us to explore the bookshelves on the classroom wall. I think it was after we sat the scholarship that we were able to make a regular selection from a crate of books on loan from the County Library. Its arrival in class always marked a red-letter day, and our excitement was scarcely containable as the large wooden box was dragged to the front, and the lid flung back.

Miss Martin at times digressed from prose into poetry, and shared with us some diverting lines she had spotted in *Punch*, entitled *Etiquette For Animals*. I recall a few:

'... should a salamander bow
To a solitary cow,
If he meets her in the village after dark?'

'... should centipedes wear wellingtons, or what?
If a lobster's out to tea,
And he's got a cold, should he
Be allowed to keep his muffler on, or not?'

In a change of mood, she read us *The Listeners*, by Walter de la Mare, a word-picture etched in silver light and shadow, still to my mind one of the most beautiful and mysterious in the language. She rang the changes again with *The Fiddler of Dooley*, a charming Irish jig of a poem with a poignant ending.

She was an admirer of John Masefield, explaining to us the meaning of Poet Laureate (a post I immediately put to the top of my own career plans) and taught us the whole of *The West Wind*:

'It's a warm wind, the West Wind, full of birds' cries,
I never hear the West Wind but tears are in my eyes ...'

as well as his more popular *Cargoes* and *Sea Fever*.

***

AT THAT TIME, schools in the Doncaster area came under the aegis of the old West Riding County Council, which, along with its renowned Education Department, was based in Wakefield. For some mysterious reason, Miss Martin occasionally deserted her classroom on school days in order to travel to Wakefield. Was she on a committee, was her personal advice sought by the Chief Education Officer, or was she merely keeping abreast of developments regarding the County Minor? It would have been impertinent to ask, so we never fathomed why.

She would suddenly announce at home time that she would be in Wakefield tomorrow, and that we should keep on working as usual in her absence. We knew that Mr Smalley would be left in charge of Standard Five, and while Miss Martin's withdrawal always left me feeling wobbly, we were used to our headmaster popping into the classroom, so he was no distant figure. He would stand before us, compact and grey-suited, twinkling in all parts. The crown of his head, his amiable pink face, his bright blue eyes peering at us over the top of his wire-framed spectacles, his teeth, his shoes, his smile, all had the same benign gleam to them. Not every bit of the time, for he could be stern; but the overriding memory I have of him is of assorted twinkles strung together to make one composite whole.

I am sure he followed his usual practice of personally bringing a new pupil into class when Joy arrived among us that November, and I expect we smug initiates displayed the normal curiosity. I knew what it felt like to join a roomful of strangers already settled into their own mysterious routine, so perhaps I was sorry for her. How remarkable that the coming of one who was to prove my alter ego should have stirred so unremarkable a response in both of us! Joy recalls being put at the back of the room, next to (she thinks) a boy called Galloway. Time was even more pressing for her in the days that followed, because her previous education had been less than orthodox.

I learned much later that she hardly went to school between the ages of seven and ten. When the war began, she moved to her grandfather's home in Bentley with her mother. For a time she was admitted to a senior school, mornings only, among a group of twelve-year-olds, because the junior school she should have attended had been bombed. Once it reopened, she started lessons there; but it was not long before it dawned on her family that she was the right age to sit the County Minor, and so she was whisked off to Kirkby Avenue.

Not only did this school (thanks to Miss Martin) have a reputation for scholarship success, there was probably a more personal explanation for the transfer. Miss Martin had once been a schoolgirl herself in Bentley, and one of her classmates had been Joy's Aunt Dorothy. This amazing piece of news, revealed to me by Joy quite lately, takes some digesting; it means that, far from having reached her early forties, as I had surmised, Miss Martin, when I knew her, was actually only about twenty-eight! Something else I discovered recently is that Joy had difficulty with 'problems' in maths, and to help her catch up, Miss Martin twice invited her round to her home to give her special grounding.

At first, before she moved to a house near the school with her parents, Joy used to go back to her grandfather's for lunch, which was quite a long way. One day, Miss Martin, exasperated by people coming late into class, vowed she would punish any further unpunctuality with the cane. Joy was terrified to find herself arriving back at school after the bell had sounded the following afternoon, but Miss Martin, for some reason, did not fulfil her threat.

**

WE GIRLS CONGREGATED in a loose sort of group at playtime, chattering, playing ball (though during the war rubber balls were like gold) and skipping, either singly or together. Communal skipping was popular in streets and playgrounds if we could get a long enough rope. We would run in and out of the elliptic arc made by somebody's mother's clothes-line, or take turns to hold the ends and thwack the rope down on the concrete in a circular motion that could 'slinch' unwary flesh. And yet, no malevolence was intended. We sang:

'All in together girls,
This fine weather, girls,
When I count ten,
We all must be in,
When I count twenty,
The rope must be empty.'

161

Or,

'On the hillside stands a lady,
Who she is I do not know,
All she wants is gold and silver,
All she wants is a nice young man'

Or something that went, with a good many double-twists of the rope,

'Salt, mustard, vinegar, pepper ...'

We avoided the boys like the plague, but they must have had access to our playground at least part of the time, because they sometimes teased from the crumbly brick walls peculiarly horrid, fawn-coloured spiders with dimpled bodies. Holding the spiders by their long legs, they would chase us girls and try to stuff them down our necks. Ugh!

Joy at first was glad of anyone who would play with her. I am sure she was soon accepted, for she was open and merry-hearted, and quick with apt jokes, which she acquired like some people collected cigarette-cards. She never forgot a punch-line, and delivered her wisecracks in a variety of convincing accents, a gift I envied.

Gradually, by osmosis as much as by direct questioning, we must have learned how much we did have in common. Both of us were only children, born late to older parents, girt with solicitude, yet accustomed to aloneness, which at times we regarded as an inestimable boon; for though eager for friendship, we were happy with our own company. We bit our nails, but were unafraid of the dark.

Books were our passport to an inner life rendered accessible by almost any opening sentence, though Joy, who had ploughed through a pile of high-minded Victorian tomes belonging to her granddad, read more widely, swiftly and voraciously than I. Her spirits bubbled more often to the surface, too, but we found (and this was perhaps the most satisfying discovery of all) that we laughed at things that seemed to strike only us as funny. Something would happen, or someone would speak, and we would glance at each other in recognition of a joint smile breaking. She would raise one eyebrow (another enviable skill), I'd respond with a grin, and we would be off, either laughing behind compressed lips, or else exploding. All very puzzling and provoking for other people, especially as we grew older, and became more sardonic. But how much of all this we recognised in those pre-scholarship days, how quickly our friendship ripened, how closely we kept within the same sphere, or how soon we first visited each other's homes, neither of us can remember.

***

MARCH THE FIRST arrived. We learned we were to sit the County Minor at Bentley High Street Secondary Modern School, and that it would take all day. If we lived near enough, we could go home for lunch, and this I had chosen to do, glad of a chance to talk to Mother about the morning's events.

I felt lucky to have been allocated a desk in the light and airy hall, rather than in one of the dark-looking classrooms, but I had no idea how well or badly I had done. As we had been fore-warned by Miss Martin, each of us had been given a number (mine consisted of four digits, I think) and told to write it at the top of our papers, so the examiners should not know who we were. This fact was to haunt me for many months after the results were announced.

I remember feeling reasonably at ease as I walked back across Bentley Bridge in good time for the afternoon session, with Mother's encouragement ringing in my ears. It was only after the whole thing was over, and we faced Miss Martin again, and swapped notes about our ordeal, that my doubts about my ability to pass came flooding back.

Still, the next few months were enjoyable, for, true to her word, on March the Second Miss Martin abandoned her iron regime and her unpopular seating plan. We should all choose a friend to share a desk with, and she spurred on our decision-making with her usual briskness.

I have called her a good psychologist, and so she was in urging us to our maximum effort. But she taught at a time when the private feelings of children were of less account than they are today. People who already had one close friend in class paired off automatically. Many of the rest found themselves in an embarrassing position, although it is hard to see how else things could have been arranged.

A girl I got on well with, called Joyce, was asked whom she would like to sit next to, and picked me. Joy also named me, for she and I had spoken of sitting together, so Miss Martin said I must choose between them.

Standing in front of the class, I prevaricated, not wishing to hurt either, and, when pressed by Miss Martin, mumbled that I didn't know.

'Come along, Janet, make your mind up, we haven't got all day', she urged.

'Well, Joy, then,' I said. But there was never really any doubt.

After that, Joyce was never unfriendly, but we went more separate ways. It had been a painful situation. And a crossroads.

***

THAT SUMMER, WHEN the scholarship results came out, we were all terribly nervous, of course, and sat frozen in our seats as Mr Smalley entered the classroom with the list in his hand. Miss Martin took up her position alongside him, and he began to read out the names of those who had passed for the grammar school, peering at us over the top of his spectacles every now and then. And this again was a cruelty of the times we lived in; no discreet letter on the doormat, or posting on a noticeboard, but a public sorting of the sheep from the goats. I braced myself to be a goat, but still hoped for a miracle, as everyone else must have done.

The list was alphabetical, and Joy, whose surname was in the Cs, was up there, triumphant. When Mr Smalley came to Sylvia Emberton's name, he read out 'Sylvia Greenwood'. I was aware of a background murmur as Sylvia and I glanced at each other apprehensively, and of Mr Smalley pausing, viewing us each in turn over his glasses, and giving a little smile. But surely it could not have been a deliberate tease?

'Sylvia Emberton.' ('Aaah!' from Sylvia). Then, 'Janet Greenwood', and a confirming nod from Miss Martin. The miracle had happened! Joy's excitement redoubled, and I was in a state of levitation.

Mr Smalley proceeded to the end of the list. It seemed quite long, but many of our classmates were not on it. In the playground afterwards, we focused our blurred impressions. 'Have you passed?' 'Yes'. 'No'. The dividing line was already drawn.

It seems harsh in retrospect, but after a vague show of sympathy, all we chosen ones could think of was our own exclusivity. We bounded home, burst in, and screamed, 'I've passed! I've passed!' Suddenly our parents knew, in the flowering of their own pride, that they were exclusive, too. I feel ashamed now when I realise what little thought I gave to the classmates who had to go home and say, 'I didn't pass.'

How did we react when the last day came, and we said goodbye to Miss Martin and Mr Smalley, and friends who might be lost to us, and the dear old school? Were there tears and backward glances? I am sure we were sad, fearful, too, but I have lost all memory of those parting moments.

I never saw Miss Martin again (Joy did, though only once) but my indebtedness to her has been incalculable. When Joy became a teacher herself, she tried to hold to her example in at least one important respect. I quote from some thoughts my old friend sent me recently:

'Miss Martin was a martinet, but of the best kind – she put our interests ahead of being "lovable", and earned our loving regard by not seeking to be liked. It is more important to be respected than to be liked, but if you can learn this, and, live by it, you are often surprised to find yourself liked, and sometimes loved.'

CHAPTER FIFTEEN — OPERATION

WHILE ALL THIS was happening at Kirkby Avenue, events were also moving at home. Georgina had got engaged to a fellow called Herbert, a stocky Welshman who worked as a miner at Bentley Colliery. He had a jovial, teasing charm about him, and I thought him great fun, rather like a big brother or young uncle. Unsurprisingly, he also had a wonderful singing voice, which he sometimes used to splendid effect in the Drum's lounge. Whenever he drew his friends together for an impromptu rendition of 'Land of My Fathers' or 'On Ilkla Moor B'aht 'At', the raw emotion in those hurriedly-blended voices made my eyes water.

Georgina asked my mother whether, after she and Herbert were married, he could come and live at the Drum. She pointed out the great advantage of having a man permanently about the place, available to help with heavy duties, such as carrying coal-hods upstairs from the cellar. Mother was hesitant and not altogether sure about Herbert, or of having him there as a fixture, but she was fond of the gentle-natured Georgina, and knew she was anxious to arrange a wedding date. So it was agreed, and the ceremony took place at St. Peter's Church, Bentley, I being one of the bridesmaids. After a reception at the Drum, bride and groom settled into the main guest bedroom, which became their marital base for a year or so.

Everything went quite well at first, especially on Sunday afternoons, when Herbert would delve into his pocket as he sprawled in an armchair after dinner and announce his intention of buying us all some ice cream. Brenda and I would stroll the quarter-mile or so to Massarella's farm with a big glass jug. We sometimes voiced reluctance once the novelty had worn off, pleading tiredness, but Herbert would jolly us into going. There was no denying he was a generous man.

Gradually, however, strains began to develop in the new domestic arrangements, and Mother discovered with mounting anger that her premonitions had been well-founded. Herbert must have worked very hard at being nice, for the alteration in him was amazing once he thought the effort no longer worth making. He started to take time off work, and to lie in bed late. His rough edges began to show, particularly at the table, where he would sometimes indicate his readiness for the meal by declaring he could eat 'two taties more'n a pig'.

His bride waited on him, ensuring that the choicest morsels found their way on to his plate. Down in the bar, he would hold court among his cronies, who deferred to him as though he were the boss. He treated Georgina so churlishly that my mother found it hard to bite her tongue; though I think her ire might have found expression when she caught him lolling by the fire as his wife struggled up two flights of stairs with two huge buckets of coal.

We had been used to family and friends coming to stay, but now Herbert made them feel unwelcome and in the way. No wonder Mother wished she had never agreed to let him live with us! But, although I had grown increasingly wary of his moods, at the time I was more preoccupied with what life held in store at the grammar school. Only later did I realise that many of the subtle atmospheric changes taking place at home had completely gone over my head.

***

THE GRAMMAR SCHOOL lay about six miles away, a great distance in our imagination, and Mother and I had no idea of its actual location, nor how to reach it. She arranged for me to be taken there on my first day by Winnie Day, daughter of one of our butcher customers. Winnie and I were introduced shortly before term started, for we happened to be with our parents when they bumped into one another at Arksey Show. She was about to enter her third year at Percy Jackson's, so the gulf between us seemed to me unbridgeable.

Equipped with all the grey P.J.G.S. uniform except the expensive blazer (Mother hoped the red jacket I already owned would be acceptable for the time being), and bearing a leather satchel passed down to me by Cousin Margaret (about which I also had unspoken qualms, for her name and address, although crossed out, were still decipherable inside the flap), I accompanied Winnie and her friend Kathleen along Watch House Lane to the bus-stop on the main road. That first walk and bus-ride are indistinguishable in memory now from countless others we made together; it is sufficient to say that the girls and the rest of their circle tolerated me remarkably well, considering they were so much older and wiser.

The school, built only five years previously, was huge. In the hall, our names were read out according to class, and I found myself in one with hardly anyone I knew. Joy had been put in another. We voiced bitter disappointment, but at least we could meet at break and lunch-times, and swap notes about the first-form syllabus, which, to my delight, included German.

For English we had to tackle *Prester John*, by John Buchan, and *Memoirs of a Foxhunting Man* by Siegfried Sassoon. The latter I found extremely boring, and recall nothing of it, but the Buchan engaged my attention, especially at the powerful climax, where the hero leaps into the torrent with the fabled emerald collar flashing fire around his neck. From this book, Joy and I, who flourished on secret codes and messages, culled a phrase ideal for warning each other that teachers or prefects were on the prowl: 'The blesbok are changing ground'.

For poetry we studied two direly pessimistic pieces, *The Lyke Wake Dirge* ('... To Brig o' Doom thou com'st at last, And Christ receive thy soul!') and Shakespeare's *Fear No More the Heat o' the Sun* from *Cymbeline*. Horrifying, both of them, for it was hard for even a hypochondriac to credit that golden lads and girls must finally come to dust.

That first day, I bundled all my text books into Margaret's satchel and struggled home with them to show Mother. She was very impressed. Up to then, in our family only Margaret (apart from Gwen, my aunt-by-marriage) had ever had such a span of knowledge made available, or been taught by teachers in black gowns. Brenda came across, curious to know how I had got on. My transfer to the grammar school made little difference to our friendship, though sometimes my homework tended to get in the way.

I think it was that winter that heavy snowfalls created misery during journeys to school. Winnie, Kathleen and I were at times waist-deep in drifts as we forced our way along Watch House Lane. The snow packed itself into our wellingtons and froze our fingers in their woollen gloves, so that when we finally got to school, some of us cried as we warmed ourselves by the radiators, so agonisingly did our extremities throb as the blood coursed slowly back.

At the Drum, with the grate still unlit, Mother and I had our breakfast near a one-bar electric fire, positioned on the table. Then came a period when the upstairs water-supply froze, so we had to 'camp out' in the downstairs sitting-room. One dark morning I fell down the stairs, imprinting the pattern of their brass treads across my nose. Mother, who had decided to switch off the landing-light as an economy measure, probably because she had bought the electric fire without consulting 'Owd Buggerlugs', was so remorseful she kept me off school for the day, and vowed as she hugged me that, hang the expense, the bulb should remain operational.

So winter progressed. At school we learned to play hockey on windswept pitches, subject ourselves to the indignities of communal showers, digest the often strange combinations served up at meal-times (like mashed potato, grated cheese, beetroot and gravy), and avoid the displeasure of the prefects. Lucy, an easy-going sixth-former, with legs as rosy as her cheeks, always called me 'Little Redcoat', so I knew I stood out among the grey blazers, and had better watch myself.
Another, of much tarter disposition, in charge of our table at dinner, complained during dessert that I held my spoon like a shovel, (true!) whereupon Joy fired back accusingly, 'Well, at least she doesn't talk with her mouth full!'

Though I was writhing with humiliation, my friend's audacity staggered me. Would I have had the wit to conceive such a brilliant riposte, or (even more importantly) been brave enough to deliver it? I doubted this very much. Meanwhile, unequal to the contest, our antagonist fell back, glowering.

So, with help, I knew I could survive. But mere survival was not my most pressing concern. Throughout those early weeks, as I became more and more enmeshed in life at Percy Jackson's, I wrestled with my greatest doubt of all.

I was afraid I should not really be there. I, Keyhole Kate, dreamy, odd, exasperatingly lacking in common-sense, how could I possibly have been clever enough to pass the County Minor? I struggled with 'Problems', and my handwriting was atrocious. How could I have succeeded where better brains had failed? The answer probably lay in the numbering system when we took the exam. Either I had misread mine and made a mistake on my entry papers, or the examiners had blundered. Day after day, I sat in class expecting someone to come in and say there had been a mix-up, and Janet Greenwood had no business to be at the grammar school. I pictured Mother's disappointment when I arrived home with the news that my place rightfully belonged to someone else.

Gradually, however, as time went by and nothing happened, I began to feel safer, and more capable, and to convince myself that I wasn't as stupid as I had feared. Maybe, after all, I was in the right school.

***

CHRISTMAS, 1944 DREW near, and we learned there would be a party, for which all three first-year classes would band together. I never was much for parties, except my own, and the thought of musical games in the hall, followed by sandwiches and trifle in the dining-room, held scant allure. The full horror of the situation did not dawn on us, however, until Miss Houghton, our form-mistress, announced that, rather than girls being allowed to stick together in one group and boys in another, we should all have a partner of the opposite sex. Hands up those boys who wished to name a girl. Ah cruel, cruel!

While the rest of us sniggered, a few bold spirits crooked arms aloft and specified their choices. We had all known those likely to be picked. There were more girls than boys in the class, and with any luck some of us might end up with a partner of the same gender. Then (oh no, oh no!) a boy called Derek stuck up his hand and said, 'Janet Greenwood, Miss.'

Miss Houghton made some comment like, 'There you are then, Janet', and there indeed I was. It was impossible to decline, even supposing I had not been dumbstruck. I felt as though my inner workings had wrenched themselves out and tumbled on the floor.

I was not one of the stars in the school firmament, those confident, bright-faced girls who were good at sport, and attracted followings, usually with one admirer in tow more favoured than the rest. Though I might envy this kind of popularity, there were advantages in staying anonymous.

Derek had been in Miss Martin's class, and now used the same bus-stop as Winnie, Kathleen and I to get to school; but this was all the awareness I had of him. We had scarcely exchanged a word. Now here he was, making an exhibition of us both by publicly naming me as his partner.

Back home, I told Mother of my predicament. She took the news far too lightly, I felt, even seemed to find it amusing. Of course I must be polite and nice to that poor lad, she said; it would have taken some courage for him to ask me (or rather, tell me) in front of the whole class, a point I had not thought of. Better, too, to know my fate than to be allocated someone willy-nilly by Miss Houghton.

But the thought of the party hung over me, and I expect it probably bothered Derek, too, for all his bravado. It was very awkward waiting at the bus-stop once Winnie and Kathleen had wormed the story out of me. They teased me, naturally, and treated it as remarkable that I had received an invitation from a boy.

I think we girls must have changed into our party-clothes at school. I remember Derek looking very well-scrubbed in a short-trousered brown suit. Two by two, we lined up in the corridor outside the classroom before being marched into the hall. Were we made to hold hands then, or did that happen during the musical games? Derek's grasp was firm, and he did not clown around or do anything to upset me, but our partnership was restricted to that one occasion, and afterwards we thankfully returned to status quo.

***

ONE DAY IN March, 1945, mother found a lump in her left breast. She was frightened, because she remembered her own mother's painful death from breast cancer, but she was also aware that Granma Carrie had ignored a similar lump for a very long time before consulting a doctor.

Mother told Aunt Clara about her discovery during one of her frequent visits to Hull, and although she had already decided to seek medical advice, Auntie urged her to waste no time. So, soon after she came home, Mother went to see Dr Singh, who had cared for my father so sympathetically nearly three years earlier. The doctor referred Mother to the same consultant surgeon, Mr Shepherd, who had operated on Dad, and he arranged for her to enter the same private nursing home, St. George's, on Thorne Road, Doncaster. Everything happened very quickly, and Mother felt that if it really were cancer, and she had 'the operation', she should, with luck, last at least another two years, to see me through to the age of thirteen.

She had only a few days to get organised. I think she must have delegated charge of the Drum to Georgina, and she asked Aunt Nancy to collect me and take me back to Cromer Street for a time. I was told that Mother was going into the nursing home for a rest, and I believed it. In retrospect, it seems strange I never suspected that she was to have an operation.

The day before Mother was due to enter the nursing home, I developed a terrible toothache at school, so bad I spent the afternoon in the sick-room. When I got home at tea-time, I was still in such agony that Mother said I must see a dentist. Together we walked to old Mr Robinson's on Bentley Road, and although it was out of his working hours, he agreed to extract the tooth, which was a big double one.

His surgery was upstairs, and I was conducted thither, leaving Mother in the downstairs waiting-room. I expect I must have had an injection, but when Mr Robinson got to grips with the tooth, the pain was so excruciating I screamed my head off. Poor Mother, who must have had far more serious matters than teeth on her mind, had one foot on the stairs as Mr Robinson started to descend, holding the offending molar in his pliers. He wanted to show Mother what a job he'd had removing it, because the root had been hooked around a nerve.

***

I REMEMBER NOTHING about Mother leaving for the nursing home, and all I know about her stay there was what I gathered later. As she was led to her room she said, 'It's not the same one, is it?' (where my father had died). She was assured that it was not.

She smiled as she described to me one oft-repeated instruction from staff preparing her for surgery: 'You'll have to take your teeth out'. Of course, they were her own.

On the way to theatre she joined in the pretence that she was off to the cinema. Such forced cheerfulness did not percolate beyond the higher reaches of her consciousness, or prevent her from repeating parts of her recently-made will as she surfaced from the anaesthetic. She remembered a voice going on and on, and thinking to herself, 'I wish that woman would shut up.' But the voice was hers, and she was told afterwards that she had said '... And to my sister, Nance, I leave my dearest possession: my daughter, Janet.'

She came round wondering whether her lump had been malignant and whether she had lost her breast, and soon realised this was so. Surgery, she learned, had been radical, involving lymph glands beneath her arm. Radiotherapy would be necessary once the wound had healed, but as far as Mr Shepherd could tell, the operation had been successful.

I think Mother was in St. George's for about a fortnight, and she did not want me to see her. I have a vague mental picture of her in a single bed in a strange room, but this would either relate to the brief period before her operation, or else be purely imaginary. Aunt Nancy came to Bentley with the intention of taking me back to Hull, but the plan went awry when I fell ill with a rash. When Dr Singh was called, he said it was measles, and I should stay at home in bed for a while.

Herbert was very put out by this development, and could not see why I was forbidden to take the train. Mother was ever afterwards convinced that he had expected she would be too ill to keep her job, and that here was his chance to inherit it. From what some of his acquaintances later let slip, he had boasted that he would soon be running things, and, as if to endorse his new image, he bought a large Alsatian dog.

Having all of us still hanging around the pub was a great irritation for Herbert, and Aunt Nancy and Aunt Clara, who had also come to lend support, found themselves in an unenviable position. They, Mrs Dunn, Aunt Elsie and Uncle Jack, and anyone else in Mother's camp, were made to feel unwelcome. Discomfort was stoked to outrage after a butcher friend brought an oxtail, a rare wartime treat, to make a strengthening stew for Mother. Georgina cooked it, Herbert ate it – greed so perfidious Aunt Clara would relate the story years afterwards with her indignation still touching top C.

Poor Aunt Nancy! Away from home, worried about her sister, entrusted with her child, and faced with Herbert's animosity. I see her now, on her knees in my bedroom, scrubbing the lino. This would be a threefold therapy, for as well as expunging germs she was passing her time usefully in a familiar task, and letting off steam through hard physical effort.

At length I was declared fit for travel, and she took me to Hull. I seemed to be there for weeks, but perhaps it was not so long. I have fragmented memories of that time: sharing a double bed with Auntie and Annette; writing letters to Mother, and composing an emotional poem for her; playing at night in the cold, dark street or in the big (now largely unused) air raid shelter near Auntie's house with Annette and her friends; reading *The Daily Mirror*; listening to wartime radio programmes (Anne Shelton singing 'I'll Walk Alone'); dodging Grandad; eating bowl after bowl of porridge and treacle, Auntie's staple in times of hunger; losing hold on anxiety while watching films at the Mayfair Cinema; parrying well-meaning inquiries from constantly popping-in neighbours; learning to keep my end up during family cut-and-thrust; making myself scarce if real rows developed.

I don't recall being either happy or worried about missing school. I was worried about Mother, and missed her and the Drum dreadfully, and couldn't wait to go home. But Mother had explained to me that Aunt Nancy was my Godmother and would look after me, and I knew this was true, even though I never felt entirely integrated into the hubble-bubble at Number 1.

When the great day came, and I finally went back to the Drum, my arrival coincided with Mother's, who was returning from a trip to town. She was sagging under the weight of a big tweed coat. I flung myself at her, and although she kissed and hugged me, it was not the bear-hug I had expected, and I remember feeling disappointed. She looked very tired, and I could tell that while she was happy about my homecoming, her mind was on other things as well.

Next morning, as we lay in bed together, she cradled me in her right arm and said that, although she had told me she was going into the nursing home just for a rest, she had in fact had an operation. She had kept this from me so as not to worry me, but now, as I heard some of the details, I realised why she had been unable to hug me properly. I think she must have still been waiting to start the course of radiotherapy, which in those days was a much clumsier form of treatment than it is now.

What I had not known at the time, either, was that a day or two after leaving the nursing home, Mother had been sitting in the office behind the lounge bar when Herbert's Alsatian came up to her and placed his head on her knee. As she put out her left hand to stroke him, he snarled and went for her, clamping the hand between his jaws. Her screams brought someone running from the bar, and Herbert took his pet away and locked him up.

Dr Singh was sent for, and came immediately. He had already advised Mother that after her operation she should keep her left arm still, and not lift 'so much as a pen' with it. Now, as he cauterised the deep tooth-marks in the palm and back of the hand, he said in his high, sing-song voice, 'I would give anything for this not to have happened.'

Mother said afterwards that the pain and swelling from the bite were worse than the mastectomy. As for the dog, his end came quickly. It so happened that Bill Day, Winnie's father, was having a drink in the bar when the attack took place. Being a butcher, he kept a gun at home for hunting game, and he went off to get it. Then Bill and Herbert took the Alsatian into the garden, and Bill shot him.

Herbert must have been as disturbed as anyone by the turn of events, but his sulky acceptance helped to drive an even deeper wedge between the two factions in our household. I do not know how soon it was after this that he and Georgina took over the management of a Bentley club, but it surely cannot have been long before they departed, with Mother's anxious blessing on Georgina. We lost direct contact with them, but heard after some years first that she had left Herbert, then that she had divorced him. This seemed a very good thing.

***

MOTHER MANAGED TO run the Drum while completing her course of radiotherapy, although the treatment was distressing, and went on for some time. She travelled to Doncaster Royal Infirmary, and it has only just occurred to me what a trial that journey must have been, for though the hospital was only about three miles away, she would have needed to catch both a trackless and a bus.

The effects of the radiography grew increasingly severe: remarkably, no hair loss, but acute nausea and weakness. But the worst part was the burning. The long scar and flat area of skin where her left breast had been became an enormous, weeping blister, which stuck to the gauze pad covering it, so that the pad, when it was raised, came away coated with a yellowish serum, leaving bare flesh beneath. One day she came home in such a sorry state that she could no longer keep her condition from me, and lifted the dressing to show me the bright red mass beneath, looking like raw steak. I shall never forget the sight of it.

Nor shall I forget the sight of my mother carrying heavy coal-buckets up from the cellar a few months later. Her wound had healed, and she had gradually recovered her strength, so it seemed that Mr Shepherd and Mr Blomfield, the consultant radiologist, had known what they were doing when they used such drastic methods on that frightening lump. She blessed them every day, I think. I blessed them too, when I thought about it, and wondered at the selfless dedication of Mr Blomfield and his team; for Mother said that although they wore special protective clothing, the effects of the radiation were such that their skins were quite yellow, and she had heard they might be unable to have children.

Paradoxically, while she was grateful for the outcome, and for the reassurance she gained from regular check-ups at the Infirmary, Mother did not like to admit she had had cancer, and pushed it to the back of her mind. 'Cancer' was a word with such dread connotations it was avoided in our family as if the very mention of it might trigger an attack. If they happened to be talking of someone with the condition, Aunt Nancy and Mother would refer to it as 'you know what', and nod pityingly. This was a common attitude at a time when so little was known about the disease.

Mother, who had always carried a tray of drinks in her left hand, learned to carry it in her right, and gave away her heavy tweed coat with the beaver-lamb collar. No prosthesis was suggested, so she stuffed the left cups of her brassieres with handkerchiefs or scarves. During the Fifties, 'falsies' (rubber cones to complement and compliment the flat-chested) came in, and she wore one of these. It was years before she able to obtain a sort of prosthetic bean-bag: a great improvement, she said.

***

STRANGELY ENOUGH, DESPITE all the ill-feeling that surfaced while Herbert was ensconced at the Drum, his family's friendly attitude towards Mum and me remained unaffected. His parents had made me welcome at their house in Bentley, and I have fond memories of his mother's bilberry pies. Later the old couple went to live near Port Talbot with their daughter, Dilys, and after Herbert and Georgina left the Drum to manage the club, his other sister, Mary, became our barmaid. If she knew we had had problems with Herbert, she never mentioned them, and was always very kind to Mother and me. So when, in the summer after Mother's operation, Mary, who had no children of her own, suggested I accompany her on a visit to the family in Wales, I was pleased to be asked, and excited by the idea of visiting my first foreign country.

I received a warm welcome from Dilys, her husband and her parents, and had a busy time. Much of it was spent in the company of a boy called Clive, Dilys's nephew-by-marriage, whom I had met the previous year at Herbert and Georgina's wedding. Clive was twelve, like me, a gentlemanly boy with wonderful brown eyes and a Corgi called Sandy, and he lived in a pub just down the road. If he had been told to look after me, he did it without any obvious signs of resentment; and, as if all these marvels were not enough, his mother took us by car to seaside places like Mumbles and Porthcawl.

When the time came for Mary to leave, Dilys wondered whether my mother would like to come for a break, and if so, whether I would be happy to stay on until she arrived. Would I not! To my delight, Mother accepted, and I remember being taken to meet her at the railway station a few days later, and admiring the stylish figure she cut as she stepped along the platform in a navy-blue, chalk-striped costume, turquoise blouse, and turquoise feathered hat.

We were given a splendid holiday, which, looking back, was a remarkable gesture by Herbert's kith and kin, considering he and my mother had parted as enemies. I can only assume that either his family knew him better than we did, or else he and Georgina had decided to keep their own counsel about those distressing events at the Drum.

I never saw those kind people in Wales again. I had high hopes of returning the following year, but when summer came round once more, Mary fancied a change, so we spent a week together at a rather uncomfortable boarding-house at Scarborough instead. How on earth did we pass the time? All I can remember is watching the Fol-de-Rols perform at the Floral Hall, and having a hair-raising switchback ride at a fairground.

Though I always found Mary a sweet-natured person, her husband had left her, a disaster Mother feared she might have brought on herself by being too house-proud. No man, said Mum, could be happy in his home life if his wife sprang forward to plump up the cushions every time he got out of his armchair.

After her divorce, cushion-plumper or not, Mary remarried, and gave up her job as our barmaid. Sad to say, our friendship cooled a little while this new situation was developing, and after our lives took different directions we gradually lost touch with each other.

CHAPTER SIXTEEN – GROWING

I WENT BACK to school after many weeks away, though I remember nothing of settling in except a nagging worry about end-of-year exams, which, as the date approached, even began to outbalance the bliss of being at home.

Still, as the situation was restored, with Georgina and Herbert gone, Mother hopeful and active, and Paddy as rumbustiously affectionate as ever, the Drum became a haven again. No worry was so bad it could not be subdued, at least temporarily, by turning a few cartwheels in the garden, bouncing a ball for Paddy across the long reaches of the living-room floor, or stretching out in front of the fire with a book. Whenever customers congregated and I was alone in my eyrie, the familiar smells and sounds carried up to me from below were reassuring: the tinge of beer and smoke, hum of voices, chink of glasses, ripple of laughter, ping of tills. This was the stuff of normality. Nothing important had changed.

Things had changed for Aunt Clara and Uncle George, though, and very much for the better. They had rented the house in Anlaby Park Road, Hull, knowing that when the war ended the owners would want it back. When it seemed the war might soon be over, they were wondering what to do when Jackson's, the big provisions and confectionery firm who employed Uncle to manage one of their Hull stores, made them a proposition. The company had a shop in Preston, a village a few miles from Hull, and wanted Uncle to take charge of it, and live there, so Auntie and Uncle went to Preston to make an inspection and could hardly believe their luck. Soon the corner shop in Stepney Lane, Hull, which Auntie had been running alone, was disposed of, and the exciting shift achieved from town to country.

It was as though a fairy had waved a magic wand, for not only was the Preston shop a local institution, it was also charmingly rustic. The frontage was of that mellow, pinky-red brick which distinguishes old East Riding villages. The private front door and sitting-room window opened directly on to the pavement in Main Street, giving no hint of the wonderful garden behind.

Vegetable patch apart, this casual Eden had grown under its own influence into a place of more intimate enchantment than the Drum's vast heart of open grassland, for here the crowding trees made even the air seem green.

I can visualise the Preston living quarters almost as clearly as those at the Drum, for they became a second home for Mother and me. The sitting-room had a white marble fireplace, its mantel the perfect setting for Granmer's vases (which Grampa had rescued from the sea). Once Auntie had installed Uncle's piano, a three-piece suite in rust uncut moquette, and a fire-screen painted with large, pale roses, it was hard to believe there was a finer room anywhere.

A narrow hall led to a living-room, kitchen, and a mysterious, dark staircase, which curved up between walls to five bedrooms and a bathroom. Plenty of space for not only Auntie, Uncle and Cousin Georgie but for Uncle Fred, Brian and Granmer as well, and for any visitors who cared to take advantage of Auntie's pressing hospitality, and the perquisites of the grocery side (for food was still on ration years after the war ended).

Mother and I could go to stay any time we liked, for as long as we liked, and sometimes when the beer ran out, and the Drum closed, and I was not at school, we would head for the Hull train, and then, after calling at Aunt Nancy's for our dinner, catch the bus to Preston. Half an hour later, we would be rising from our seats and clinging on like grim death as the bus rounded the ancient church, fearful of missing our stop.

Then it took only a few steps across the street to reach the shop (still bearing the name of the previous owner, Francis Myers) and walk through the unlocked private door; and immediately we cleared the threshold, my fancy tells me now, we sensed with a lifting of the spirits, as we breathed in the scents of cheese and bacon, that the process had begun. An antique phrase describes it best: the sloughing off of care.

***

AS SOON AS I could, I made for the garden, running across the yard, flanked by various out-houses (including the stable in which my soft-hearted Uncle George learned to fatten piglets for the Ministry of Food, staying indoors when his protégés departed for slaughter), then through the gap in the wall to the grassy area, and the orchard where gnarled old trees yielded in the fullness of time a bountiful harvest of apples, pears and plums.

One particular apple tree held a swing, on which I spent untroubled hours alone (Brian and Georgie eschewed it). But when Annette came, which she often did, we took turns. Sometimes we would stand gazing across the hedge at the open fields around us, and plan our lives, wondering whether we might marry. On the whole, we preferred the idea of a spinster life. We would live together in the lonely cottage we could see in the distance, and Annette said I should write stories which she would run with (we pictured her tiny figure sprinting across the horizon) to send off to publishers from Preston Post Office.

The Greenwoods soon felt at home in their new surroundings, even Granmer, I think, though she did not go out much. She liked to potter in the house, but

Auntie saw to the cooking, and a good-natured girl, Audrey, came in to do the washing, ironing and cleaning. Uncle Fred travelled on the bus to his work in Hull as a sign-writer. Georgie and Brian joined the village school and Aunt Clara and Uncle George became popular local figures. They could not help but make friends, for as well as being in charge of doling out nearly everyone's rations, with the help of two assistants, they were indefatigable socialisers, and soon had the measure of Preston's pubs. They patronised all three, but their favourite was The Nag's Head, known as 'Owd Woman's', run by an idiosyncratic elderly couple, the Dunstans, whose customers overflowed nightly into their personal parlour.

'Owd Man' Dunstan was a slow mover, who spent much of his time sitting down. If there was a beer shortage, he would take up his position on a bench outside the pub, pretending to be a customer. Desperate drinkers whose usual haunts had run dry would sometimes alight at the bus-stop opposite, hoping to slake their thirsts at The Nag's Head. But no matter how their tongues hung out, 'Owd Man', strongly protective of his regulars, would tell newcomers that the beer was 'off' (meaning undrinkable). How many believed him is a matter for conjecture.

Normally, 'Owd Man' occupied a chair by the parlour fire. Georgie and I used to be taken in to join the regulars when Auntie and Uncle called for their frequent nightcaps, but rambling adult conversation and a dark Victorian atmosphere were not to our taste, and we were immensely bored.

I remember 'Owd Man', sitting there in his cap, asking me once, 'Do you like crud cheesecake?'

'Pardon?'

'DO YOU LIKE CRUD CHEESECAKE?'

'Yes', I quavered, not sure what it was.

'Got any of that crud cheesecake left? Fetch some for little lass', he said to his wife, who obliged. I was relieved to find it was actually 'curd cheesecake', as I had suspected, and a good home-made one at that.

'Owd Woman' herself was a squat bundle of tightly-packed energy who ran the pub on kindly but no-nonsense lines, with her taller, thinner sister drifting wraith-like in the background. The three old dears had been young in a very different world, and their recollections might have been worth hearing. But I was at the wrong age, alas, and though I hope I managed to feign interest, I was not really listening.

I much preferred to be back at the house, playing with Georgie's toy farm, poising the little white duck on its mirror pond. I was allowed to take charge of the farm, but though I liked watching the Hornby train bustle round on its track, I never felt I had the right to touch it, or (not that it bothered me) the Meccano. The boys and I had a kind of arms-length relationship, for I was a girl, which was a pity. We saw

179

quite a lot of each other, though, for they would come to spend long holidays at Bentley in the summer, and with Annette we made a cohesive enough quartet.

Brian, coolly detached, and nearly two years older than I, was indisputably our leader, and I regarded him with shy admiration. Georgie, six months my senior, was diffident, quiet and coddled, and seemingly not the stuff of heroes. He had never recovered the dignity he lost in my eyes when Aunt Clara turned out his trouser-pockets after one of my birthday parties and found he had stuffed them with sandwich-crusts.

Such resourcefulness had tickled Auntie. 'I always cut his crusts off, Dorrie', she explained as she and my mother laughed together over the incident. But when Mother repeated the story, hardy souls who never experienced cut-off crusts, and were even told to eat the burnt bits 'to make their hair curl', scoffed at such namby-pambyism. They subscribed to the opinion that this was typical of the way Aunt Clara spoiled Little Georgie, until Mother pointed out that Georgie had a weak constitution, and his appetite needed coaxing. She might have added that poor Auntie had already lost one son.

In close alliance, Brian and Georgie were great teasers, sometimes poking gentle fun at Granmer if she appealed to them to quieten down, clear up after themselves, or come and get their dinner while it was hot. Any show of mild defiance (and it was very mild) would make her catch her breath with a peppy 'eh-eh-eh', and threaten to become vexed. But she never minded being beaten at cards or dominoes, just laughed and wiped her eyes. Sometimes Brian, Georgie and I preferred building tunnels with the dominoes, or constructing houses with playing-cards. Draughts I drew the line at, for I always ended up looking stupid. The boys liked jigsaws, but my interest in these was half-hearted: they were never my idea of a good time.

When my cousins came to stay in Bentley in the summer holidays, a certain pattern developed. We used to play tracking in the garden shrubberies, climb trees, make camp in the grassy clearing under the big willow. There we lit fires to boil up crab-apples in tin cans, and heated water to mix custard-powder, a disastrous combination. We would, against Mother's strict instructions, lift the iron lid of the well in the stable-yard and chuck pebbles down, down, down to fret the distant glim of water. Often we would stroll through the gate and along the lane to Pipering Wood, with Paddy bounding joyfully ahead. Georgie must have missed his own dog, Gyp, a cream Labrador who had been his shadow ever since either could remember.

The boys were good at making catapults and bows-and-arrows out of wood and bits of string and elastic, and pea-shooters from hollow stems. We went birds'-nesting, and occasionally further afield to Bentley Park, where, at the ornamental pond, tiddlers and sticklebacks yielded themselves up in large numbers to anyone with a fishing-net and jam jar.

Georgie and Brian enjoyed, nay, had a mania for, collecting railway engine and car numbers. I frequently found myself stationed alongside a road or on top of a bridge, memorising passing registration-plates. At Doncaster Railway Station we would stalk the platforms for hours, on the look-out for engines hitherto unspotted. At least some of them had names, which gave them a kind of identity. My eager cousins carefully listed their cars and engines, poring over them, totting them up, and comparing them with those amassed by their friends. It was a great triumph to have spotted a prize like the Flying Scotsman, for rivalry was keen, and cheating frowned upon, and quite pointless to the serious collector. But I was no such one, and though often pressed into service as an extra pair of eyes (and weak ones at that) found the whole business achingly boring.

Sometimes, when they stayed at the Drum, we would visit one of the town's two swimming- baths, occasionally meeting up with Gordon and Dennis. I hated the echoing vault of nasty-tasting cold water, full of unappetising bodies, and the sodden changing rooms with their insecure doors and slippery duck-boards. Despite having my chin held by Annette, and sometimes Dorothy, I could not swim, and floundered madly. I was conscious of my stick-like body, and my scratchy, bottle-green, woollen costume with its long, knicker-like legs. The costume was conspicuously trimmed with orange and yellow braid, and was miles too big for me, having been passed down from a much larger friend. It ballooned when I got in the water, and sagged as I left it, trying to drag me back with its dead weight. Forty-five years on, less frumpily garbed, I learned to swim in Australia.

***

IN PRESTON, I can bring to mind only two occasions when I tagged behind to meet my cousins' friends. Georgie once took me to the village 'cinema', really a hut in a field, for a Saturday morning film show. The other, even bigger, event was the celebration of either V.E. (Victory Over Europe) or V.J. (Victory Over Japan) Day in 1945.

I was in Preston for whichever of these two momentous dates it happened to be, and remember tramping through the cool night air towards a gigantic bonfire. Suddenly we were in a crowd, closing in on the spectacle, dodging its sparks, scorched by its breath.

What followed is a blank, though I do recall how excitement kept welling up inside me, mingled with relief. Worrying about the war had been a responsibility I was glad to shed. Now it was After The War. Peace was here.

But what did it mean, the End Of The War? I dredged down into my pre-war memories, and came up with the taste of the bacon from my father's plate (wartime bacon tasted fishy). And of course, there would be bananas. And no more air raids or blackout. Further than this, imagination simply could not go.

***

IT MUST HAVE been around this time that I began to revise my opinion of Georgie. He had always looked embarrassed when Aunt Clara was being particularly protective, especially when her voice rose to its highest register. Too young to respond with gracious deflective tactics, he would wriggle his shoulders, muttering, 'Don't fuss, Mum', and a flush would rise up through his cheeks right into his ears.

Because he and I had been thrust together from childhood, there being only six months (and in the early days, only a few streets) between us, in shared play, outings and parties we had accepted each other unquestioningly, if not with great enthusiasm. Then he started to grow tall, less 'chesty', more considerate and confident, even quite good-looking, with his velvety, silver-fair head and very blue eyes. The vulnerable sticking-out blades of bone on the insides of his knees, so evident in schoolboy short trousers, disappeared inside long ones. He lost some of his awkwardness, began to wield a dryish wit, and handled his mother's fussing with good humour. Perhaps he took his cue from his father's own reaction to Auntie's maternal clucking (a grin at the audience and a mild 'Aye, all right, Clara.')

My cousin's long fingers had always shown patience in the construction of model ships and aeroplanes, and he now spent some of his spare time helping out at a local garage. He became known as Young George, or George, went off on long bike-rides, developed a tan, got himself tentatively acquainted with an admiring girl. Suddenly, he was a young man of dash and presence, and we started looking on each other as proper people, not just cousins thrown together. In a strange way, I was both more and less at ease with him.

But all this took time, a process not fully worked through or appreciable until he was fourteen and I was thirteen, just before he died.

***

THE DRUM HELD its own festivities to mark the war's end, the biggest taking place in the little-used club-room reached by the iron staircase on the side of the building. This event was for local residents, not just pub customers, and I popped in for a few minutes because I was curious to see how the place acquitted itself under party conditions. Normally its windows presented a blank, mysterious stare when we gazed at them from the living-room across the inner well. Sometimes Annette, though the club-room was consistently shut up, thought she saw movements behind the dusty glass, or, even worse, faces peering out. Such impressions lent wings to her nervous fancies, and she remained convinced the room was haunted. It fell, I think, into complete disuse, and although some years later Bruce Woodcock, the European Heavyweight Boxing Champion, who was a Doncaster lad, wanted to set up his gym in it, and do outdoor training in the garden, he and the brewery failed to reach agreement. Mother was disappointed, regarding it as a very short-sighted decision.

Far jollier was the downstairs concert-room, with its stage and painted backcloth, and it was here that the Home Guard battalion held their Victory Dance, which I was thrilled to attend. A highlight for me was taking the floor with a plump, middle-aged gentleman who was attired in a navy-blue siren-suit like Winston Churchill's. My partner's ample girth tapered down through surprisingly agile legs to a pair of twinkling feet that spun us through the old-fashioned waltz with centrifugal force. I remember his kind, pink face bending over me, his warm, woollen shoulder, his absent-minded smile.

An old man got up on the stage and sang:

'I saw the old homestead, and faces I knew,
I saw England's valleys and dells ...'

I think this was the occasion, too, when the Home Guard presented my mother with a silver brooch in the shape of a Union Jack, set with tiny red, white and blue stones, as a mark of their regard, and to commemorate the End of the War.

***

SUCH JUBILATION WAS all very well, but there were serious matters to attend to. Peace did not mean the end of exams, and mine were soon upon me. I have a strong recollection of lying in bed one Saturday morning, worrying about them. (Mother sometimes spoiled me at the weekends by letting me lie in with a book, bringing me marmalade or jam sandwiches, and tea.)

Yet when I mentally ran through my list of classmates, and asked myself who was more likely to do better than I, only two names occurred to me, Peter Whiteley and Godfrey Outram. I felt somewhat calmer then, and when at last, after due trial, the class positions were announced, these same boys had come first and second, and I third.

I never did as well again, but I had ensured a place for myself in the top form the following year. Joy also moved into 2A, and I spent the rest of my school life sitting next to her. As for Whiteley and Outram, who ended up in the desks immediately behind us, they generally managed to outstrip us in overall markings, being better at maths and science.

Exams remained a worry for me, especially towards the end of each school year. During escapes to the Don Cinema, I would lose myself in the film, only for troubles to resurface as the lights went up, the interval music jerked into play (usually 'Whispering Grass'), and the gauzy orange curtains swished across to hide the screen. Some nights, as well as depressing thoughts of unfinished homework, and tests, and difficult teachers, and being made to teeter on high parallel bars in the school gym, or to try to clear its vaulting-horse, other fears crept in. Was Mother's cough/headache/backache a serious sign? Were those red spots between my fingers really scarlet fever?

Such nervous anxieties were, however, peripheral to the main concern of making sure the Drum's privilege tickets were not wasted. The pub had a standing arrangement with the Don to display its posters in return for free tickets, and as the film changed twice a week, my companions and I were spoiled for choice.

But there was a snag. In order to gain entry to our pleasure-palace, we had first to beard, and overcome, the dragon, a box-office salesgirl who seemed to hate us. I see her now, her square, peevish face and precisely curled hair, crisp blouse and manicured nails. If it was a 'U' film, the fingers bearing those nails grudgingly pressed the button controlling the slit from which the tickets sprang, and no comment was forthcoming. But if it was an 'A' film, we were supposed to be fourteen to see it without an accompanying adult, and the dragon was entitled to issue her challenge.

At town cinemas, we might try asking grown-ups in the queue if they would say we were with them, and sometimes they agreed; but at the Don we adopted different tactics, pleading that we had special right of entry because of our free vouchers. If a queue had built up behind us, this often worked, but sometimes we were turned away.

As success was unpredictable, we started to pretend we had reached the stage where one of us was fourteen. Although our adversary glared in disbelief, she had to let us in. We were convinced she bore us a personal grudge, but maybe she was only trying to protect our innocence, or feared a telling-off from the manager.

Shame on us, we smirked every time we threw down our gauntlet to her Ladyship in the glass box, and, if we won the round, whispered and wriggled in triumph once we were in our seats. But it was a glad day when Brenda actually reached fourteen, because we knew that from then on, right would be on our side.

The dear old Don, where Joy and I, too, submerged ourselves in dreams, was demolished long ago, its charmless brick shell not worth preserving. But I am still grateful for the solace I found there, which is why I will always revere its sacred memory.

***

THOUGH BRENDA HAD passed the magic number fourteen, she was small, and bureaucracy took some convincing, even when she proudly demanded a penny fare on the trackless instead of a ha'penny one. Such a milestone, though financially crippling, we younger ones could not wait to reach.

This did not mean, of course, that we were careless about our money. I kept mine in a tin box and counted it several times a week. When I started at Percy Jackson's, Mother decided she would give me five shillings (twenty-five pence) a week, and out of this I should pay for my school dinners (two-and-a-penny, roughly ten pence), school milk (I think this cost fourpence, or just over two pence), and the threepence I had volunteered to donate to the Guild of Help.

The Guild was a charity our form-teachers had asked us to support when we started at the school, and although I was never sure what it did, I felt Mother would wish me to be generous, and that I should act accordingly. So I made my rash commitment of threepence a week, and was disturbed to find that those who held their hands up after me mostly proposed giving a penny or tuppence. (There was one girl, though, Pat Dalton, who amazingly promised sixpence, and stuck to it.) I was left with pocket money of two and fourpence, which I saved in the tin box to buy books and other treats, and Mother's Christmas and birthday presents.

The new books were lovingly marshalled in my bedroom, and over the years the collection widened to include works by Dumas (*The Three Musketeers, Twenty Years After, The Count of Monte Cristo*), Victor Hugo (*The Hunchback of Notre Dame, Les Misérables*), Dickens (*Pickwick Papers, Oliver Twist*), Scott (*Ivanhoe*, especially appealing because it was partly set in 'that pleasant valley of England which is watered by the River Don'), Robert Louis Stevenson, and the Brontës.

But I still kept the old books I had brought from Hull in a wash-stand in the playroom. I wish I had them now. I gave or threw them away along with my dolls and other toys when we left Bentley. Teddy I would have kept, but he had already been lost by visiting children, and though I was well into my teens by the time he disappeared, I conducted a fruitless search for him in the garden, with tears rolling down my cheeks.

185

When I first knew Brenda, we used the playroom a lot, and it was big enough for us to split down the middle with a length of string to make separate 'houses'. We called the landing with its numbered doors Claremont Avenue, and ran our homes and our children, Rosie and Sheila, and Sally and Jeniffer, with motherly pride and rigour. If we grew weary of the domestic scene, and it was raining, we polished our tap-dancing routines, or played three-ball in a corner of the living-room, juggling three tennis balls against the cream-washed wall until, over the months, a pattern of grey blotches developed. When we tired of this, we practised doing handstands against the wall.

Gradually, our interest in dolls waned, and I began to realise, having reached the age of ten or so, that it would never revive. (Brenda must have felt like this for far longer than I, but was probably too kind to say so.) Yet after I betrayed those fixed-smile personalities I had treated as flesh and blood, and shut them in the playroom to gather damp and dust, I was seized by a sense of melancholy and loss.

***

AT SOME STAGE, Brenda acquired a big, two-wheel bike and let me share it, yelling instructions as I bumped around the cinder-track in the garden. I could balance on the straight, but fell off at every bend, ineptitude which made her cry with laughter.

But once Brenda was eleven, six months after we became friends, she stopped coming to play on Tuesday nights. She joined the Girl Guides in St. Peter's Church Hall, and Tuesday night was Guide night, when all manner of exciting things happened. I listened with envy to tales of uniforms, and tracking, and Morse-code, and 'camp-fire' sing-songs in the hall over mugs of cocoa, and working for badges, and keeping the Guide Promise. ('I promise to do my best to do my duty to God and the King; to help other people at all times; and to obey the Guide Law.')

I longed to be a Girl Guide, too, and place myself under the jurisdiction of the Captain, who Brenda said was lovely. It seemed a long, long wait until I should be old enough, but at length, before I was quite eleven, thanks to a special dispensation obtained by Brenda, the call came.

But Mother was unsure about letting me out on dark, wintry nights, even with Brenda, and begged me to put off being a Guide until spring. She was so pleased with the way I swallowed my disappointment that as a reward she took me to see the film 'Reap the Wild Wind'. It was a tale of storm and shipwreck, the drowning of a beautiful stowaway, and the hero's battle with a giant squid. My terrified enjoyment was tinged with guilt, for, to tell the truth, when actually faced with becoming a Guide I had felt nervous. Supposing I should prove no good at it? Postponement meant more welcome breathing-space.

My eventual entry into St. Peter's Girl Guides coincided with a parade. What it was for I cannot say, most likely St. George's Day, but I do know that I yearned to be part of it, though of course I had no uniform. Then Mother took matters in hand. The marchers were due to assemble on a Sunday morning outside the Don Cinema, and with only a day to go, she borrowed Brenda's Guide tunic and bought a length of dark, navy-blue cotton in Doncaster Market. She cut out my tunic using Brenda's as a pattern, and stitched it up on her machine, with me, for once, eager to be fitted.

The main business done, she turned to accessories. On Brenda's recommendation, a folded triangular bandage, dipped in saxe-blue dye, became the tie. The lanyard was easy, lengths of white string twisted together, but the hat was more of a problem, until Mother remembered a navy felt trilby-type she had in her wardrobe. Shrunk and moulded to roundness over an upturned basin placed near a steaming kettle, this looked authentic enough once its brim had been cut down. Lastly, I needed a brown leather belt, for which Paddy surrendered his lead. He hated it anyway, and though rarely used, it was a bit chewed.

When morning came, and I stepped out behind the band with the Guides, Scouts, Cubs, Brownies, and all the other marchers, I felt proudly in keeping. 'She looked as good as anybody,' I heard Mother tell someone later.

In Bentley, another procession, which Brenda and I liked to watch from a distance, was held each year to celebrate the crowning of the Catholic Church's May Queen. The chosen girl, majestically robed and attended, was paraded through the High Street along with a statue of the Virgin Mary, and it was a sight to make folk of all persuasions gather. One year Brenda knew the queen personally, which imparted an even greater air of mystery to the ritual.

Although Brenda's mother had been brought up a Roman Catholic, and Brenda herself had been Christened in the faith, the old ties had been relaxed sufficiently for my friend to join the Protestant flock at St. Peter's. But Brenda always seemed perfectly normal to me, whereas Catholics were a race apart, who prayed to idols and were full of strange superstitions.

Years later, I worked with a Catholic journalist who told me that in the Yorkshire mining village where he grew up, Protestants would cross the road to avoid him. No such strong antipathies were flying around Bentley in our day, as far as I could tell, but Mother, saddled with prejudices passed on by her father, had handed her wariness of Catholicism down to me.

It seemed so alien a religion that I thought I could tell its adherents simply by looking at them. I wondered what it felt like to be a Catholic and to have to go to their ugly church, and I was fervently glad I need not confess my sins to our Vicar, Mr Campbell.

Joy, by contrast, inclined to Nonconformism. I remember going with her to a concert at Bentley Road Methodist Church in which one of her mother's friends was singing solo. The prospect of the lady's stage appearance intrigued us, because we had already heard her rehearsing at Joy's home, with Joy's mother accompanying on the piano.

Certain scenes engrave themselves on the memory despite being of no great import. I cannot explain why the sight and sound of this confident soprano, giving her all in the front room at Earlston Drive, lives on inside my head. True, Joy and I found it a testing experience to sit a few feet away, able to see the glistening tongue rolling its 'r's and stressing its consonants as its owner intoned so feelingly about a girl called Dorothy May.

Not only was I all too ready to giggle at the high-pitched intensity of the poor lady's delivery, I could not help thinking she seemed all wrong for the song – too old, too strongly-built and (I realise now) too artful. I am sure Joy thought so as well, though we never put it into words. Still, we could not laugh and shame her mother, who bent so graciously over the keys.

Through careful avoidance of each other's eye, we stayed poker-faced, even though tragedy was building. The song's last line proved almost too much; we learned that 'the angels had taken Dorothy May', news that might have meant our undoing had it not also signalled our release, and liberty to grin as we applauded.

When it came to the concert in the crowded church hall some nights later, we relapsed a bit. Not overly so, mind you, for we were surrounded by chapel-folk who took such matters seriously, and knew Joy as her mother's daughter.

***

THE PIANO AT Number 49 Earlston Drive was the magnetic core of our own singing sessions during my visits in those early days. I always got a hearty welcome from Mr and Mrs Cuffling, Joy's parents, whenever I walked the two trackless-stops to their home, and was usually whisked into the front room for conversation, and perhaps a slice of raisin pie. Both parents took a loving but firm hand in Joy's upbringing, and while it was obvious how proud they were of their sparkling, clever daughter, who had come into their lives quite late, they had laid down in their own minds a pattern of expectations which Joy strove to fulfil. She had more constraints upon her than I did, for there was only my mother to worry about me, and she had the Drum on her mind as well, and all the distractions this entailed.

I tried to live up to Mrs Cuffling's idea of me, in the way most of us do when we value a person's good opinion, presenting the facet we think they expect of us. I tried to be more ladylike, more reflective of Mrs Cuffling's genteel manner. I was still working on my accent, endeavouring to rid myself of Hullisms (although even now I still occasionally say 'I aren't' instead of 'I'm not', a grammatical slip which always amused Joy). Mrs Cuffling spoke with scarcely a trace of Yorkshire, never dropping her aitches as my own mother sometimes did.

Once, during one of the sporadic arguments I had with Mother, I said as much to her, and was immediately sorry when I saw how much it had hurt her. I often did hurt her, but those particular words I have never forgotten. There was a period, as I reached my teens, when we had quite bitter rows, and she would rightly accuse me of wilfulness, or selfishness, which boiled down to the same thing.

We were both born under the sign of Scorpio, which might, I suppose, be advanced as a reason for our flare-ups. Certainly our similar personalities were destined to clash, even without the tensions commonly experienced in mother-and-daughter relationships; I impatient to try my wings, she anxious to guide and protect me. Wearied of verbal fencing, we would subject each other to cold silences, which were far worse than the rows, until one of us put out a tentative feeler and received a grudging response. Then harmony was restored very quickly. That was the way we were made.

In all the disagreements we had, only once or twice do I remember Mother bringing my father into the equation. It would have been so easy for her to make him her ally, so easy to say, 'You wouldn't do that if your father was here', or, even more damningly, 'That would have disappointed your father.' But she resisted the temptation. Had she not done so, she would certainly have undermined me.

Such forbearance, when at times she must have been very worried, or very angry, astonishes me now. I was well into my teens, and seeing a boyfriend she disapproved of, when she said, 'If your father had been alive, you wouldn't have had so much freedom, you know. He would never have thought anybody good enough for you.'

I don't suppose Mother and I were in the least unusual in having squabbles and 'atmospheres', but I never heard tell of any in the households of my friends. In that era, no-one was encouraged to indulge in heart-searching or amateur psychology, and Joy and I, and Brenda and I, and Winnie and I never gave much thought to one another's home backgrounds. Such things were not discussed, and it was not done to ask personal questions that might prove too awkward to answer.

When, in the third year at the grammar school, we heard a rumour that Joyce Hildreth's father had died the day before my birthday party, we did not expect

Joyce to turn up for the fun and games. But turn up she did, a little puffy-eyed, but otherwise seemingly quite herself. In the face of such normality, no-one, not even Mother, dared raise the subject (after all, how can one ask, 'Is it true you've lost your father?' of a twelve-year-old who has come to enjoy a party?) So we carried on as usual, although we were all extra nice to Joyce.

Next day, Mother learned that the rumour had indeed been true, but Joyce never mentioned her father when we saw her in school, and so neither did Joy and I. We were a very close three-some, but some territory was just too private to be strayed upon. Also, I remembered my own embarrassment in similar circumstances.

**

THE WARMTH OF the welcome I always received from Joy's parents still radiates across the years. Mr Cuffling, if he was not working the night shift as a crane-driver in a glass-factory (a job that seemed to me a contradiction in terms), or doing his garden, or out on his bike, might be in the kitchen, and might have a joke to tell us. The only story of his I recall was about a member of a village football team who turned up to play in a match at a lunatic asylum and encountered one of the patients in the garden. The 'madman' started to chase the terrified visitor, who ran for his life. In the end, exhausted and breathless, he turned to face his pursuer, who leaned forward, touched him on the arm, and said 'Tig'. I thought it quite funny, and laughed. Today, being politically incorrect, the joke makes me laugh even more.

When he was feeling more serious, Mr Cuffling liked to quote a verse from *The Rubaiyat of Omar Khayam*:

'The moving finger writes; and, having writ,
Moves on: nor all thy piety nor wit
Shall move it back to cancel half a line,
Nor all thy tears wash out a word of it.'

Mrs Cuffling was fond of word-play (as in 'It isn't the cough that carries you off, it's the coffin they carry you off in', a melancholic nugget that drew an uneasy smile from me). I did not always grasp her puns immediately, but followed her with alacrity when she said, 'Shall we have a tune?' and led us into the front room, where the piano stood against the wall like an old friend waiting.

A lifting of the lid, a riffle through the song-book, a few tinkling notes of introduction, and the three of us would be borne on our own harmonic air-stream to a land 'where daisies pied and violets blue and ladies'-smocks all silver-white and cuckoo-buds of yellow hue did paint the meadow with delight.'

From there we might go on to harken to the lark as it at heaven's gate sang, or to stand beside a brooklet that sparkled on its way, and see beneath the wavelets a tiny trout at play. Joy and I would blend to a joint soprano, underscored by her mother's contralto, and we would all smile and nod at each other, and Joy would arch her eye-brow and look quizzical, and we would all be quite charmed by the noise we made. We knew we were happy as we ran through those sweet, old-fashioned airs, but now I find it easier to put our feelings into words: we were serene, and our delight was unalloyed.

CHAPTER SEVENTEEN

– STILL GROWING

WHEN I JOINED the Girl Guides, I was put into the same patrol as Brenda, the Robins. Guiding was a happy business with serious undertones. There was the Guide Law to be learned before one could be properly enrolled, along with the correct form of saluting, and in due course we were expected to master Morse-code and various other skills, such as tracking and knot-tying, and try to win badges.

Committing numbers and words to memory seemed to be a constant requirement of childhood, no matter where we found ourselves, at school, at Sunday School, and now in the Guides. At school we learned our tables by rote (I can still see Norman Williamson's rhythmic nodding as we 'timesed' high numerals in Miss Martin's class). We memorised the money table ('twenty pence one-and-eightpence, twenty-four pence two shillings'); avoirdupois weight ('sixteen ounces one pound, fourteen pounds one stone'); poetry (anything from Christina Rossetti's *Boats sail on the rivers/And ships sail on the seas*, and favourite Psalms, like *I shall lift up mine eyes unto the hills*, to Keats's *St. Agnes Eve! Ah, bitter chill it was*, and Shakespeare's *I know you all, and will a while uphold/The unyoked humour of your idleness*.

Some phrases stuck to the memory without direct effort, like wet newspaper blown against a lamp-post ('Come unto Me all ye that travail and are heavy laden, and I will refresh you', or 'Will you walk a little faster?' said a whiting to a snail, 'There's a porpoise just behind me, and he's treading on my tail.') Great tides of words, some workaday, some lyrical, flow like unbidden music through the channels of the brain. The best retain their potency. Did Tennyson realise what strong magic he was making as he jotted down *The Lady of Shalott*?

But hard concentration was needed to absorb other concepts, like the Catechism and the Ten Commandments, and we browbeat ourselves with these every week at Sunday School. ('What is your name? – N or M. Who gave you this name? – My Godfathers and my Godmothers in my Baptism; wherein I was made a member of Christ, the child of God, and an inheritor of the kingdom of heaven.' I still wonder who N or M were.)

Like the Commandments, the Guide Law made ten requirements of us, although nowadays they have been modified to six. Some of our high intentions sound old-fashioned today. 'A Guide's honour is to be trusted. A Guide's duty is to be useful, and to help others. A Guide smiles and sings under all difficulties. A Guide is pure in thought, word and deed.'

We had a lovely Captain, as Brenda had promised me, and a jolly Lieutenant, too. Both were unmarried, but courting, in fact Captain was going serious with the Boy Scout Leader. Captain lived with her mother and brother in Watch House Lane, and one week Brenda was fizzing with a great idea. She and I should call for Captain on Guide night, and walk with her to the church hall, a distance of about half-a-mile. I was reluctant, but Brenda persuaded me, and we duly turned up on Captain's doorstep and rang the bell.

We were received with great surprise by Captain's mother, who said her daughter was just home from work and getting ready, though she still hadn't had her tea. We were invited into the kitchen, where Captain was putting on her tie, and when she saw us she thrust down the last of her sandwich and evinced pleasure at our arrival, despite being as surprised as her mother. I don't remember anything about our walk together, but although I expect we created a gratifying stir among the other Guides when we told them we had been in Captain's house, and talked to her mother, and walked all the way to the hall with her, we never did it again.

The cocoa was strong and so was the singing at the camp-fire sessions, which always ended the Guide meetings in the church hall kitchen. ('She sailed away on a lovely summer's day on the back of a crocodile' was one of our favourites, and 'We are Indians tall and quaint in our feathers and war-paint, pow-wow, pow-wow' was another.) I suppose it must have been after the war when we had the chance of attending a real camp, but Mother was unsure about the idea, and I did not try very hard to persuade her to let me go. As so often when I was prevailed upon to opt out of a risky venture, my regret was mixed with relief: camping would be tough, and I knew I was probably too fastidious to enjoy it. Afterwards, when I heard talk of what fun it had been, I wished I had been braver and more insistent.

Lieutenant, a tall, dark, rather heavy-chinned young woman with hairy legs but a charming disposition, played the piano enthusiastically when it was time to rehearse us for a public concert. Brenda and I nursed secret ambitions about dancing careers, but singing in a Guide choir was a start. Quite rightly, it made no difference that Brenda could not stay on key for longer than a few notes. The whole company lined up for 'Jerusalem', 'Bless This House' and 'All Men Must Be Free' from 'Pomp and Circumstance.'

To Brenda's dismay, on the night of the concert her mother refused to allow her to appear in short white socks because it was the middle of winter, and Mrs Newland was afraid her daughter would catch pneumonia. I cannot claim to remember this embarrassing turn of events, but Brenda has never quite got over the shame of being the only Guide on stage wearing three-quarter-length grey socks.

She and I had begun to despair of ever showing the world how hard we had been training with the tap-dancing when we had a stroke of luck. Mrs Wylie, a parishioner who was producing one of the periodic shows in the church hall, wondered whether we would like to take part. We could do one of our dances, working out the steps ourselves, and she would sew us some special costumes.

Up to then, we had created flimsy outfits from any scraps of material we could find, and they sometimes came to bits as we were dancing. That Mrs Wylie, a busy mother of twin boys, should go to so much trouble on our behalf was astonishing. We glowed our gratitude when we visited her home to have our new skirts and boleros fitted (blackout material came into its own again, trimmed with bright braid). She even made us pill-box hats. Armed with short sticks, and with Brenda setting the pace, we acquitted ourselves to our own satisfaction on the big night, though our début seemed over far too quickly. Later we had a photograph taken at Roberts' studio in Doncaster, one arm draped across our partner's shoulder, the other held aloft. Brenda's pose seems natural, whereas I look as though I am asking permission to leave the room.

One of Brenda's friends did go on professional tour as an acrobat, and when her troupe was appearing at the Grand Theatre in Doncaster, Brenda and I went to see her in all her spangled glory. She had invited Brenda backstage after the performance, so, picturing glamorous scenes from Hollywood films, we both made our way there via the symbolic stage door in a state of high excitement. She was a nice girl and greeted us warmly, but her shared dressing-room, situated along a dark, dank corridor, was as forbidding as a dungeon, and not very clean. It made the small changing areas in the Drum's concert-room seem delightfully light and airy.

Most little girls are stage-struck, but not many have a real stage to frolic on. Mother let us use the concert-room when the pub was closed, and Brenda and I spent many hours there, entertaining an imaginary audience. Sometimes there might be a group of friends or relatives staying at the Drum, and we could prevail upon them to come and watch us. Applause was guaranteed, but it was disconcerting when they laughed in the wrong places, like the time when our paper moon fell down while Annette was singing 'Wrong'. She was very distressed, and never forgave me for using spit instead of proper glue.

We became so used to making free with the concert-room that I, for one, grew quite blasé, even wishing ungratefully at times that we could change the scenery, and not be forever committed to performing against a background of terrace, balustrade, and garden. Plays with indoor scenes caused problems, never more so than when we put on *Cinderella* in aid of St. Peter's Church spire.

The spire was in need of repair, and a fund had already been launched. What if we were to support this noble cause by presenting something special, and charging our audience real money? Mother was in favour, and I got down to writing a script in rhyming couplets, which I took through with me to Hull to teach Annette her lines. I insisted on rehearsing her at convenient times throughout the day, every night before we fell asleep, and on the train going back to Doncaster. She thought me a slave-driver, and said so, but on the whole she indulged me.

Annette shared our passion for putting on shows, and we needed her very much for *Cinderella*. She was a bonny little girl with a winsome treble (even her sarcastic family had to admit it) and her solo rendering of 'I'll Be With You In Apple-Blossom Time' was a heart-stealer. I knew she would make a splendid Fairy Godmother.

She remembers one of her speeches:

'Ah Cinderella, fair and true,
A husband I will give to you,
He is the fair prince of this land,
And he will ask you for your hand.
You have been kind to all you met,
And that you never will regret,
So sleep, and when you wake, know this –
I've sealed my promise with a kiss.'

There was a lot more to be learned, for as I had naturally cast myself as Cinderella, and was on stage most of the time, Annette was required to double up as Dandini, besides appearing (under protest) as an Ugly Sister. Brenda took on the second Sister, but her main role was Prince Charming (wearing wellingtons for the hunting scene).

A fair-sized audience was whipped in, including one or two of our cleaners and a few supportive customers. The takings amounted to well over a pound (100 pence), and Mother made this up to £1 12s 6d (about 160 pence). It was a proud day when Brenda, Annette and I walked round to the Vicarage and handed the cash to a grateful Mrs Campbell, our Vicar's wife, though it was a disappointment that Mr Campbell himself was not there to hear the story of how we had raised the money. Afterwards, though, whenever we glanced across the roof-tops at the reassuring cone of grey slates, we felt pleased we had helped to keep it up.

***

IN THOSE DAYS, St. Peter's Church was the focal point of my life. It signposted the right ways to go about things which, though often expressed in outdated English, were translated at Sunday School and Guides into ideals that were more straightforward: forgiving your enemies and turning the other cheek; honouring your parents (or in my case, parent); not trying to wriggle out of a bad situation by shifting the blame on to others; keeping your word; pushing bad thoughts out of your head; doing unto others as you would have them do unto you (a hard order, this, for it included being nice about another person's prowess or possessions even if you were green with envy).

The staples of life were also beautifully simple. Bread was either white or brown; potatoes were potatoes and apples were apples, and we did not normally ask what variety; cheese was either Cheddar or Cheshire; spaghetti came in tins, and was eaten on toast; rice was found only in puddings; salads consisted of lettuce, tomatoes and cucumber, topped by Heinz salad cream, with radishes, spring onions and cress as optional extras. Mother broke out sometimes, though, with what she called Russian salad – all the ingredients chopped up small in a sugar and vinegar dressing.

Certain conventions were written in stone. Blue didn't go with green, or black with navy-blue or brown; nice girls guarded their virtue; smart women always wore hats and gloves; murder was a hanging offence; illegitimacy was a stigma; dead people were usually buried, not burned; would-be suicides were prosecuted, and successful ones consigned to unhallowed ground unless it was decided that the balance of their mind had been disturbed; the King was our natural ruler, spiritually boosted to do the job by being God's anointed; and we were the greatest nation on earth, with an Empire on which the sun never set. New clothes had to be kept for special occasions, and it was unthinkable to hang washing out on a Sunday, or for a child to call a grown-up by their first name. Even adults addressed each other as 'Mister' or 'Missus' unless invited to be more familiar.

The rules and guidelines of those far-off days were strangely comforting, except to the rebellious, which we all were at times. But mostly, we lived according to formula, within the framework. We accepted. We knew where we stood.

***

TUESDAY NIGHT REMAINED the highlight of my week for some time, because Brenda and I were eager Guides. She became Patrol-Leader of the Robins (two white stripes on her breast pocket) and I her Second (one white stripe). We were even asked for a very brief period to take temporary charge of the Brownies, so proudly substituted our saxe-blue ties for tan ones, and presented ourselves an hour earlier at the Church Hall in order to boss the small fry around, without much of a clue what to do. (Brenda was less bossy than I, for she loved children.)

But, as my mother reminded me from time to time, in a maddening phrase I vowed I would never use, 'all good things come to an end.' Gradually, Brenda and I became disenchanted with the Guides. I think it must have been because Captain and Lieutenant both left to get married, and after that things were never the same.

Captain had already gone through the terrible drama of her brother's suicide. He was still at school, and I had seen him sometimes in Watch House Lane in his blazer and cap. They were a red-cheeked family, and his were as rosy as his sister's, which had given him a merry look. I could not imagine how anyone could be brave enough to take their own life, especially one so young, and hoped he would not be denied his bit of hallowed ground.

***

AMONG THE CUSTOMERS in Butchers' Corner a new face appeared one night. The newcomer was compactly-built and smartly suited, and when he removed his trilby hat he revealed a modicum of fine brown hair, and a bald crown polished to a tremendous sheen. He had a longish face with rather a lantern jaw, steady hazel eyes, and broad, capable hands with surprisingly well-shaped nails. Standing with two of the butchers who were his friends, he watched my mother as she served behind the lounge bar, and was impressed. He lived in lodgings a ten-minute walk away, and soon he became a regular.

One night when Mother was short-staffed and there was a crisis with the beer, this unassuming man, whose name was George Henry Burton, offered to descend to the cellar and sort it out. No well-meaning amateur, he, but one long seasoned in the licensed trade, conversant not only with changing and tapping barrels but with all the myriad other things to do with running a pub.

George Henry had been born in the Derbyshire mining village of Killamarsh, near Sheffield, one of nine children whose mother was called Ardoin, though I cannot remember how she came by this unusual name. The only other thing I know about her is that before every Christmas she would make an enormous batch of big plum puddings, which she lined up on a shelf in the pantry. One was earmarked for Christmas itself, and the rest, each with an individual's name on its wrappings, were saved for family birthdays. It was a fine thing to smell your own pudding boiling up in the copper when your turn came, far better than having a cake.

George Henry became a miner in the family tradition, and he blamed the loss of his hair on constantly washing the coal-dust out of it. He did not like being a miner, and gravitated to working in a pub near Doncaster. I believe the story was that he had transferred to Askern Colliery, and later seized the chance of a job at the Askern Hotel. The owners were a delightful couple, Mr and Mrs Froggatt, and over time he became their right-hand man, taking charge in their absence, and being treated as a member of the family.

George Henry must have seemed a confirmed bachelor by the age of forty-four, when Mother and he first met. She gathered, when she got to know him better, that he had once been engaged, but then the young lady had found somebody else. He had made his home at the Askern Hotel, bought himself a wire-haired terrier called Rags, and a car, and driven down to Eastbourne alone every year for a holiday in the Glastonbury Hotel on the sea-front.

This establishment boasted a refined menu, and he was fond of relating how he had once ordered a dessert called '*le petit bleu*' (he pronounced it 'lar pettit bleeoo') and 'when it came it was BREAD-AND-BUTTER PUDDING!' (Here he would bend to laugh and slap his knees, because he still found the memory of his disappointment so amusing.)

When the war arrived, George Henry gave up his car (his dog had died) and was recruited to drive a food lorry, visiting farms to collect vegetables. This was how he came to leave Askern and base himself in Bentley. He found a room with Mr and Mrs Harold Hickman and their grown-up daughter, Doreen, in Old Hall Road, and Mrs Hickman took him under her wing. Once more he was accepted into a family, and the ties were so strong that when he began to spend time at the Drum, helping Mother out, or simply enjoying himself in Butchers' Corner, Mrs Hickman was pained by rumours that he had fallen into the clutches of a widow in the licensed trade. Her protective instincts were aroused, and she marched round to the Drum and confronted my mother, demanding to know what was going on.

Mother, who had accepted George Henry's help gratefully while characteristically keeping him at arm's length, was astonished and indignant that Mrs Hickman should think the relationship had blossomed into something more. (She saw the funny side later, though.) The two had a candid discussion, which cleared the air, after which Mrs Hickman departed feeling reassured. From that day, the Hickmans were our friends, and I started to walk to their home on a Sunday, often staying for lunch or tea. Mrs Hickman had been an orphan who was never taught to read and write, but she was a great baker, and each weekend covered her kitchen surfaces with pastries, and cakes, and sponge flans holding tinned pears and peaches in lakes of red and green jelly. And every year, knowing how much my mother loved lilies-of-the-valley, she picked a shoe-boxful from her garden, and sent them to the Drum.

At first I was very suspicious of George Henry, and not at all welcoming. Mother had come to rely on his cheerful willingness, and for a long period he was content to help in the cellar, or behind the bars, without any expectation of being paid, even though he had given up his driving job by this time, and was living off his savings. But then Mrs Dunn pointed out that Mother was not the only lucky one; John Smith's brewery was benefiting from George Henry's goodness of heart as well. So Mother made it all fair and official by putting him on the staff list, part-time.

He was so modest and uninsistent that he would never push himself forward, being happy to be regarded as a family friend, though his admiration for Mother was evident. He could be infuriatingly stubborn, but was by this same token utterly dependable, and the most patient man I have ever known. Generous by nature, he took to spoiling me, giving up his sweet ration to supply me with chocolate. Over time, there were larger gifts: he bought me my first watch, a hockey-stick, a bike, and an opal ring (promising to get me a manicure set if I ever stopped biting my nails). But it was all done quietly and without fuss, usually through Mother.

There was never any question in my mind that George Henry was buying me things to make me like him, although of course it helped. Even as I railed against the strengthening bond between him and my mother, it was obvious, from his relaxed, avuncular dealings with Annette, Dorothy, Brenda, Joy, Winnie, and other young visitors, that his approach (he addressed us all as 'ma duck') was ingrained and automatic. He came from a line of child-indulgers, for all the Burtons I ever met displayed this same doting attitude, rarely finding fault with those of tender years in the belief that they could do little wrong.

At the beginning, I looked upon George Henry not just as a rival for my mother's affections, but as someone who, even more disturbingly, was trying to take my father's place. They were two very different men, George Henry being easy-going and pleasantly uncomplicated, whereas my father had been much more tightly-wound. But I had loved and known him from the viewpoint of a cherished daughter. We had spent long hours together high in each other's estimation, exceptionally in tune. Now death had torn him from us, how COULD Mother think of supplanting him with somebody else? She tried to reassure me, saying that George Henry could never take Dad's place, nor would he wish to; he would certainly never come between her and me.

Because he worked behind the lounge bar on Sundays, and we did not close until two o'clock, when much clearing-up and replenishing of pumps and shelves remained to be done, it seemed only right that George Henry should come upstairs afterwards and share our Sunday dinner. Sometimes, if the weather was fine after we had eaten our roast joint with three veg and Yorkshire puddings (the left-over puddings with sugar and raspberry-vinegar) he would suggest a bus-ride to Selby. There we would inspect the beautiful Abbey, and have afternoon tea at the impressive Londesborough Hotel.

There was never any hint of more than extremely close regard between my mother and this new man in our lives, with a gradually perceived understanding that one day, in the unforeseeable future, they would probably marry. Both were bound by the strict mores of an earlier generation. My mother had always been guarded in her dealings with men, and George Henry possessed patience beyond the masculine norm. Having waited forty-four years to discover his destiny, he seemed agreeable to delay matters further until the time was ripe for its fulfilment. I never saw them kiss unless they were bidding each other a long goodbye, as when Mother and I went to Germany in 1951, and George Henry took charge of the Drum in order to make our trip possible. So there was no undue 'familiarity' to distress me; beyond the ease of trusted friendship, no advantage taken. Both took into account my reservations about a second marriage, and though they toyed with the idea of running a country pub together, they postponed any decision mainly because of me.

But it is also true that Mother enjoyed her independence after twenty years of coping with my father's cautious attitude to money. She made the most of being able to spend as she wished, and gradually acquired a settee, china-cabinet, tea-set, gas-cooker, washing-machine and dining-chairs, as well as clothes for herself and me, without having to justify herself to Dad, or bow to his superior knowledge of the business world. She had grown used to being in charge of her life, organising staff, doing the books, ordering stock, and managing the Drum. George Henry understood this; he was happy to take a back seat, and did not try to rush her – or me.

***

LESS THAN TWO years after Mother had her mastectomy, at the very point when she had been half expecting the cancer to recur, she was taken very ill. It was the notorious winter of early 1947 which none who endured it will ever forget. Roads and rails were blocked with snow, and normal life was disrupted. I remember hearing that some of the school buses had been unable to get through to Percy Jackson's. This did not concern me, though, for Mum had no-one to give her close personal attention but me, so she cast her principles aside and kept me off school.

She was in bed for what seemed many weeks, but was possibly two or three, burning with fever, wringing with sweat, and for a long time bringing back every bit of food or drink, even water. I did my best to look after her, and tried to keep cheerful, but as days went by and she failed to show much improvement, a feeling of desolation crept over us both, and we had the occasional weep together.

George Henry had stepped into the breach. He took over the running of the Drum without any of the bossiness Herbert would have shown, and his calm masculinity wafted reassurance during his visits to the sickroom. (I think Mother must have somehow managed to supervise the paperwork.) He bought a second-hand wireless and plugged into the overhead light-fitting so we had something to help us while away the hours.

Up to then, we had lived without a wireless, and I had been invited to Winnie's home on Friday nights so we could bite nails and roll eyes together during *Appointment with Fear*. The programme was famous for the suave menace in the voice of Valentine Dyall, who introduced it with the phrase, 'This is your story-teller, the Man in Black'.

I don't know whether Mother and I listened; perhaps Mr Dyall's dark tales were too depressing when there was sickness in the house. But it was good to be able to lose ourselves in *Music While you Work*, *Forces' Favourites* and *Have a Go*, though these distractions did little to help Mother physically. She struggled along the corridor to the lavatory as usual, and did not so often bring back her tiny meals into the handsome, gold-patterned chamber-pot, but she felt very weak and helpless. I did, too, and one night worked myself up into a fine fit of hysterics, sobbing, as George Henry gave me a comforting hug, 'I ... want ... my ... father.'

It was the only time I ever knew him to be the slightest bit brusque with me. He said, 'Come on, ma duck, this isn't doing any good, you know', and gave me an even firmer hug. I knew I must have hurt him, and felt ashamed.

Neither of us ever referred to the matter again, and I never apologised. But I had known perfectly well what I was doing.

***

OUR WONDERFUL DOCTOR Singh had been killed in a car crash at the junction near the Gaumont Cinema in town, a huge loss to his patients, and his practice had been taken over by a jovial Celt called Dr. McKeown, whose personality was as different from his predecessor's as it was possible to imagine. Mother got to know the newcomer when he became part of the group in Doctors' Corner, and now she had fallen ill he began to call at the Drum professionally. When the usual medicines did not work, he listened to her fears about cancer, and suggested a consultation with Mr Shepherd, the surgeon who had carried out her mastectomy.

Because Mother was not fit to travel, it was arranged that the great man should come to the Drum. An appointment was made and I was kept busy before his arrival, ensuring that Mother and her bedroom, the landing, lavatory, stairs and bathroom were as immaculate as one would expect to find in a fastidious household.

'And please set out clean towels in the bathroom,' said Mother, 'because Mr Shepherd will probably want to wash his hands.' (He didn't.)

He came with Dr McKeown, and I can see them both now, striding along the landing. I hardly dared to look at Mr Shepherd as I stood there, an apprehensive thirteen-year-old, but I recall he was a pleasant-faced man. Dr McKeown wore a thick jacket and wellington boots, and as he walked past me he gave me a very broad wink. From that moment, the cloud that had enveloped us began to shred.

I waited in the living-room. Mr Shepherd did not take long to make his examination and give his opinion, which was that he could find no sign of cancer. Neither, as I recall, did he think it necessary for any further tests. As soon as I heard him and Dr McKeown tramp back along the landing and down the stairs, I flew into the bedroom and learned the glad news, which turned me quite light-headed after so many anxious days. Mother already looked different, and declared ever afterwards that it had only taken a visit from Mr Shepherd to make her feel better immediately.

Slowly and steadily, her strength returned. In the meantime, George Henry borrowed a car belonging to his friend, Mr Chris Beresford, and took me with him on some errand, driving cautiously along slushy roads edged with impacted snow. It was strange being out of doors again, especially in such an unreal world; stranger still to be in a car with George Henry. I admired the confident way he handled the vehicle, for I was unused to private transport, apart from Winnie's father's van.

I did not ask to be allowed to steer, as Winnie's father sometimes permitted Winnie and me to do when we went out with him in the van to deliver meat. We had to steel ourselves to enter some of the scruffier houses in the mining villages, where bare-bottomed children with snot 'candles' hanging from their nostrils ran round the streets, and bikes and prams rusted in overgrown gardens. Later, working on a local newspaper, I ran such gauntlets yet again.

George Henry could cook as well as drive, and to tempt Mother's appetite he produced one of her own special dishes, cod in brown gravy, sucking his teeth and inner lip as he bent over the frying-pan, which was his way when he was concentrating. Possibly he had a cigarette on the go as well, for he was a heavy smoker.

The copious snow caused chaos throughout the country when it melted, the River Don over-topped its banks, and Bentley and nearby Toll Bar were badly flooded, with rowing-boats brought into the streets to make dramatic rescues. Amazing tales were told in the Drum's two bars, and when Mother was strong enough, and the floods had abated, George Henry borrowed Mr Beresford's car again and chauffeured us around the stricken areas, so we might see for ourselves how high the water had risen by the tide-marks on the walls.

Now at last the harsh winter was all but over, and our fears for Mother's health had been set at rest. With so much to be thankful for, she and I picked up our separate threads again, and I was surprised at how soon things got back to normal.

CHAPTER EIGHTEEN – JOY

THE PERCY JACKSON Grammar School, Adwick-le-Street, more commonly known as Percy Jackson's, or PJGS, with its pupils sometimes scornfully referred to by their enemies as Percy's Piglets, was named after a former Chairman of the West Riding Local Education Authority when it opened in 1939, the year the Second World War began. Its founding Headmaster, Mr Field, who is remembered by me only for having announced that school dinners would go up from 2s to 2s 1d a week (still only about ten pence) slipped away at the end of my first year.

Joy remembers more about Mr Field. She recalls how, at our earliest assembly, he told us that now, for the first time, PJGS had a fifth-form that had come right up through the school from year one. And we sang 'Pioneers', which Mr Field said he wanted to make the school hymn, though for some reason this never happened, and we rarely sang it. It was aired, however, at his final assembly, a declaration of intent which sounds high-flown today:

'All the past we leave behind,
We take up the task eternal,
And the burden and the lesson.
Conquering, holding, daring, venturing,
So we go the unknown ways,
Pioneers, O pioneers.'

Mr Field was succeeded by Mr Elliott. A dark-haired, upright figure he, probably in his forties, bearing himself on to the hall stage with scarcely a flicker of his shoulders; eyes of peculiar intensity, set in a permanent stare; voice never needing to be raised to instil in us the fear of retribution. He was not unfair, and sometimes allowed himself a small smile, especially if praising sporting prowess. The true man we could not know, because I cannot think his authority was ever called into question.

Senior Mistress Miss Banks, was almost as awe-inspiring, though behind her back we called her Fanny; she was probably in her fifties, with a pillowy bosom as controlled as Queen Mary's and grey hair that was Eton-cropped, in stern contrast to the delicate pink of her features and the warm brown of her (often unamused) eyes. I thought she had just a look of Granma Carrie.

The school building itself, only five years old, was short on tradition, daunting in size until one had mapped it out, with facilities undreamt of by 'little first-years' from the sticks. It had a library and lecture-theatre; chemistry, physics and biology labs; rooms for art, geography, boys' woodwork, boys' metalwork and girls' cookery; a gymnasium with showers; warm cloakrooms; a wash-room with a central drinking-fountain and a long line of comfy lavatories; and the unaccustomed green of playing-fields rolling by classroom windows (fine for sunbathers, less tempting to reluctant hockey-players). No tennis courts were laid, though, until after I left, and there was no swimming-pool.

The school motto was Keep Troth, and Joy and I thought it very limp. Who had chosen it? Was it Sir Percy? (He had been knighted.) We would far rather have had something like *Semper Fidelis* or *Honi Soit Qui Mal Y Pense*, and wondered what 'Keep Troth' was supposed to mean. Tell the truth? Keep your word? We snorted our disapproval. But when, after many years, I thought again about those two words on our old school badge, I realised how very profound they were. So profound, in fact, that most other mottoes hinge on them, fancier versions of the same truth. Shakespeare has their measure in Polonius's advice to Laertes: 'To thine own self be true ...'

PJGS was a separate world we entered each weekday morning and quitted by late afternoon, completely divided from the world of home, peopled by characters we never expected to see out of context, apart from our own special friends. The school stood about six miles from the Drum, but it might as well have been six hundred for all the contact my mother had with it, though the occasional letter was sent. (At that time we had no telephone.)

During my five years at Percy Jackson's, I can remember only one visit she made there. An open night was held in our fifth year, a startling innovation. At last our mothers (Joy's father was working) would meet teachers who, as mere initials on school reports, had been at the mercy of our descriptive whims. Together the pair of them would descend from the bus and, after passing the house where Miss Smith, (music and history) was in 'digs', make their way through the school gates. They would skirt the bungalow occupied by our caretakers, Mr and Mrs Cray, awesome figures in their own right (Mrs Cray supervised school dinners, Mr Cray was long-suffering about rescuing balls off the roof) and enter our seat of learning by the hallowed main door. Then Joy and I, fussy as two-tailed dogs, but with an edge of nervousness, would take charge of our mothers and show them around. Thus do worlds collide.

Working-class folk ranked teachers almost as high as doctors and solicitors, thought they 'knew best', and treated them with deference. Even those like Mr Good, who could not keep order, were accredited with vastly superior brains and an exhaustive knowledge of their subject. Perhaps the poor young man was more vulnerable because the black gown only half-concealed his boyish frame, so that he seemed like an older brother eager to inspire us with poetry and literature; perhaps it was because, while teachers' first names were generally shrouded in secrecy, he signed himself 'John T. Good'.

On open night the staff stepped briefly down from their pedestals and chatted affably to our parents on almost level terms. Mum and Mrs Cuffling, for their part, were unusually quiet, and did nothing to embarrass us. Joy thinks that at the end of the fifth year our parents were invited to see us receive our School Certificates, and it seems likely that Mother also came to watch me perform as Lavinia in Shaw's *Androcles and the Lion*. But I simply cannot remember.

The workings of a grammar school were a closed book to my mother, and she left the solving of its mysteries to me. There was never any 'Have you finished that essay?' or 'Shouldn't you be revising?' or 'Don't you think you ought to spend more time on your geography?' If applied to for help, she would give it, and she was always very interested in anything I cared to tell her. But she knew I needed no extra spurring. The one (irritating) question she always asked when I got home was, 'What did you have for your dinner?'

***

WHEN JOY AND I moved together into 2A we had planned our strategy, and in the scramble for seats managed to bag ones right at the back, where we could whisper, pass notes, or read under our desks without being pounced on. This happy state of affairs, wangling seats at the rear as we moved around the school for different lessons, continued until we reached year three, at which point I decided to shed my hated spectacles and rely on Joy to tell me what was on the blackboard. All went well until the half-yearly exams, when I was alarmed to find that some teachers preferred chalking up questions to handing out test-papers.

Vanity proved my undoing. The imposed silence was total, the blackboard was a blur, and though, by turning my head sideways and screwing up my eyes, I managed to make out some of the words, it was a slow process. Numbers presented an even greater problem. When the results were announced, mine were disappointing, according to some of the comments on my report.

I realised I had been stupid, and talked things over with Joy, who agreed it was time to become more serious, and swap our quiet backwater for seats at the front of the class. Henceforth our form-room pitch was right under the teacher's nose. Yet though she had reacted sympathetically, in point of fact Joy had envied me my glasses. She said spectacles gave one's face character, and she intended to have a pair when she was older, even if they were only plain glass.

I had always been absent-minded, but I grew worse when I got to the grammar school, constantly forgetting where I had put my belongings. Panic often set in at breakfast-time, and I would launch a desperate sweep through our living quarters, with Mother and Mrs Atkinson dancing attendance. Mrs Atkinson cleaned our rooms, and was as clever as Mother at locating missing objects, and less given to exasperation. Once we had found what I needed, and I had clattered downstairs to catch the bus, the two ladies would calm their nerves with a pot of strong tea.

Joy, who climbed aboard at an earlier stop, would be upstairs with the girls in the double-decker 'special', keeping me a seat, and during the half-hour journey we would get down to our German or French vocab(ulary), or compare our maths homework (she was cleverer at maths). Sometimes the general standard of appearance when we dismounted at the other end was a disappointment to Miss Banks. We were a fledgling grammar school with as yet no proud traditions, and she complained during one assembly that certain girls had been seen arriving in head-scarves, 'looking like potato-pickers.'

The nicest room in the school was the library, where Miss Banks was in charge. Though she stamped dates and filed tickets with her customary decisiveness, if we kept our voices to a murmur we felt welcome there. I was unacquainted with libraries, apart from being aware of the one at Boots, and now for the first time I might wander through a room set apart for reading, and prise whatever took my fancy from tiers of colourful bindings. In memory I can still run my eye along the shelves and pick out some of the titles: *I Sailed with Christopher Columbus, From David Copperfield to David Blaize, Mr Midshipman Easy, The Stalking Horse, The Boots and Josephine* ...

One day I picked out a rather dull-sounding title, *The Inimitable Jeeves*, and after reading it, I passed it to Joy, whose enthusiasm was even greater than mine. From then on we devoured as many books about Jeeves and Bertie Wooster as we could lay our hands on. We were enraptured by The Drones' Club, and Gussie Fink-Nottle, and Sir Roderick Glossop, and Bertie's strong-minded aunts, and laughed until our sides ached.

One of our most absorbing games was enacting scenarios of our own devising, taking turns to be Jeeves. Joy went on to admire the wider works of P.G.Wodehouse, but, expose myself as I might to the shenanigans at Blandings, or the exploits of Psmith or the Efficient Baxter, none of them, in my opinion, was a patch on Jeeves and Bertie.

There was, though, another fictitious character who had us literally rolling on the floor, although volumes of his adventures were hard to come by because they were so popular they were often dropping to bits. Miss Banks ordered the prefects who helped her run the library to round up all books with loose leaves and battered covers, and place them on the repair shelf, and we were forbidden to take anything from this section.

Joy and I would creep up to it when no-one was looking, hoping to spot a treasure, and if we saw the familiar, washed-out maroon binding and faded black lettering of one of Richmal Crompton's *William* books, we would sneak it off the shelf. Getting our prize past Miss Banks was a challenge, particularly if it was bursting out of its jacket, but more often than not she would stamp it, though she might look suspicious. Our triumph once we had reached the corridor was blatant; but perhaps we had not really fooled her.

Joy taught me that there was humour to be found in almost any situation, and find it we did, even if our laughter was self-mocking or rueful. In the first year, with no special friend to share classroom experiences, I had been quite a bore according to the summary on my end-of-year report – 'steady, reliable, and unobtrusively efficient as form almoner.' (The task involved collecting the Guild of Help money. Goodness knew why I had been selected, but I probably looked anxious to please.) Alliance with Joy made me less reverential, and life became much greater fun; in her company I felt more confident, less tightly-wound.

But as I reached adolescence, I grew more contrary and less able to laugh at myself, and was seized by a sort of fatalism, modelling myself on Hollywood drama queens like Bette Davis, Joan Crawford, Barbara Stanwyck and Susan Hayward, and practising a brittle style of conversation. There were times when Joy and I lost patience with each other, and enjoyed some steaming rows, usually about quite trivial things, although their effects soon wore off, thank heavens.

All this might have given us an air of self-absorption, because Mrs Wood, one of the cleaners at the Drum, whose granddaughter was in our class, indicated as much to Mother. She said their Kathleen had told her that Joy and Janet were stuck-up, and did not mix.

Mother raised the matter with me, more in regret than anger, and did not harp on it. I could not believe quiet Kathleen had said such things about us, and although I was so nonplussed I could only make indignant noises, I might also have pointed out that Joy was very popular with the rest of the form, who knew it took only one witticism from her to enliven a turgid lesson; whilst I (due, I suspected, to some secret machinations of Joy) had inexplicably been elected form vice-captain. (Not that I ever had to do anything: the captain, Avril Moore, was never away, and in any case there seemed to be no actual duties.) As for not mixing, why, we often joined in playground games, or huddled among the gang who collected in the porch on rainy lunch-times, hoping to catch a bit of tittle-tattle, or a discussion on the latest Hollywood film.

I told Joy about Mrs Wood's remarks and she felt equally miffed; but when we thought about it, we realised that maybe we did seem a bit stand-offish, because most of our spare time was taken up by reading and writing, pastimes not to everybody's taste.

Surely we could not be the only ones to laugh at private jokes, or invent a new alphabet for coded messages? It was true that I sometimes walked past people on the other side of the street, pretending I hadn't seen them, but there were seven possible reasons for this:

One: I was shy or afraid of the person, or felt inferior.

Two: they were boring.

Three: I disliked them.

Four: I did not see them due to my short-sightedness.

Five: I could not be sure it was really them for the same reason, and feared making a fool of myself.

Six: I avoided meeting the eye of certain contemporaries due to a mutual wariness. The origins of our aloofness might be lost in the mists of time, which made it even more ridiculous, but I did not know how to mend matters.

Seven: I was in a hurry.

No matter what the reason, I knew I had the perfect excuse – poor eyesight.

But at school, things were different, and it took me a while to forgive Mrs Wood even though Mother and I still enjoyed her gifts of home-made ginger parkin. In any case, her comments rang no changes, and Joy's passion for reading still had me gobbling to keep up. Without her urgings, for instance, would I ever have tackled so much of H.G. Wells? I became as gripped as she by *The Time Machine*, *The War of the Worlds*, and his gruesome *The Island of Doctor Moreau*. Our devotion to Sherlock Holmes, and to a lesser extent Father Brown, began in those days, and we consumed a lot of Alexandre Dumas and L.M. Montgomery.

Joy, a page-turner of lightning speed, blazed through dozens of different authors, with me in tow. We did not invariably agree on their appeal, and I considered her rather cool towards some of my pet writers, such as Louisa M. Alcott and Mrs Henry Wood. I don't think I ever dared lend her *The Flower of the Family* or *Jessica's First Prayer*, two other gifts from Mother that were indisputably maudlin, but I had the triumph of introducing her to Hugh Walpole's 'Jeremy', and she really fell for him.

We tried writing novels ourselves, though neither of us ever got beyond the first few chapters. Our short stories did not turn out much better, but we had more stamina for poetry. Mr Good encouraged our efforts, and if we screwed up our courage to knock on the staff-room door and leave our scribbles there for him, he took the trouble to put his criticisms in writing. Once or twice he gave us poetry books.

Limericks, or fun-poking songs to the tune of 'Much Binding-in-the-Marsh', a favourite radio programme, were joint, less serious, endeavours. On wet days we passed indoor breaks by inventing adventures for two fictional schoolboy heroes, taking it in turn to wind on the plot. Each contribution had to begin with the next letter of the alphabet, and it was hard to be innovative once we reached X and Z.

When Brenda got immersed in the world of work, and joined Doncaster Wheelers' Cycling Club, where she met Stan, her future husband, Joy and I were usually the ones to use the complimentary tickets at the Don Cinema, though sometimes we ventured further afield to the pictures in town. We would wander down the long arcade at the Ritz in Hall Gate, and call at its dark little sweet shop to buy Horlicks or Ovaltine tablets, or tiny licorice Nippits, for real sweets were still rationed.

Close as we were, we did not live in each other's pocket, and respected each other's privacy. School and socialising apart, because we were only children we still needed space and time to ourselves. We never totally let down our guard. I do not believe, for instance, that I ever gave her an inkling of how much I missed my father. We never made any serious disclosures about our home lives, moaned to each other about parental strictures, or compared notes about our budding adolescence, maybe because we were concerned for our dignity. We were far from goody-goody, and got into scrapes, as, for example, when Miss Banks gave us lines for being late for dinner, or when we were caught copying homework. But self-analysis was not yet in fashion, and soul-baring would have spoiled things.

In the fourth year we made friends with a girl called Joyce Hildreth, and became a trio. Joyce had much the same sense of humour, and was willing to join in our alphabetical tale-spinning, but she did not seem to write stories or poetry. She was an all-rounder, particularly good at science, which made us wonder afterwards why she had opted to join our language form. In fact, she went on to read a branch of chemistry at Cambridge University after winning a State Scholarship, so either she had been spoiled for choice at age thirteen, or else thought she needed the Latin.

I lost touch with Joyce after I left school, and when I saw her again a few years later it was on a Bentley trackless. I asked her about the recent Boat Race, and she told me how she had been among a group of undergrads cheering on the Light Blues from the riverbank. Another time, Mother told me Joyce had called at the Drum and was disappointed because I was out working that evening. Despite the fact that my old friend had made an effort to see me, I could not believe that we would have much in common now that she moved in such exalted intellectual circles, because I did not feel good enough for her any more. So I made no effort to return her call, which shows how foolish I was in those days, for it never occurred to me that she might feel upset at being so unpardonably shrugged off. It was one of the most stupid decisions I ever made, and I have regretted it for fifty-five years.

A certain diffidence had developed between Joy and me during our fifth year, possibly due to a cautious acceptance of our growing interest in boys. Things had taken a serious turn in the fourth year when an old acquaintance from Kirkby Avenue days approached me on behalf of one of the boys in 4S, the science form. Would I accompany him to a Dramatic Society party?

The idea set me all of a flutter, but I accepted. During a Christmas get-together for all fourth-year pupils, Bobby had discovered I could dance, which was why he was now asking me to this party. He was my first date, and I remember the event in some detail, even to the dusky-pink spotted dress and navy and white sling-back shoes I wore. I think this was the first time I borrowed Mother's lipstick, though she told me to wipe some off because it was too bright.

In the school hall, Bobby and I took to the floor for a succession of foxtrots, waltzes, quicksteps and tangos, accompanied by a small band on stage. I had learned the rudiments from Hilda, one of our live-in girls at the Drum. Together we had fast-footed over our living-room lino, or scuffed our shoes on the rough stretch of concrete at Hexthorpe Flatts, where music was broadcast for outdoor dancing, a popular wartime activity.

But now there was a problem: the rhythm to which Bobby and I were moving came not from records, or our own humming, but from my cousin Gordon and three of his pals, who had been hired as instrumentalists for the party. If Gordon and I were astonished to see one another, what was even more aggravating was that he and Bobby were astonished, too, because they lived near each other.

Realising we would come in for much teasing, from the rest of the band as well as from Gordon because they all knew us (they had been to my fourteenth birthday party), Bobby and I performed our gyrations and ate our supper with an even greater sense of constraint than we might otherwise have felt. However, once free of those eight glinting eyes, we chatted amicably on the bus going home, and my host walked me courteously down Watch House Lane, though it was well out of his way. The evening, despite its obvious drawback, had been a success, I thought, but Bobby did not ask me out again.

Joy, for her part, started seeing a sixth-former she got to know during our fifth year while she was helping with the production of *Androcles and the Lion*. He played

Caesar, and seemed immensely mature. She never took me into her confidence about their meetings, for we were both becoming a bit cagey as our paths began to diverge. School Certificate was approaching, it was time to choose what we wanted to do with our lives, and as we had different ambitions, a parting seemed inevitable.

Before the exams, the open night took place when our mothers came to school to meet the teachers. By this time I had been offered a job as a trainee-reporter on a local weekly newspaper, *The Doncaster Chronicle*, a chance I had seized with no hesitation, for I had wanted to be a journalist for some time. The idea had first taken root as I followed the adventures of Sylvia Starr, a character in a comic who travelled the world as a foreign correspondent, never failing to get her scoop, even when exposed to the most appalling dangers. Of course I knew there was no comparison to be drawn between an existence like Sylvia's and working for the *Chronicle*, but I had been granted a start, and if I ever did get posted abroad my French and German might prove useful.

Unlike Joy, I had never nursed a desire to teach, so even before I was offered the newspaper job it seemed pointless for me to stay on in the sixth-form and try for a university place. Mother tentatively suggested I might enjoy working as a nurse, or in a bank, and put out a feeler at the Westminster Bank when she went there to deposit the Drum takings. Unbeknown to her, however, I had entered a short-story competition run by *The Yorkshire Evening Post*, and to my delight and incredulity a letter came from the Chief Sub-editor at the paper's Doncaster office, inviting me to call and see him.

Mother was amazed when I showed it to her, and equally excited, and when the day came she accompanied me to town, leaving me outside the premises in Scot Lane, where both the *Chronicle* and the South Yorkshire edition of *The Yorkshire Evening Post* were produced and printed. Wearing my best red tartan frock, I was shown up to the Editor's office, where Donald Clayton, Chief Sub and Acting Editor, sat with my story on the desk before him. Sadly, he felt the plot was somewhat weak as a competition entry (an unlikely tale about a sheepdog who rescued his master from a snowdrift) but he thought it well-written. What did I want to do when I left school?

When I told him I wished to be a journalist, he said there was a vacancy for a junior on the weekly paper, and if the *Chronicle's* Editor agreed, it could be mine. And no (in reply to my anxious question) the offer would not depend on my passing my School Certificate, though of course he hoped I would do so. I floated on air down those shabby old stairs, and ran out to meet Mother and tell her that, fingers crossed, I was going to be a newspaper-reporter, and to heck with nursing or banking. She seemed happy that I had found a job I really wanted, and once confirmation came after a second interview, and I was taken on at two pounds a week, we felt settled in our minds about the wondrous turn events had taken.

Doubts were raised, though, at the school open night, when Miss Williamson, our English mistress, said she thought I would do better to obtain a degree in English before trying to enter journalism. Her advice was to stay on in the sixth-form, and apply for a university place. Mother and I discussed this, and she wondered if I was sure I was doing the right thing by leaving school. But jobs on newspapers were as hard to get then as they are today, and I felt I would be crazy to turn down the rare opportunity the *Chronicle* had given me, so I chose to ignore Miss Williamson's well-meant counsel, and Mother left the final decision to me.

The School Certificate exams took place in June, and as I was not due to start work until August 1st, once they were over I had the same feeling of disengagement as the rest of our group. We were like castaways bobbing in the slipstream while the ship of school sailed on, for we were no longer needed on board. It was a very odd experience, not having to catch the bus every day, not doing the usual things or seeing the usual people. Joy and all those who planned to move up to the sixth-form could not have been affected by the same sense of finality that haunted leavers like me, but we did all return for a last assembly, when the hymn, 'Lord Dismiss Us With Thy Blessing', which I had always found mournful, seemed more poignant than ever.

In the weeks before this tearful farewell, Joy and I seized our chances to relax in the old, happy way. We had become fond of playing tennis at Bentley Park, and were flattered when Peter Whiteley and Godfrey Outram, the two cleverest boys in 5L (who, when they sat behind us, had seemed interested only in our marks) asked if they could join us.

Chopping the ball towards them across the puddly red court, we addressed them no longer as 'Whiteley' and 'Outram', but as 'Peter' and 'Godfrey'. What an amazing change! After years of cool appraisal, sizing up the opposite pair, our wariness had started to desert us. It seemed that now, too late for me, the barriers were finally coming down.

Amid all the flux and flurry of my strange new life on the *Chronicle*, I often experienced a feeling akin to homesickness which I can only call schoolsickness. I missed the routine, the people, the building, the good things and even the bad things about PJGS. While I pecked out my Church Calls on an ancient typewriter, I pictured my old contemporaries.

As privileged members of the small sixth-form, they would be using the library as their classroom, and the sun would be streaming in as they sat around the wide oak tables. They would be wearing prefects' badges and, when they strolled the corridors, be regarded with reverence by the lower forms. They would be on chatting terms with the teachers, have lots of free periods, be under no obligation to do games or P.T., but be able to take advantage, if they wished, of two brand-new tennis courts. Comradeship would be strengthened by in-jokes and socialising. Best of all, they could study their three favourite subjects with a depth of concentration that was in itself a luxury.

I missed Joy enormously, Joyce, too, and many other faces that kept popping into mind. I remembered the quiet encouragement of Mr Good; the avuncular ease and humour of our popular French and German master, Mr Rockett ('K. R.'); the tolerance of Mr Cunnington, who had said, as he caught us passing notes during maths, 'Now Joy, now Janet, put the little pieces of paper away, dears'; the way Miss Campbell, the Edinburgh graduate who spoke French with a slight Scottish accent, blushed if embarrassed; no-nonsense Mr Horsfield, who tried to teach me about imponderables like stocks and shares, and sines and cosines, and had one blue eye and one brown; Miss Mills, who could be sidetracked from Latin translation into talking about spiritualism; Miss Hanson, who we thought must have been shell-shocked during the war because the chalk regularly broke in her shaking hands when she wrote on the blackboard; poor Miss Williamson, who always looked as though her mother had sent her to school without brushing her hair, and whose mild blue eyes flooded with tears during one class detention.

I missed watching the boys playing cricket in their whites during hot afternoons on the school fields; singing carols at Christmas assemblies, and posting cards to friends in classroom letter-boxes; identifying dinner by its smell as we passed the dining-hall; witnessing the Staff Dramatic Society in action (their productions of *The Ghost Train* and *Charley's Aunt* had been electrifying).

I missed doing P.T. exercises, and rope-climbing, and turning upside-down on wall-bars, and netball. I even missed the dreaded Standard Tests of running, jumping and throwing a cricket ball, by which we tried to gain points for our school houses, and I recalled with nostalgia those freezing hockey matches which always resulted for me in bruised and bumpy shins.

While there was much to learn about many things when working on a newspaper, and life was certainly busy, and sometimes exciting, I was sad that my hold on French, German, Latin, English literature and history was lost. I was even sad that I was no longer required to struggle with maths and science. On the *Chronicle* and *Yorkshire Evening Post*, I was being tested and stretched in a different way: learning to spot a story, think in headlines, write to format, pare down extraneous matter and accept brusque criticism.

While I did not have serious doubts about choosing to drop my formal education at the age of fifteen, I sometimes gave a backward look towards the might-have-been. I returned to school three or four times, to cover a speech day, see Joy as Miss Prism in *The Importance of Being Earnest*, and a production of *She Stoops to Conquer*, and also to collect an English prize, awarded, ironically, by our rival weekly, *The Doncaster Gazette*. As I chatted to Mr Good after receiving it, I was unaware that he had slipped a new copy of *The Century's Poets* among the books I was carrying, with a note wishing me well. I was surprised to find these during the bus-ride home, and still treasure the gift as a link with my old mentor.

My break with PJGS was more or less complete, apart from the snippets of school gossip I gleaned from Joy. I had cut myself adrift and was a stranger, so it was natural that I should feel distanced, as well as envious, as I listened to her revelations about life in the sixth-form on the increasingly rare occasions we saw each other. Nevertheless, the magical bond of our friendship has ever since remained unbroken, and in times of trouble we still draw on each other's comforting words, and fiercely-biased loyalty.

CHAPTER NINETEEN – PADDY

INSIDE THE WORLD that was the Drum, family, friends, customers and staff ebbed and flowed in endless permutation. The cleaners arrived at eight in the morning, the barmaid at just before opening time, the cellar-man, if we had one, according to less specified arrangements. By eleven o'clock, one or two customers might have gathered outside the main entrance, waiting for the grained-oak double door to split asunder at the magic hour.

Wednesday was the barmaid's day off, when Mother ran the pub on her own until three o'clock closing. When I got home from school about half-past four, I was sometimes sent over to old Mr Bostock's corner shop to buy a loaf, and his thin wife might be serving. Her voice was thin, too, and how ill she looked, with her red-pinched nose and skin like watered milk.

If there was none of Mother's baking left in the enormous meat-safe we used as a pantry, I might buy myself a small Lyon's fruit pie in its individual cardboard box, or else one of the strange, dome-shaped, chocolate-coated buns I only ever saw at Bostock's. They reminded me of tortoises, though this resemblance did not put me off.

There was a proper baker on Bentley Road, called Mr Philips, but he only opened when he felt well enough, and if his supplies had come through. It was often hard to tell if his shop was open, so untrumpeted were its contents and so bare its brown shelves. If we happened to pass on a good day and spotted some treats in his window, we were inordinately glad, for his Madeira and caraway-seed cakes, his puff-pastry lemon and jam tarts and his short-crust fruit pies were manna in our mouths.

Because I had school dinners, tea was a light affair: a boiled egg, or sandwiches spread with home-made jam, or tomato sprinkled with sugar, my great favourite. After our meal in front of the big black range, there might be time for a game of hide-and-seek with Paddy. Mother would cover his eyes and I would hide, and if he found me three times he got a biscuit. I always lay flat on the table when the third turn came, and he would make a great to-do of seeking me in all sorts of unlikely places, panting and giving excited little woofs. At last, all other avenues explored, he would balance on his hind legs with his front paws hooked over the end of the table, and peer at me, barking to signal his pleasure and surprise. It was obvious to Mother and me that a dog of such intelligence knew what was expected of him, and was playing up to us.

Biscuit eaten, he and I would go downstairs to collect *The Yorkshire Evening Post* from the doormat. I had to fold it and place it gently between his painfully-decayed teeth before he was able to bound back upstairs and deliver it proudly to Mother. She would spread out the paper, trying not to touch the smears left by his noisome slaver, and sit with it in her armchair until just before six o'clock.

During those precious minutes before she went down again to the bar, she expected to be left in peace, so I would settle to my own reading. Thinking back to those Wednesday tea-times, I can still hear the background noises that bore so lightly in on our tranquillity. Coke shifts in the grate; pages rustle; a sash window rattles; a knee-joint cracks as Mother recrosses her legs. But the most emotive sound is the tiny fizzing noise she makes when she sucks her lips and inner cheek in concentration.

For long periods, Mother, Paddy and I were the only ones sleeping at the Drum, but it never bothered us. We went to our beds without a qualm, and even though I sometimes had to get up in the middle of the night to go to the lavatory, and risked being chased by the Witch At The End Of The Landing, such imaginings owed more to force of habit than genuine fear.

If I went to Hull, Mother and Paddy were on their own. The little dog was happy knowing she was just up the corridor from his sleeping quarters in the living-room, and she felt safe knowing he would alert her if he heard a noise. He was a phlegmatic sleeper usually, thank goodness, but I remember one particular occasion when we were roused by his barking.

Someone was ringing the bell, banging on the door, and shouting. Greatly alarmed, Mum and I got up, flung open the window above the side door and stuck our heads over the sill. With difficulty we made out a dark figure, crying that he needed brandy because somebody had collapsed. He gave a name which Mother recognised, so she hastened down to get the brandy, with Paddy and me whining our warnings in the background.

I remember her once indicating that, with alcohol and cigarettes on the premises, money in the safe, and only a Yale lock and metal crossbar to secure each of the four outside doors, it was quite wonderful how no-one had ever broken in. Yet while the size and darkness of the Drum could be awesome at times, even to someone like me who called it home, I don't recall being troubled by thoughts of thieves and vagabonds. If such thoughts occurred to Mother other than on that one occasion, she never revealed them, being strong-minded and not inclined to 'nerves'.

It is a fact that sixty years ago people worried far less about personal security than they do today. One individual could look after all the Drum's customers on a weekday lunch-time, even though it entailed walking at least twelve yards to get from behind one counter to another, passing each time through a heavy swing door, and cutting through the office at the back of the lounge bar where stock was kept. Asking for trouble, one might think now; yet as far as I know, nothing was ever stolen. (Mind you, if anyone had opened a till, there would have been a tell-tale ping.)

One night when the Drum was closed due to a beer shortage and Mother and I were returning from a trip to the pictures, the silent building, bulking doubly black against the night sky, seemed unusually mysterious and menacing. I remember remarking, 'Doesn't it look big and dark?' which must have confirmed Mother's own impression, for later I heard her say to someone, 'If that's how it struck me, how must the poor little lass have felt?'

Though Paddy usually stayed upstairs with me whilst Mum was working downstairs in the evening, he would sometimes descend to the bars, where he had the reputation of being difficult. Regulars avoided him, apart from a favoured few, but strangers would often try to be friendly. If they attempted to pat him, he was liable to warn them off by baring his brown fangs. Mother always maintained that his suck was worse than his bite, and we reckoned his teeth were too soft to do much damage. Still, a suck might have led to blood-poisoning, if the power of its stench was any gauge.

He did not suffer anomalies gladly, in fact, they alarmed him, and he made no bones about standing barking in the street at anyone with a physical or mental defect. People with a limp, or a silly laugh, or a funny voice, or anybody who tried to ingratiate themself with him when they were persona non grata, drew reproof bordering on hysteria. He could also take against some folk for no apparent reason. One of our barmaids was aware that he hated her, and delighted in baiting him, tittering as she stretched out her hand, 'Come on, Paddy, come on then, good dog ...' Mockery was another thing that got him on the raw; you could tell this by the way his legs went all stiff as he let fly with the barks.

It was embarrassing if we walked past anyone with a walking-stick, or in a wheelchair, for he singled them out with a crescendo of loud yelps. One of the shopkeepers opposite the Drum, poor Dickie Burbanks, had no roof to his mouth, and his efforts to speak drove Paddy demented. Such incidents had a sort of slapstick edge to them which I had a struggle not to laugh at sometimes. Yet I had to admit that while my darling dog had many noble traits, his lack of compassion for the afflicted was a definite minus. Except towards his chosen circle, he grew even testier with age.

Once when my cousin Gordon called at the Drum while on leave from the Navy, and made to fondle Paddy in the bar, a customer warned, 'Watch him, sailor, that dog can get nasty.' Gordon laughed, and proceeded to stage a mock fight with Paddy, going, I expect, through the usual routine of ruffling his ears, shaking a fist under his nose, rubbing his back fur up the wrong way, and altogether giving him a rollicking good teasing.

Paddy would look fierce on these occasions, and dance around, and pretend to growl as he went for Gordon's wrist, jaws a-quiver with the effort of not actually biting it. When he had had enough, he usually signalled pax by rolling over to have his tummy tickled, which made one of his back legs go round and round in an involuntary scratching motion. But until this point was reached, the customer had been right to feel nervous. How could he know that the Drum's most notorious resident had adored this particular stranger since puppyhood?

Upstairs among the family, Paddy was biddable. One might almost have called him subservient. When he first came to live with us at the age of one, I had sometimes treated him like my teddy-bear, wrapping him in a shawl, balancing a doll's bonnet on one of his ears and pushing him around in my dolls' pram. His patience did not last, but it was harder for him to escape than it was for Pussy Willow, the cat, who fought with teeth and claws against such humiliation, and was out of the pram in a flash.

Dogs are game for adventure. Paddy's joie-de-vivre only wavered if something went wrong, as, for instance, when he was ordered to get on his mat. This was a small, oblong door-rug in a corner of the living-room to which he was banished if he overstepped the mark. He would slink to it and sit shivering, with his back against the wall, and over time, the rubbing of his coat made a black shadow impossible to wipe off.

He dreaded baths, and regarded 'Would you like a nice bath, Paddy?' as an even more distressing phrase than 'Go on your mat!' To tease him, we would sometimes run water into the kitchen sink; not that he would ever have been allowed in it. When he had rolled in something really horrid, and was impossible to live with, we would get out my old wooden bath-tub, and at the sight of it, he would try to leave the room, though he must have realised that we would catch him, and that struggling was useless. Nevertheless, it took two of us to hold him down and lather him. With face and undercarriage rinsed to a beautiful shade of honey, he would wriggle out of the towel, preferring to dry himself by sliding his body frenziedly across the coconut-matting. Once outdoors, we knew he would look for something else to roll in to rid himself of the shameful smell of soap; he favoured horse-manure, but this was much rarer than his staple embrocation, dog-wee and dead birds.

Throughout his fifteen years of life, I think he went only two or three times to the vet's: as a puppy, to have treatment for the abscess which rotted his teeth, and again in middle age, to have a couple of his most painful teeth extracted. His final journey was to the Dogs' Home. If his nose seemed dry or his head hot, Mother would dose him with Karswood Dog Powders. We would open his mouth gingerly, not because we feared he would bite us, but because his breath was so fetid, and slip a powder down his throat. 'Look up and smile the Odol smile,' Mother would say to him, echoing a toothpaste advertisement of the time.

He ate what we ate, waiting patiently until we had finished our dinner and the remains of it were scraped on to his enamel plate: vegetables of all kinds, mashed potatoes (being a 'real Irishman for his murphies', according to Mother) and lots of her delicious gravy, which she always flavoured with Burdall's Gravy Salt. As often as we could we gave him bits of our precious meat ration. Dog-biscuits were no good to him. He had fish and chips on Saturdays, and was always pleased to have a saucerful of tea dregs, which Mother said were good for distemper.

It was important to remember that the ceremony of setting down his plate required the incantation, 'WHAT a nice DINNER for a WOGGIE', and there was often pudding to follow. On days when we had nothing to give him, we would walk across to Mrs Whitley's shop (Mrs Whitley had died long ago, but the shop was still referred to as hers) and buy him a tin of Tom Piper Stew.

This diet must have suited him, for as a young (and not-so-young) dog he was always bursting with energy. I fondly recall how he used to accompany me up Broughton Avenue. The terraced houses had tiny gardens separated by walls about three feet high, and sometimes he would set himself a hurdle course along this frontage, jumping walls just for the hell of it.

One afternoon he gave us a terrible fright, and I still feel horrified when I think of it. The weather had been hot, and Mother and I had gone out, leaving one of the sash windows on our first-floor living-room wide open. As we rounded the street corner on our return to the Drum some time later, oh good Lord, there stood Paddy high above on the narrow sill, front paws almost on the edge. He got very excited when he saw us, but we dared not shout to him for fear he might try to jump down.

I am not clear what happened next. Was someone else with us? Was George Henry there, or Cousin Dorothy, or Mrs Dunn? I think Mother stayed below, quietly telling Paddy to go back. Could we catch him if he fell? Would he crash on to the railings or the concrete? Would he land on his feet like a cat?

I remember running upstairs as softly and quickly as I could, seeing Paddy still framed in the open window with his back to me, and approaching him with great caution, for there was little space for him to turn around. Perhaps it was I who hauled him off the sill, perhaps it was somebody else. All I knew was that he was safe, and I buried my face in his fur, and thought I would never take him for granted again. He seemed surprised, and wriggled.

Like any male, Paddy found displays of emotion embarrassing; yet let us pay the slightest attention to Pussy Willow, and he would chase him round the kitchen. But though they had some terrible fights, I do not blame these for driving Willow away, for he had always been exceptionally independent, even for a cat.

Gradually, we saw less and less of our fierce tom, and sometimes he went missing for weeks. Then one day he dragged himself home with a great gaping wound along his back where fur and flesh had been torn away. How he came to be so horribly injured we could not imagine, but we nursed him as best we could, and he seemed grateful, and for a time became our household pet again. But as soon as the wound started to heal he went back to his wild old wanderings, and slipped away one morning, never to return.

***

BAD BREATH NEVER appeared to get in the way of Paddy's love life. Periodically he would disappear for twenty-four hours, and we guessed he had been pressing his suit with a bitch on heat. Once I was introduced to one of his putative pups. He was always a bit sheepish when he came home after a night's courting, and wagged his tail at ground level.

As he aged, he got so cranky we were a bit fearful about letting him out for his usual strolls. He had always been free to roam the neighbourhood, and would challenge other dogs no matter what their size. Even when his back legs stared to wobble, he still had the idea he was cock of the walk. A bigger worry was that he had become less tolerant with children, and would give a warning growl if they tried to touch him, but only because he was afraid they would jar his head and set his teeth aching. As he had never bitten anybody to our knowledge, and probably couldn't, there seemed no real danger of his hurting anyone.

One day, a man in uniform called at the pub and asked if he could see our dog. He was an inspector from the R.S.P.C.A., and Mother naively assumed he was in the area giving old animals a check-up or something. She took him upstairs, where Paddy lay in front of the fire, chewing a marrow-bone. (Actually, he was sucking it, for chewing hard things made him yelp.) It was a Friday, cleaning day for our living quarters, and Mother was particularly glad that the furniture and brass had been polished, and the room looked its best. No family dog could have had a more cared-for setting, or been better done by.

The inspector was more interested in examining Paddy, which he did in a most thorough manner, and Paddy let him run his hands around, and check his mouth and ears and under his tail, without raising a single objection.

'He seems very well for his age. There's no neglect here,' said the inspector.

"Neglect? NEGLECT?' I can still hear the stupefaction in my mother's voice as she repeated to us later exactly how she had responded to such an outrageous suggestion.

Someone, it seemed (the inspector was not allowed to say who) had reported to the society that there was an old dog at the Big Drum who was neglected. This kind of allegation had to be investigated, but he had seen for himself that in this case there was nothing to worry about, and that, even at the age of fifteen, Paddy was still able to enjoy life. However, when the situation changed, the inspector was sure Mother would do the kind thing and not keep the old boy hanging on, but have him put to sleep.

Mother was so upset, incredulous and angry that as soon as the man had gone she rang me at work to tell me about it. The knowledge that some anonymous person had contacted the R.S.P.C.A. to accuse her of neglecting her dog was deeply hurtful. She could only think that Paddy might have turned awkward with someone, so they had taken steps to get him out of the way. She had her private suspicions as to who that person might be.

But we never found out who the informant was. Meanwhile, Mother made no secret of her indignation, and hoped that whoever was responsible for calling out the inspector would hear his verdict over the Drum grapevine: Paddy Greenwood was officially pronounced in good shape for his age, and his owners were congratulated on their care of him.

After a time, when Mother told the story she was able to give it a more cheerful, consolatory slant by remembering what a 'picture of contentment' Paddy had looked when the inspector called. Wasn't it lucky that the living-room had just received its weekly spit and polish, and that there was a fire going, and Paddy happened to have a bone? Indeed, the circumstances could hardly have been bettered. Here was a well-fed, happy dog toying with a bone before a fire and displaying no sign of bad temper, even when intimately handled by a stranger. (Had he been cold and hungry, he might have been less obliging.)

So that is how Paddy and Mother won the day. But while there was balm in justification, it was not pleasant to think there might be an enemy out there, keeping an eye on us; and though the episode eventually slipped into limbo, Mother was still indignant on the rare occasions when she thought about it. Even so, the passage of time had made her more philosophical, and I remember her once observing: 'All I can say is, whoever reported me didn't know me, and didn't know my dog.'

***

223

NOT MANY MONTHS after the inspector's visit, Paddy began having serious problems with his back end, a weakness common in old dogs and cats. It was distressing to watch him trying to make his legs work as he lowered himself clumsily down the stairs, which he had to do in order to get outside to relieve himself. Then he would drag himself upstairs again. On occasion, his descent was too slow for him to get through the side door in time, so we started to carry him down. Though his back legs and bottom had shrunk, he was still fairly heavy, but George Henry, whom he loved and trusted, could pick him up and cradle him like a baby.

Then Paddy began to lose control of his bowels. Dog-like, he found reassurance in being close to us when he fell asleep on the living-room matting. I remember him lying up against my feet and feeling a warm discharge ooze softly on to my slipper.

It was time to be kind. One Saturday morning while I was at work, George Henry and a friend took him by car to the Dogs' Home. I had wondered how I would say goodbye, knowing I would not see him again, and in the event I did it quickly, because he was gazing as cheerfully as he always did up into my face.

'Do animals go to heaven?' I asked as a child. If you need them in yours (or if they need you in theirs) the answer must be yes.

CHAPTER TWENTY – BEL

BUSY AS SHE was, Mother enjoyed having people to stay, and so, usually, did I. A special, fragile guest was Granmer Greenwood, who visited us once or twice a year. She would be brought to Doncaster from the village of Preston by Uncle George and Aunt Clara in their car. They would drop her off at Uncle Jack's and Aunt Elsie's, where she would stay for a fortnight's holiday before coming to the Drum to spend another two weeks with Mother and me.

As the years progressed, and Granmer passed from her seventies into her eighties, she became increasingly frail, and needed assistance to reach the lavatory or her bedroom in the larger-than-life expanses of the Drum. When bedtime came, and I had helped her out of her armchair, she would link her arm in mine, and the hand she rested on my wrist was like an empty glove. Together we would jerk along the corridor, she slightly hunched and cruelly stiffened by 'rhumtic', as she spelled it in her letters. She was hesitant about leaning on me during these slow journeys, so I had to keep reassuring her that she was not dragging me down. Her tiny frame as she clung to my arm had the lightness of balsa wood.

Although she bit her lip, and uttered mouse-like squeaks now and then because of the pain, and screwed up her face in an effort to make her legs go, I never knew her to grumble. Sometimes she sighed, 'aye ... aye ... aye', such a quiet sigh. Sometimes she laughed, but her laughter held no bitterness: I can best describe it as rueful. The tears that filled her eyes seemed to spring not just from frustration, or the humour of her situation, but also from incredulity, as though she could scarcely recognise the self she had become.

I treasured Granmer's company not only because I loved her for herself, but because she was my father's mother, and enjoyed talking about him. 'Oh, he did love you,' she would tell me. 'He thought there was nobody like you.'

She rarely criticised anyone behind their back in my hearing, and I cannot remember her ever correcting me, even if she was sometimes a bit querulous with mischievous boys. Though legends still circulated in the family about her iron will, she seemed to me just a very sweet old lady. We were always in harmony, she and I, not least in one very important aspect: we agreed that my father had been an exceptional man.

He had not inherited from her his careful way with money, for she was a delightfully generous person. She had by this time only a very small income, but she loved giving presents, and would sometimes try to thrust a ten-shilling note into our hands, and be grieved when we declined it. Of course, she had few demands on her purse, living with Aunt Clara and Uncle George. She owned four frocks, as I remember (a black, a navy a jade-green and a grey), one black coat and one or two hats, all of which she had had for years and seemed perfectly content with.

Asleep in an armchair, Granmer would curl her fingers around her straight little nose. I used to assume it was to stop herself snoring, but years later, as I clasped my own, less shapely, nose one night in one of my regular efforts to warm it, I suddenly realised that she must have suffered from the same circulatory problem as I.

When she was awake, her eyes would dart restlessly around the room, as very old eyes tend to do. But I think she was not really seeing our faces, the furniture, the walls, the floor, but other things, and other faces. There must be comfort in letting your thoughts drift backwards once you are no longer consulted about your opinion, and have finally relinquished your matriarchal sanctions.

One duty, however, she could not shed. She still worried about us, mostly unnecessarily, as, for instance, when in my earlier years she had bought me a battery-powered night light in the shape of a frosted-glass parrot because she thought I would be frightened to be left alone in a dark bedroom. Mother told her that I was not afraid, because such an idea had never been encouraged to enter my head, but I liked the parrot and kept him long after his workings went rusty.

Being a natural worrit, Granmer probably had a shoal of anxieties floating around inside her own head as she sat out her final days. I hope her thoughts were not all as disturbing as the warning she once gave me about the danger of sniffing flowers. She had heard, she said, of a girl whose nose was eaten away by an earwig that had climbed up one of her nostrils while she was smelling a rose. It was years before I discounted this terrifying story, and I am still a wary sniffer.

Mostly, though, we who were young and strong, with our life-juices merrily flowing, were unperturbed by Granmer's gentle frets. The family had never taken her concerns entirely seriously (especially if related to motor bikes, or the need for glass parrots) although she must surely have been allowed some latitude while she had two sons serving in the French battlefields. But that was a long time ago, during the Great War, and now her apprehensions had faded to background murmurs.

Very old age had its own colours, too: silver for hair, pink for eye-rims, purple for lips and gums, pale yellow for complexion, blue for hands where veins criss-crossed beneath transparent skin. Even so, it was easy to guess how pretty my grandmother once had been.

The thing that most saddened me was that because Ma, as the grown-ups called her, had become rather deaf, she was unable to hear and respond to affectionate teasing. Thus she became the unwitting butt of family jokes and fun-poking, which, though not malicious, gave her a poignant air of isolation.

I used to look at her and try to imagine how it must feel to be so old, and helpless, and near death, and to picture myself like her. But I was quite unable to conceive of anything so preposterous.

***

ONCE AUNT CLARA and Uncle George had bought their car out of Uncle's pig money, they often motored over to spend weekends at the Drum. No driving test was necessary at that time, though Uncle had been briefly coached by one of his friends in the village. He never seemed wholly confident behind the wheel, but did his patient best, egged on to be cautious by Auntie, who was a nervous and authoritative passenger. 'George, you're going too fast.' 'Look out, George, there's a dog crossing the road.' 'You took that corner a bit sharp, George.' 'George, there's another car trying to get by.'

Uncle Fred accompanied them now and again, and during one of these journeys to Bentley the three were puzzled by enormous heaps of excrement lying in the road. So huge were the piles that Uncle George had to steer round them, and Uncle Fred joked they must be elephant-droppings. 'And sure enough, it WAS elephants, because when we'd come a bit further there they were, marching along with a circus,' shrieked Auntie when, on arrival at the Drum, she regaled us with the story. And who could wonder that her decibels rose, overwhelming the dry comments of the Uncles? It was, after all, a rarity to find elephant-dung near Thorne, and the event deserved every last particle of humour wringing out of it.

Sometimes Aunt Clara and Uncle George would bring friends with them. I can't remember where we all slept, but we managed to squeeze in somehow. There were six available bedrooms at the Drum, though one was mainly used as a store-room. It contained some of the things we had brought from Hull, still in their packing-cases, and I recall Mother once unwrapping a few, and revealing a silver-plated tea service, coated in Vaseline, which my father had smeared on to try to prevent oxidisation.

Opposite our living-room, across the landing, was a large room which must have once been intended for the relaxation of the guests who patronised, or were expected to patronise, the Bentley Hotel (as the Drum was originally known) when it opened in 1913. We imagined the facilities had been designed for commercial travellers, who would be shown to their meals in the first of the two large kitchens, and sit around the long table together while the maids brought out dishes cooked on the two big ranges.

But by the time we went to live there, the residents' lounge was ignored and empty, a strangely peaceful place of bare boards and sun-blistered window-frames.

A small box of books in one corner was the only reminder of possible former occupants. I pictured a group of commercial travellers relaxing before the fire after a day's hard selling with *The Best Short Stories of 1928*, or *The Wizard's Light* (a tale of a lighthouse keeper's daughter, modelled on Grace Darling), or Jeffrey Farnol's *An Amateur Gentleman*. (Naturally, I read all the books I found there, though these are the only three titles I remember.)

But maybe the First World War changed everything, and travellers rarely or never came to stay. The room held no vibrations. Set into a corner of the building, and lit by four curtainless windows, it was too bright to be haunted. Even so, we made no effort to use it, no matter how many visitors we had, because it was so big, and needed too much refurbishing.

***

WHEN I WAS about twelve, I asked to have a bedroom of my own, and Mother agreed I could use the one next to hers. But I had to move back into her room if we had visitors.

Once, while we were sleeping together, she summoned her courage to tell me that I should not to be worried if I found I was passing blood. I would soon be starting a monthly cycle, the purpose of which was to 'clean my body out.' While this explanation was true as far as it went, Mother could not bring herself to enlarge on the subject, though the memory of her own terrifying experience had convinced her that she must broach it. Granma Carrie had been too embarrassed to mention the matter at all to her young daughter, so Mother had been caught unawares, and feared she was bleeding to death.

Growing older obviously had its problems, and Mother had some new ones of her own. Why did I cluck so disapprovingly as I watched her standing at her dressing-table mirror, tweaking out grey hairs? Perhaps it was because I had heard somewhere that for every grey one plucked, two more would grow.

The dressing-table was not the kind you could sit at, being of a low-slung Thirties design. So familiar was the furniture in my parents' bedroom that I had never paused to wonder whether I liked it; but as I grew older I realised that, despite its comforting associations, I could not admire it. The varnished brown wood was reminiscent of that jellied meat called brawn we saw at the butcher's, and those pitted chrome drawer-handles were really quite ugly. I preferred the mahogany bedroom-suite my parents had bought on their marriage, and with it now at my sole command (visitors permitting), and my books and a jug of wild flowers on the table, I savoured delicious aloneness in the handsome double bed.

The room, however, was not without its drawbacks. For one thing, the pub sign hung directly under my window, creaking and groaning if a wind got up, and keeping me awake. The front door was beneath the window, too, and it was the habit of certain customers to gather there at closing time on Saturdays and rend the night air with their singing.

In their cups, these men waxed unashamedly sentimental. They enjoyed giving us the old songs, encouraging us, for example, to Keep The Home Fires Burning and Pack Up our Troubles In our Old Kit Bag because it was A Long Way To Tipperary. They warbled longingly of Nellie Dean, Sweet Genevieve, That Old-Fashioned Mother of Mine, and similar household names. Lost loves merited descants ... ah, what poignancy they conveyed!

Rising above the ragged chorus I could detect the peculiarly piercing treble of Percy Atkinson. He was a lovely man was Percy, married to one of our cleaners, and utterly self-effacing in normal circumstances. But after a few drinks he felt an urge to serenade the stars, preferably with an accompanying choir, and underwent a startling transformation.

Not only was this new Percy a persuasive whipper-in, he was adept at reclaiming the interest of any chorister whose enthusiasm might be fading. Just as they announced they were thinking of going home to bed, Percy would remember a song as yet unsung, or a favourite due for another airing, pitch up the first few notes, and stop them in their tracks.

My hopes would rise whenever there was a break in the proceedings, a scraping of feet and calls of 'good night'; then Percy would start things off again. By this time I was so exasperated that for two pins I would have thrown up the window and emptied a bucket of water over their heads. 'You will do no such thing!' cried Mother in alarm, when I told her how tempted I had been.

I don't know whether the singing worried Granmer when she was using my bedroom: even without any kind of disturbance she had nights when she 'just closed her eyes'. Aunt Bel might have been more affected, although I do not remember her complaining.

Aunt Bel was Mother's cousin, a maiden lady who came from Hull for a holiday with us every summer. She and Mother resembled each other quite closely, for both had inherited the dark hair and eyes of the Swift side of the family, though Bel's eyes were more hazel, and she was younger and thinner. She was also rather nervous and fluttery, much less incisive than my mother. I pitied her lack of husband and children, and the boring life she must lead, sitting day after day on an assembly-line at Reckitt's, dropping paper discs inside the screw-caps of Brasso tins. But this very pity made me impatient with her for not taking life by the scruff of the neck and insisting it provide her with more excitement.

I was never rude to Aunt Bel, of course, was grateful for the generous gifts she always brought, accompanied her on walks (at Mother's instigation), and tried to make conversation at meal-times. But it took me a long time to realise how much Mother's invitations must have meant to her, and to feel ashamed of how begrudging I had been about them.

I suppose Aunt Bel must have been in her late forties by the time she started coming for her holidays. She did not look like a spinster, for she had a pleasant face and an eye for smart clothes. She had a talent for giving particularly nice presents: dinner-plates and dessert-dishes for Mother, at a time when table-ware was hard to come by; a dress for me, of coffee-coloured *crêpe-de-chine*, with a gathered neckline, and a discreet scattering of rhinestones on the bodice.

What a thrill to unwrap it from its tissue-lined box and find that, rather than buying me a practical, everyday frock, she had chosen one decidedly more fetching. 'I thought it would be nice for special occasions,' she said, smiling at the unusual warmth of my kiss. I kept the dress for years, even though I never found many opportunities to wear it.

Aunt Bel enjoyed her holidays. They brought a flush to her pale cheeks. Mother made a point of taking her about a bit, maybe arranging a coach-trip, or a visit to the Grand Theatre. There was sure to be a Monday night outing to the cinema with Mrs Dunn, followed by supper at Ye Olde Barrel Café in French Gate. This was an ancient building with narrow passageways, flagged floors and enormously thick walls. The rich stife of fish and chips hanging inside could not quite overpower the foist of antiquity, though it did its best; but I was not yet at the stage where I could savour either of them properly.

Aunt Bel seemed to thrive on company, and was not averse to a small tipple in the lounge. On days when Mother was busy, she would take herself off to town, stepping briskly around the shops in a fashionable coat and hat. Really, she was very easy to entertain.

During their joint visits to Doncaster Market, did Mother wheedle Bel into patronising the shellfish stall, or at least persuade her to stand by while she herself indulged? There was nothing my mother liked better than lining up with other devotees at the gleaming white counter; scanning the tiny saucers of mussels, whelks and cockles, and picking out a particularly fine-looking arrangement (usually whelks); dousing them with salt and vinegar; eating them with her fingers while avoiding the gaze of passers-by; then choosing another saucerful, maybe mussels this time.

Although Mother, if need be, would approach the stall alone, she felt braver if someone went with her, especially as the fishmonger's wife was not one for small talk. This lady's eyes and hair were the same beautiful shade of copper-brown, and she had a thoughtful face, far too thoughtful, in my opinion, for such cold, wet, smelly working conditions. I certainly would not have liked her job, any more than I liked being a customer in those early days. But to please Mother, I persevered, and though I always found whelks gristly, in the end I developed a taste for mussels and cockles. We would stand munching together in impish collusion, having what Mother called 'a good fuddle', and before we moved on, would wipe the vinegar from our hands (and arms, if it had run inside our sleeves) with one of Mum's lace-edged hankies.

Sharing a set of grandparents gave Mother and Bel much common ground. During one of their chats, Mother seized the chance to ask Bel whether there had ever been a man in her life, and learned that ... er, yes ... there had been someone. She had met him during a stay at a convalescent home. Mother relayed this information to Aunt Nancy and me, and we were all three quite cheered by it, since it meant Bel had at least a might-have-been to look back on.

For fate seemed to have dealt unkindly with Bel. She had, I think, two or three brothers, and a younger, vivacious sister, all of them married. But Bel it was who found herself living at home with her parents until they died, in much the same boat as her aunt, my Great-aunt Jinny.

Jinny's case was rather different, however, for she had the memory of a tragic engagement to sustain her. Her beloved Jack was killed in the Great War, and because Jinny could never bear to replace him, she remained a spinster (quite a jolly one), ending her days as housekeeper to her bachelor brothers, Jim and Billy. When Mother and Aunt Nancy counted up, they found it amazing how many Swifts had eluded the married state.

At the start of the Second World War, Bel was living in a flat. The Blitz made her nervous, so she was glad to accept an invitation to move in with Jinny, Jim and Billy. After Jinny died of womb cancer, Bel stayed on at the terrace house in Haworth Street to look after the two old men, and she continued living there once they, too, had died. Although she kept in touch with her sister and brothers, it must have been quite a lonely life.

Following her retirement from Reckitt's, she spent a lot of time walking to and from the centre of Hull along Beverley Road. It was noticed that she muttered to herself as she strode, a peculiarity common enough among those who have no-one at home to talk to. On Sunday evenings, regular as clockwork, Bel would call at Auntie Nancy's house in Cromer Street for supper, and sit drumming her fingers as she talked ... talked ... talked. Stories circulated in the family about her eccentricities ... that when she decorated her front room she painted around the piano because she couldn't move it ... that she darted behind the trees along Beverley Road to avoid people ...

Worst of all, the rumour spread, and was confirmed by an item in the local paper, that she had appeared in court for shop-lifting. Poor Bel, the inspired present-giver who haunted Hull town centre, who had been among the first to send gifts and cards for both my children when they were born – had her love of shopping taken a wayward turn? Or was her arrest a terrible mistake? It was impossible to arrive at an answer, for no-one broached the delicate matter with her, not even Aunt Nancy. I cannot remember the outcome of the court case, but now I am more disturbed by the thought of the fear and shame Bel must have felt than ever I was at the time.

When Malcolm and I took Thea to Hull as a baby, we called on Bel, who admired our daughter, but did not invite us in. For a few years after my mother died, we exchanged Christmas cards, but then Bel's stopped coming. I wrote to her once or twice without getting a reply, and we heard she had entered a residential home. Sometimes one of my cousins would meet Bel's sister in town and learn the latest news of her, and we gathered she was being well looked after.

Years went by, then a friend wrote to tell me Bel had died. I worked out that she must have been well into her nineties. So a long life was Bel's, though hardly a merry one. I hope that once she arrived at the home, she felt among friends: she deserved to.

Chapter Twenty-one
– Ebb and Flow

NOW AND AGAIN, Aunt Clara and Uncle George brought Harry and Maggie Johnson for a weekend at the Drum. They were old family friends, and Mother remembered a time when she and Dad had their first grocery shop in Hull, and Maggie and Harry were courting. Maggie had only one blouse to her name, so she would wash and iron it in Mother's kitchen before she went out to meet Harry.

After they married, the Johnsons used to get a weekly order from my father. Then Maggie stopped one of Dad's wholesalers in the street and asked if she might buy direct from him, sooner than pay shop prices. My father heard about this manoeuvre and took strong exception to it, pointing out to Maggie that his profits were his livelihood. How long his discomposure lasted I have no idea, but the friendship did survive. No doubt the fact that Harry Johnson and Uncle George were great pals furthered the healing process, for both belonged to the same concert-party, and Harry, who was a 'natural' on the piano, often led family sing-songs in my grandparents' front room.

Harry Johnson set up on his own as a butcher and did very well. He and Maggie moved to a semi-detached house in Huntley Drive, a 'better' part of Hull. Whenever she mentioned their address, Aunt Clara would breathe 'Huntley Drive' in reverential tones. (Mother was impressed, too.) I never went to the house, but I heard it was 'a little palace'.

By the time I remember her best, Maggie had a wardrobe of beautiful clothes, including at least one fur coat, and of course she and Harry owned a car. They were jokey, fun-loving and liked a drink, perfect company for my aunt and uncle when it came to the social whirl.

The Johnsons had a son, Young Harry, who was a few years older than I, and fond of reminding me of it. To him I was an irritating little girl who knew nothing, and needed taking down a peg or two. Though I did not regard this view as particularly surprising, I was irked all the same, and found the lightly mocking tone he tended to adopt with me absolutely maddening. The fact that he had slight trouble sounding his 'r's lent him an added air of condescension.

One example of his cockiness which, for some reason, is still etched on my memory, occurred when a crowd of us were sitting around the long table at the Drum, having Sunday dinner. Young Harry was being especially infuriating, riling me even when I was not his target. But his mother rewarded him, as proud mothers do, with peals of admiring laughter.

That was how I saw things then, but later my perspectives shifted, giving me an entirely new slant on Young Harry. I came to regard him not simply as a 'Big I-Am' but as a young man of courage, hiding his anxiety behind a show of bravado, indulged by his parents because they guessed what probably lay ahead.

He had seemed to lead a leisured life, and in time fortune smiled on him to such an extent that we heard he had acquired a car and a fiancée. But though I was aware he had a weak constitution, I was not told until quite a late stage that a shadow had been hanging over him.

I am not clear about the sequence of events, nor how old he was when he needed his first operation, but I know that Young Harry had a tubercular kidney removed, leaving his parents haunted by the dread that the disease might spread to his other one. Although they appeared to make light of the situation, and got on with their lives much as usual, the possibility must surely have crossed the mind of the patient himself.

Not long after his twenty-first birthday, Young Harry fell ill again, and it was found that his remaining kidney had indeed become infected. Such a diagnosis amounted to a death-sentence, for in those days organ transplants and dialysis were unheard of, and little could be done to help him. Aunt Clara kept us posted about his illness, then his death. I confess I do not remember much about the circumstances, probably because I was too self-absorbed, being at a selfish age. I imagine Mother went to the funeral in Hull, but, as usual where such morbid gatherings were concerned, I did not accompany her, and she did not expect me to.

I could not mourn as a friend, for at our rare meetings Young Harry and I had seemed mostly at odds, and I had not really liked him; but I was sorry for his parents, and for him as well because his life had been cut short. I also felt depressed at being reminded, if ever he sidled into my thoughts, that youth was no protection against dying.

***

I NEVER SAW enough of my cousin Margaret. Being six years older than I, she lived her life on another track. Of course, her interests were more mature. But the main reason I saw less of her than I did of Dorothy and Annette was that she, being the eldest of Aunt Nancy's three girls, had greater demands placed on her time and energies.

Margaret was the quiet one, kind, patient and even-tempered; clever enough to win a scholarship to Newland High School, where she held her own without ever feeling she truly belonged; conscientious when it came to scrubbing floors and running errands for Great-aunt Jinny and Great-uncles Jim and Billy, chores which formed a major part of her out-of-school activities.

Though Aunt Jinny's regime was strict, and she regarded Margaret's help in the house as a natural entitlement, she and the uncles were fond of their young 'tweeny', and took her under their wing. All the same, it was quite a hard, hurried sort of life, not least because on school days Margaret had a very long way to run in order to throw down one of Aunt Jinny's hot dinners. But I never heard her grumble (though she might have done out of my hearing). Often she would sleep at Aunt Jinny's, another reason why she mostly seemed to function at one remove from Cromer Street and the Station Inn.

Margaret was easy-going, true, but she was perfectly able to stick up for herself in family fratches, and as happy as the rest of us to laugh at other people's foibles. Oh yes, she could be 'sarky'; but hers was the sort of sarcasm that owed more to wry amusement than a desire to be cutting. If her tolerance were pushed to its limits, then she would fight back. But though she was never slow to voice her opinion on matters of principle, she normally preferred a quiet life to a showdown.

It is therefore very hard for me to picture my usually equable cousin, not once, but on two different occasions, marching up to the house of one of her father's paramours, breaking the unwelcome news that Mick Sykes had a wife and children, and introducing herself as his daughter. What was more, she told the sceptical women who separately answered her knock, he kept his family short of money, and was behind with his maintenance payments (the main reason for her visit).

At no time did I feel the edge of Margaret's tongue. She teased me, of course, and as a spoilt only child I was fair game. But while I might sometimes take umbrage against Dorothy and Annette, whom I matched more in temperament, and boost my adrenalin by having rousing spats with them, Margaret and I never quarrelled. I cannot remember her even being sharp with me. She stayed calm in the face of my shortcomings, and made allowance for my pamperedness.

So I loved Margaret to come and stay, but her visits to the Drum were rarities. By the time we went to live at Bentley she had passed the age of fourteen, which was then the minimum school-leaving age, and her mother's straitened circumstances meant she had to get a job. She found one near home, at Wilkinson's butcher's in Melwood Grove, and said goodbye to long school holidays.

As she grew older, Margaret did voluntary work as a Red Cross nurse when she wasn't serving or delivering meat. She also acquired followers. I remember a time when she seemed torn between two soldiers, one called Bob and the other called Norman. How pleased I was when she came for a short break at the Drum, and how quickly my delight turned to chagrin when Norman arrived a few hours later, and whisked her back to Hull.

He had been given unexpected leave, and hopped on a train to Doncaster as soon as he heard where Margaret was. (Perhaps he knew about Bob.) 'But she's only just got here', I protested to Mother through angry tears. I do not recall Mum's exact reply, but I think she said something about love.

It was not long before Margaret married Norman at the family church, St. John's, with Dorothy, Annette and me among the bridesmaids. By now I had forgiven Norman. He and I got on surprisingly well, and while Margaret was in hospital having their first baby, and he was at a loose end, and Aunt Nancy didn't know what to do with me, he took me to the Ferens Art Gallery, and bought me something to eat (fish and chips, I think). I was thirteen, and felt a bit self-conscious walking through Hull on my own with a uniformed soldier; but he had a sister nearly my age, so I expect this kind of situation was nothing new to him. Despite, or perhaps because of, his teasing, I enjoyed myself.

The baby was a girl, and Margaret and Norman went on to have three more girls and a boy. They spent all their married life at Number 3 Cromer Street, next door to Aunt Nancy, and after he left the Forces Norman went to sea on fish-trawlers.

***

AT THE TIME Margaret's resistance was beginning to crumble, her sister Dorothy, three years younger, seemed to share my own doubts about lowering one's guard when it came to the opposite sex. A natural sceptic with a tongue to match, she saw no reason to disguise her scorn for the poor cadets struggling to display their fighting skills in our garden. Although, as I hark back now to those innocent days, I am struck by the unworthy thought that perhaps the mockery she hurled through our open kitchen window might have been ever so slightly flirtatious.

By the age of fourteen she had started work at Rose Cottage Post Office. Once upon a time, I fancy a real Rose Cottage must have stood at that point on Beverley Road, but it had been replaced as Hull spread outwards by a line of suburban shops. The sub-post office occupied part of a pharmacy, and while I found its lack of rustic charm disappointing, it was handy for Cromer Street, being only a few minutes' walk away.

Like Margaret, once she started work Dorothy began to change. On her visits to Bentley, as the years went by, she was no longer content to accompany me to town, or walk to Pipering Wood with me to pick bluebells, and she lost all interest in ballet. At one time she had found it fun to pirouette across the living-room lino with Brenda, Annette and me, as, with outstretched arms and crooked-up fingers, we hummed 'The Skaters' Waltz'. Now all that must have seemed very juvenile to her compared to quick-stepping and fox-trotting with young Servicemen on the dance-floor at Beverley Road Baths.

What she did enjoy, when she was old enough, was serving in the pub, something which, though I tried it once or twice, never really appealed to me. I was nervous, for working behind the big lounge bar was a bit like being on show in an arena. Dorothy, on the other hand, soon mastered the various skills that bar-work involved; in particular, how to pull a pint so its 'head' was neither so high it tumbled off the top of the glass, nor so low that the customer grumbled about getting more froth than beer. And, if my mother was as strict with her as she was with me, my cousin would also have been told never to breathe on glasses when polishing them, nor to carry a tea-towel over her shoulder, which was unhygienic, bearing in mind hairs, and scurf, and greasy necks.

Dorothy was fastidious, in any case. She was also quick with the repartee which is a key requirement for serving behind a bar. Neither did she have difficulty in dealing with anyone who tried to be clever, though it was important not to be too crushing. Mother also thought it unwise for a barmaid to anticipate a regular customer's order by placing his drink on the counter before he asked for it. Once, when Georgina had done this, she had provoked the sharp response, 'Oh, you know what I usually have, then', which Mother took as a warning that some people did not like their drinking habits being noted.

Dorothy absorbed all such advice with ease. Another great point in her favour was that, thanks to her job at the post office, she was good at adding up. In fact, she had all the right credentials, and Mother wondered if Aunt Nancy might let her come to live with us and work at the Drum full-time. I would have been very excited had I known about this proposal, and when Dorothy told me about it years later, she said she had been nothing loth. But Aunt Nancy was not in favour, and the idea was dropped.

Naturally Dorothy had her admirers, including one Bentley lad who lived at a fried-fish shop with his mother and sister. Even though the shop was closed when Dorothy was asked to tea, the mother heated up one of the vast fat-friers to cook fish and chips just for the family. But despite being fond of her food, and tickled by the incident, my cousin was not tempted into a closer relationship.

She met the love of her life on a dance-floor in Hull. Walt was in the Merchant Navy, and, when only sixteen (having lied about his age), he had served on a ship ferrying supplies to the Normandy beachhead after D-Day. Later he worked on Hull tug-boats, eventually becoming a tug-master. They married at St. John's, had four daughters, and celebrated their Golden wedding in 2000.

***

IT IS TRUE that although I regarded boys as a race apart, there were one or two who stood out as exceptions to the rule, and whom, had the unlikely chance ever presented itself, I could imagine myself kissing. But in the main, boys seemed rough and unknowable, and my schoolgirl crushes were confined to film stars like John Payne, Errol Flynn (as Robin Hood), Richard Greene and, above all, Tyrone Power.

Brenda had her own heart-throbs, in particular, Dennis Morgan. 'Oooh, isn't he *lovely*?' she would coo as we sat together in the Don Cinema watching one of Dennis's films. I believe it was his wavy hair she had fallen for. Privately, I preferred the dark sleekness of Tyrone's hair; as for his wonderful brown eyes, how could she possibly resist them?

Hollywood was our dream, and maybe there was a way to get there. We pored over successive copies of a magazine that I think was called *Picturegoer*, though I cannot recall how we got hold of them. At the back of the magazine, which was devoted to the film world, were long lists of names, in very small print, of girls who nearly all seemed to live in Los Angeles, and wanted English pen-friends.

That was it! We could establish a correspondence with two of these girls and they would invite us to visit them. No doubt they were quite used to living in the same vicinity as Dennis Morgan and Tyrone Power, and to seeing them sometimes walk by. The thought of brushing past our heroes in the street made us weak at the knees, though I suppose we knew there wasn't really much chance of it happening. We were fairly confident, though, about seeing film studios like Twentieth Century Fox and Metro Goldwyn Mayer, even if we were only able to stand outside.

We realised, of course, that we would have to invite our pen-friends back to Bentley, and wondered what they would make of it. Coming from such a glamorous setting themselves, they would probably find ours very boring. But we put off worrying about how to entertain them until the time came.

Eagerly we combed the columns of names, picking out the most likely, though what criteria we used I have no idea. Seated at the Drum's long table, we composed our letters, setting out our personal details, and mentioning our favourite American films. We posted each envelope with every hope of a swift reply, and when nothing happened we tried again, choosing different names this time. But in the end, having received not a single answer, we became disenchanted, scrapped the project, and resigned ourselves to never going to Hollywood.

***

BRENDA AND I did not dwell on our disappointment, maybe because we guessed if our dream had come true it might have led to complications. Though everyday life was largely uneventful, there was less chance of anything going wrong on home ground. Bentley was a sprawling mining village we knew only in part; but Doncaster town centre in the 1940s was as familiar to us as the backs of our hands.

Twenty years later, the desecration began. Fine old buildings were pulled down and graceless modern ones thrown up in their places, leaving mere vestiges of that pleasant market town which began its charted history as Roman Danum, and later offered a selection of hostelries to stage-coaches bumping through along the Great North Road. In those days its high street was described as one of the finest between London and Edinburgh. Today, a mental stroll around the Doncaster I knew has me almost weeping with rage.

Of course, old 'Donny' had its awful bits. One of them was the Bentley trackless terminus, a concrete edifice with walls so rough they looked like forked-up butter-icing, unaccountably turned grey. Leaning against them could be painful. From there it was only a few yards to the end of North Bridge at its junction with French Gate, which had originally been the main road into town. Below, further back along French Gate, stood the Black Boy, a pub of dubious reputation, and the old Greyfriars Swimming Baths, still in use, though a new pool had been built at the other end of town. Ye Olde Barrel Café, renowned for its fish and chips, was somewhere in this vicinity.

A little higher up French Gate, towards Clock Corner, crouched a bow-windowed tobacconist's, which, threatened with demolition some years later, was saved for Doncaster Museum, along with its fittings, by an enlightened local historian. Old bow windows featured now and again along the main thoroughfare, which, after French Gate, became High Street, then Hall Gate. On the west side of French Gate was Davy's, a baker's and confectioner's that sold the most delectable cream cakes, and had a first-floor restaurant where waitresses in fancy white aprons and starched tiaras served strong tea or coffee in silver pots, and the air was rich with the savour of toasted tea-cake.

A little further along, displaying an appropriate coat-of-arms, was the Angel and Royal Hotel , a place of dark mystery I came to know later as a gathering-ground for journalists' union meetings. Queen Victoria had stayed there in 1851, and the old Angel had been granted the 'and Royal' as a result. But even such a proud connection could not save the building, and it was demolished to make way for an Arndale Centre, then later redeveloped yet again.

Along this pavement, too, reared the ornate frontage of the Regal Cinema. The poor old Regal was not in the same class as the Picture House, Palace, Ritz or Gaumont, and the films it advertised were never the great Hollywood hits we longed to see, though Brenda and I resorted to it occasionally if the queues were too long elsewhere. I remember watching something called *Rainbow on the River* there, starring a cherubic-faced boy called Bobby Breen, and maddeningly, I am sometimes revisited by Bobby's sweet soprano singing the title song, and have to stop myself singing it too. If you have swallowed too much treacle, and been as aggravated by somebody's saintliness as we were by Bobby's, you have no wish to remember. Long before we emerged from the Regal's dark shades, we had reached the same mournful conclusion: we had wasted our pocket money on rubbish.

***

ALMOST DIRECTLY OPPOSITE the Regal stood the pillared Guild Hall, home of Doncaster Borough Police and the Borough Magistrates' Court. Not far past it along French Gate was a dairy shop, with its name in large golden lettering set in a glass panel below the shop window, and assistants behind a counter of white marble, ready to cut cheese, slice bacon and pat butter to personal requirements.

Boots the Chemist was near Clock Corner, with two entrances, so we could nip through the store from French Gate and come out at right-angles in Baxter Gate, or vice versa, glancing at the splendid display of leather handbags, and wishing for time to browse in the lending-library, where the spines of Boots' books were punched with distinctive eyelets. Joy and her mother were enthusiastic borrowers.

Clock Corner was the town's most notorious landmark, for the handsome clock marked a crossroads that, by the 1950s, was a nationally-recognised bottleneck. Doncaster's Town Moor Racecourse was home to the St. Leger, last of the English Classic horse-races, and once cars became popular after the war, the traffic build-up in the town sometimes stretched back as far as Red House, seven miles down the A1.

This was when P.C. Haigh came into his own. A Doncaster Borough policeman with a way of directing traffic that bordered on genius, he took his stance at the offending junction and worked his essential magic. Further along on High Street were the banks, the most imposing being the Westminster, where Mother deposited the Drum's takings twice a week, and collected change for the tills. I often went with her on Saturdays, and passed time as she queued by inspecting the tall Roman jug that had been dug up from the bank's foundations and put on display. Walking around its glass case, customers could admire the astonishing find from every angle. It had a yellowish glaze, unmarred, as I recall, by a single chip or crack.

Onwards then up High Street, and past the end of Scot Lane, with, opposite, the eighteenth-century Mansion House designed by the famous architect James

Paine, and one of only three in the country, so safe from developers. A little higher up stood a scarcely less noteworthy building: Parkinson's double-fronted, bow-windowed shop, source of the famous Original Doncaster Butterscotch.

Samuel Parkinson had begun his business at 50-51 High Street in 1817. The small oblongs of toffee had a taste all their own, and I still have one of the gold and white packets they came in, printed in blue, and bearing the Royal coat-of-arms. It says: 'As supplied by permission (and to no other party was the same granted) to the Queen and Royal Family on their visit to Doncaster in 1851. And extensively patronised by the Nobility, Clergy and Gentry'.

By one of those twists of fate which posterity often finds baffling, Parkinson's shop closed down around the 1960s, and remained empty for years. Apart from his butterscotch, Samuel Parkinson had been known for his excellent baking-powder, and the business he founded had enjoyed a reputation as one of Doncaster's leading confectioners. Lidless mince pies, topped with white icing, were a speciality, though the mincemeat, poking up through its sugar coating, reminded me of squashed flies.

There was a restaurant, too, with a black and white chequered floor, and the comforting wink of brass and copper reflected in dark, polished wood. Once it had been a meeting-place for the discerning, but something must have happened to change things, perhaps a yearning for newness. Eventually, after years of scandalous neglect when the threat of demolition hung over it, arousing strong feelings amongst conservationists, the building was saved. The company who took it over preserved the Georgian frontage, and thankfully, when I last saw it, it still had its picturesque bow-windows.

Past the end of Scot Lane on the left were Williamson's chemist shop, H.L.Brown, the jewellers, and a turquoise-painted confectioner's and café, the Lyceum, which sold amazingly large cream puffs (an office treat when I started working, for the *Chronicle* and *Yorkshire Evening Post* office was just around the corner). A bit higher up stood a clothes shop called Evans, devoted to larger ladies, and one of the dummies in its window drew tactless comments from passers-by, including Mother and me.

The model was always decked out in the latest style from the far extreme of the outsize range, so shoppers with similar dimensions might know they were catered for, and take heart. But instead of a smile of reassurance, the face atop the vast body wore an extremely grim expression, as if she realised that nothing in her constantly-changing wardrobe could do much to improve her appearance. We never saw her naked, for in those days all bare mannequins in shop windows were discreetly covered with paper.

One night, as Joy and I walked by on our way to the Ritz, and the dummy glared back at us, wearing a particularly awful outfit, Joy murmured, 'You, too, can look like this!' Six little words, falling sweetly into place to make the perfect slogan! We laughed so much we could hardly get up Hall Gate, and I still regard it as one of her finest witticisms.

***

THE REINDEER HOTEL, located somewhere opposite Evans's, was another fine old pub eventually demolished in the name of progress, along with the Wellington, which stood next to the Red Lion in Market Place. The Welly had an entrance in Bower's Fold, an alley leading into Silver Street, with Pinny's, a delightfully old-fashioned haberdasher's, on one of its rounded corners.

The fine Victorian Corn Exchange still stands in the Market Place, and at one time a somewhat eccentric figure would loiter nearby, selling bags of Teale's home-made humbugs from a tray slung round her neck. I cannot put my finger now on exactly what was strange about her, though I have a blurred mental picture of a thin, woolly-hatted person with a sharp manner. Her humbugs crumbled sweetly on the tongue, but had a chewy core.

During the war, the Corn Exchange housed a Government-subsidised British Restaurant. Mrs Dunn, who was used to working in canteens, looked upon it with favour, but when I went there with her and Mother I was put off by the starkness, and need to queue, and disgusted to be served two large, pale, cold pilchards with hot boiled potatoes and lettuce, just like the worst school dinner. Sunny Bar led off the market, and there stood Sleaford's, famous for its puff-pastry curd cheesecakes, which were said to be made with extra-special, secret ingredients during Leger Week.

Leger Week fell during the month of September, when Doncaster became part of the international horse-racing scene, and the owners of some of the town's grand houses rented them out to wealthy visitors. I remember, as a schoolgirl after the war, walking to the Race Course among a happy, chattering stream of people. Here and there along South Parade and Bennetthorpe, groups were gathered at stalls manned by professional gamblers eager to demonstrate something called the Three Card Trick. But I averted my eyes from the legless beggars who made their way through the crowds on low wooden trolleys, using their hands to push themselves along. And though I stopped to listen to Ras Prince Monolulu, the famous racing tipster in his huge, feathered headdress, I kept to the back of his audience, for he had a way of singling people out, remonstrating loudly if they made to move off without buying one of his slips of paper. 'I've gotta horse ... I've gotta horse! ...' It was a cry that has come down in racing history.

How lovely, and open, and green, and sweet-smelling it was up by the Race Course, and round by Sandall Beat and Flint Wood, edging into countryside. But I was more familiar with the bustling commercial area of town, and the quiet short cut by way of St. George Gate, which we sometimes took to get to the Bentley trackless. Rounding Beetham's pub on the corner of Baxter Gate after an onslaught on the market, we would pass the Waverley Hotel and the Public Library, and cross in front of the Parish Church and its gravestones, with the Technical College in the background. There was a passage that ran down the side of the Guildhall and brought us out near North Bridge, and though we avoided its shadows at night, it was a well-trodden path by day.

As I grew older, St. Sepulchre Gate became my favourite town centre street. It contained Hodgson and Hepworth's, a wonderful grocery, cake-shop and delicatessen, with a splendid café upstairs (not that we were among its patrons) and a cosmetic section on the ground floor that sold Atkinson's beauty products. Once I started work, I latched on to the promises made by Atkinson's about their face-cream and powder, but I must say I was disappointed with the results, which did little to disguise my spottiness. Maybe nothing would have done at that stage. Blackheads were a problem Annette, Dorothy and I tried to erase by squeezing each other's pores, but neither Brenda nor Joy was troubled by greasy skin.

Opposite Hodgson and Hepworth's was a large chocolate-shop we sometimes visited after school to use up our sweet coupons. Occasionally, as fifth-formers, Joy and I would make for Taylor and Colbridge's, a neighbouring book-buyers' haven, where one felt constrained to whisper. Even so, we were at ease there, losing ourselves among the shelves of green leather-bound Olive Classics, and the blue ones published by Nelson. They cost, I think, five shillings each, and we normally had a particular author in mind when it came to splurging our pocket money.

It is strange how certain minor incidents engrave themselves on the memory. I recall how, one tea-time, Mother and I were hurrying through town towards the Bentley trackless, laden as usual with shopping so heavy it was almost pulling our arms off, when a car drew up alongside. The window was lowered, and a courteous voice asked if we would like a lift.

Behind the wheel was Mr William Peel, one of our most respected customers, who lived in Watch House Lane, and was, I think, a builder. His car was impressive, and we were pink with delight as we sank into its deep leather upholstery. We mouthed frequent protestations of gratitude as he steered towards Bentley, and smiled through the windows, hoping to wave to people we knew, though I don't think we saw anyone.

Mr Peel sat on a cushion to drive, for he was very tiny, with a face as crumpled as an old pixie's. I don't suppose he thought twice about giving us a lift, and indeed he pointed out that he had been going our way in any case; but I have not forgotten his kindness, and our gleeful ride home.

***

THOUGH MR PEEL was in a good line of business and had quite a big house, even he did not live in one of the handful of detached properties on Watch House Lane. Dr. Erskine did, of course, and his double-fronted home seemed to me like a mansion. The Jenkinsons, who ran a garage on Bentley Road, occupied a detached house opposite the Drum, and our Girl Guide Lieutenant lived in another further along.

Many of the other houses in the lane were thirties-style semis with rounded bay windows, while the streets running off at right-angles were terraced. From this mixed community, and from further afield, the Drum, like any truly popular pub, drew customers from various walks of life. Butchers, doctors, coal-miners, factory-workers, grocers, teachers, pensioners, businessmen, and one or two gentlemen of 'private means', regarded it fondly as their local.

All were characters in their way, but some tickled my curiosity more than others. So reserved was Mr Peel that had he not given us a lift in his car, I might never have remembered him; but people like Big Eva are much harder to forget.

Everyone expects big people to be jolly, and Eva was, despite the fact that she had been left to bring up a young family when her husband was killed in the 1931 Bentley Pit Disaster. Perhaps she had turned to food for comfort. She made jokes about herself, and seemed content to be as big as the notorious model in Evans's shop window, though her wardrobe was far less varied, for I never remember seeing her in anything but a dark grey, double-breasted coat.

She had trouble clasping her hands together across her stomach, and I used to worry about the size of her coffin. Yet her hair, which she wore in a bun, was still brown, her face was smooth, and she had surprisingly trim ankles for one who had no choice but to waddle. Mostly she drank half-pints of bitter in the ladies' tap-room, but sometimes she would be among the privileged few who occasionally stayed back in the lounge after closing time, and then she might have a 'short' as she joined in the singing around the fire.

Licensing laws were strict, and it was forbidden for alcohol to be sold after hours, but now and again Mother would permit a 'landlady's private party'. In my teens, I was infrequently one of the group, chilled and sleepy once the fire faded, bored by much of the conversation, but pleased enough to sip a port-and-lemon,

244

or a Babycham, or a small gin, which Mother said was helpful for a certain time of the month. I liked to hear the old ballads, especially when my Mother and George Henry sang solos and duets.

In response to requests, Mother would run through some of her father's favourites, or Irish or Scottish airs like 'I'll Take You Home Again, Kathleen', and 'It's Oh, How I'm Longing For My Ain Folk'. George Henry, who had a pleasant tenor, would be prevailed upon to give us 'The Last Chord' and 'Excelsior'. Songs from both World Wars presented a chance for everyone to sing, and while there was no piano, the sound we all made was far from disagreeable, though sometimes so loud we shushed one another, in case the police were listening outside, and came in for an explanation. Even though no money had been rung in the till, it could have proved an awkward situation.

***

ONE OR TWO of our customers had foreign connections. Mr Oliver Glass had a charming Peruvian wife, a grown-up son, and a home in Bentley, where his employers, the Cementation Company, were based. After the war, most of his time was spent abroad, helping to supervise construction projects. When he was home on leave he would bring Mrs Glass into the lounge, and if I was passing through they always gave me such a warm greeting that I would go shyly across to have a word with them.

Mrs Glass was dark and vivacious, with a very strong accent, and Mr Glass was a quietly-spoken English gentleman with an avuncular twinkle and a face and hands burned brown by distant suns. He offered to write to me when next he went abroad, and was as good as his word.

I have no idea how many letters he sent, only a few, I think. I still have two of them, penned in the most beautiful hand on airmail paper, describing conditions in the part of the world where he was working. Replying to an adult is always difficult for a child, and I tended to put off the chore, until one day Mother would say, 'Isn't it time you wrote to Mr. Glass?'

Of the two letters I kept, one, dated September, 1947, came from a camp in Venezuela, 6,000 feet up in the mountains, where Mr Glass was involved with building a dam. The other, posted in October, 1948, and apologising for not having been in touch for nearly a year, is from Peru, and was accompanied by a postcard, showing the beach at Lima.

As well as referring to the local scenery, exports, and the price of food and other commodities, Mr. Glass's letters encouraged me in my efforts at school.

In one he congratulated me on my progress in French and German, stressed the importance of Latin as an aid to other languages, and said, 'We shall have to go in for a little Spanish when I get home' (a suggestion that horrified me). But I think the chief reason he took the trouble to write was because I had once told him I was 'doing' South America in geography.

Another great traveller was Mr Harby, but with him I had no contact or conversation, finding him rather forbidding. He was retired, and once banana-boats began accepting passengers again after the war, he sailed off to the Canary Islands every winter. Mrs Harby, meanwhile, remained at their home in Bentley Road, giving piano lessons.

Mr Harby never brought Mrs Harby into the Drum, and I don't think I ever actually saw her in the flesh, but I pictured her as rather fierce, because she was said to be good at getting people through exams. Dear Mrs Straw, my own piano-teacher, was far less demanding, thank goodness: indeed, she was such a chatterbox that, during many of our sessions, more tongue-wagging went on than finger-exercises. I listened enthralled to anecdotes about her youth, her husband, Granville, her old dog, Punch, her wide circle of friends, the crises that sometimes beset them, and the meals they regularly enjoyed together. So unstoppable was her flow during one particular lesson, that when my time was up she realised neither of us had played a single note, and asked me to tell Mother she would not be charging on this occasion. However, I must not give the impression that Mrs Straw was a careless tutor, or that her tendency to chat prevented her more dedicated students from achieving top grades, for this was not the case. She would have realised very quickly that I was not exam material, and that if I learned to tinkle a few tunes from memory, that would be as much as I could manage.

Her conversational teaching style suited me very well, and if she showed signs of breaking off the stream of small talk, and turning her attention to matters musical, I would sometimes try to sidetrack her again. The reason I egged her on so shamelessly was because, once my initial eagerness to learn to play the piano had evaporated, I became very lazy, confining my practice sessions in the Drum's big smoke-room to an hour or two after closing-time on Sunday afternoons. But even though I was stuck for months on the waltz from *Coppélia*, Mrs Straw displayed exemplary patience, welcoming me into her front room as warmly as she welcomed her more conscientious students, whose number included Joy.

I used my bicycle to go to Mrs Straw's. George Henry had bought it for me, a spanking new Rudge, and though I was excited about owning my first two-wheeler, I knew Mother was not convinced it was a good idea, fearing I might have an accident. Then Joy and her father, to whom cycling was routine, offered to take me for a spin around Cusworth, a gesture that did much to improve my morale.

I endeavoured to live up to the demands of my gleaming black metal steed; I even tackled a sixteen-mile round trip to Askern with Sylvia Emberton in an effort to prove that I was getting the most out of George Henry's gift, for I did not wish to seem ungrateful. But while Brenda loved whizzing around on a bike so much she progressed to a model with gears, and joined Doncaster Wheelers, and while Joy regarded her machine as a useful form of transport, my heart was never really in cycling.

Propelling the rather heavy Rudge began to seem too much like hard work, and in the end, after demonstrating to my own satisfaction that I had tried my best, I allowed my interest to wane. I confined my pedalling to Tuesday evenings, free-wheeling part of the half-mile journey to Mrs Straw's with *Coppélia* in my saddlebag, and puffing back up Bentley Road while mulling over her latest confidences. But though she could be sharp in her assessments, because she was one of the most direct and unsentimental people I ever knew, she was also one of the kindest.

Like Mrs Harby, Mrs Straw never crossed the threshold of the Drum, apart from one red- letter day when she and Mrs Cuffling, Joy's mother, entered by the private side door to have lunch with my mother. Mrs Straw had previously invited Mum and Mrs Cuffling for a meal at her house, and this was a return gesture on my mother's part. It was also, I am fairly sure, the only time that Mrs Cuffling ever saw our home, which, when I think about it, is astonishing.

Our private quarters were exactly that, and the only customers who came upstairs were the ladies who made the sandwiches for darts-league matches. The filling they used was a combination of grated cheese and raw onion, to which I took strong exception, especially when the miasma floated along the corridor to my bedroom. 'Ugh!' I would cry rudely, holding my nose as I stalked past the kitchen door. 'Lo-o-ovely,' they would call after me, amused by my airs and graces.

***

DOWNSTAIRS, I WOULD sometimes run across Mrs Fryer. The soft spot I had for her was not entirely due to the fact that she used to bring me her sweet coupons. I would have liked her anyway, because she was always so cheerful, and did not make a burden of being old, and treated me as a friend worth talking to.

When I first knew her, she had a deaf husband at whom she needed to shout, and I assumed this was the reason for her corncrake voice, so hoarse it made my throat feel sore. Then Mr Fryer died, and she started to come into the pub alone. Hitching her arthritic bones with difficulty into one of the tub-chairs, she would eagerly launch a conversation, still with that rasping delivery. She was so small her legs dangled, which gave her an engaging girlishness, despite her grey, Eton-cropped hair and grizzled eyebrows. But the most noticeable thing about her was the roguish gleam in her eye.

If Mrs Fryer's refusal to give in to old age filled me with admiration, I was even more impressed by how Billy Leach's grandmother defied the advancing years. She had a house in Cheltenham, and Billy had been sent to live with her in order to attend a school with more rigid discipline than Percy Jackson's, where his commitment to his studies had been disappointing. His grandmother sometimes accompanied him back to Bentley during the holidays, and came into our pub with Billy's parents. I knew them quite well, because Mr Leach taught Standard Four at Kirkby Avenue Juniors, and they had invited me to their home in Watch House Lane when first I came to live at the Drum, and continued to encourage Billy and me, who were the same age, in our rather awkward friendship.

Though she seemed to be in her eighties, Billy's grandmother was a tall, striking figure. Her eyes were large and strangely iridescent, which I now realise might have been due to cataracts. Her hair was dyed black, her long finger-nails were painted red, and her make-up did its best to conceal the ravages of time.

She wore the latest fashions: furs, fine stockings, high-heeled shoes. She made me realise that old age could be glamorous. I was fascinated, and vowed that when my turn came, I too would paint my nails, and dress in style, and have four-inch heels, and smell of expensive perfume, and adorn my fingers and wrists with rings and bangles. I, too, would refuse to Let Myself Go.

As we grew older, Bill and I started to see a bit more of each other. One night, when we were saying a chaste goodbye in the shadows outside the Drum, Big Eva and friend lumbered out and, oblivious of our presence, relieved themselves on the grass with giggles, sighs, loud gushings, and other awful noises. When they had gone, Bill and I tried to laugh off our embarrassment. But I could not face him after that, and perhaps he felt the same, for very soon our friendship came to its quiet end.

CHAPTER TWENTY-TWO

– AT PRESTON

EVERYTHING WENT SPLENDIDLY at first for Aunt Clara, Uncle George, Cousin Georgie, Uncle Fred, Cousin Brian and Granmer when they moved to the village of Preston, near Hull, at the end of 1944. They all got on as well as ever; indeed, sharing the spacious living quarters at Jackson's shop was much less demanding than squeezing into the three-bedroomed semi-detached house they had previously occupied in Hull. Peace between nations also seemed likely, for the war was plainly drawing to its close.

The six had nicely settled into their new accommodation in Main Street when they heard my cousin Gladys was about to marry; whereupon Aunt Clara, hospitable as ever, invited the newly-weds to spend their honeymoon at Preston, even though Gladys's choice of husband had proved controversial.

He was a charming Irish soldier, and a Roman Catholic. Gladys's father, my Uncle Jack, and her step-mother, Aunt Elsie, were horrified when she told them she intended to marry a Catholic and convert to his faith. Sixty years ago, such a division existed between the Anglican and Roman Churches that any change of allegiance usually provoked a seismic shock, even among people who, like they, were not regular worshippers.

But Gladys and Paddy were in love, and married in a Catholic Church in London. Uncle Jack and Aunt Elsie declined to attend the ceremony, and though later they came to know and like Paddy, at the time they were extremely upset.

Being of a romantic turn of mind, Aunt Clara felt sorry for the newly-weds, and Granmer, who had a particular bond with Gladys because she had helped to bring her up, was eager to see her again, and make her a gift of some specially-hoarded linen. I suppose the honeymoon invitation must have ruffled Uncle Jack and Aunt Elsie, but any disapproval they might have felt was only temporary, thank goodness.

I happened to be staying at Preston at the same time as the honeymooners, and what happy days they were. Paddy was the quintessential Irishman, and there was no doubt in my mind why Gladys had fallen for his bright blue eyes, delightful (though sometimes impenetrable) brogue, and gently-teasing manner. He had such an easy way with people. Once he and Gladys took Brian, Georgie and me on an outing to Hull, and though I am vague as to what we actually did, apart from visiting the pier, I remember feeling tremendously indulged.

When Paddy was demobbed he and Gladys moved to Hartburn, near Stockton-on-Tees, and soon had three children, Anne, Susan and John. Gladys used to bring them to stay with Aunt Elsie and Uncle Jack, and they would call at the Drum to see Mother and me. Sometimes Paddy would come, too. But after Gladys gave birth to two more daughters, Brenda and Jennifer, the visits to Doncaster tailed off, and following Uncle Jack's death, Aunt Elsie made trips to Hartburn instead.

Then, one terrible day, Paddy was killed in a road accident, and with her children still young, Gladys had a long, hard struggle to bring them up alone. More recently she lost her son, John, to cancer, and in October 2007, my cousin herself died at the age of eighty-eight, leaving behind a large and close-knit family.

***

GLADYS'S WEDDING WAS not the only cause of family dissent, for a rift developed between Uncle Fred and Aunt Clara and Uncle George. Uncle Fred, now unattached, though not yet divorced from Aunt Gwen, had struck up a relationship with a local lady named Ivy. When tongues in Preston started to wag, Aunt Clara and Uncle George signalled their concern, and the situation grew more and more uncomfortable. For years my two uncles and aunt had shared a home without friction, but now Uncle Fred, who was, after all, entitled to see whom he pleased, found it unbearable to have Aunt Clara and Uncle George keeping an eye on his activities, and offering unwanted advice, however well-intentioned.

He decided to move from the living quarters at the shop to an ancient, two-roomed cottage a few doors away, which had been standing empty for some time. Brian accompanied him, and Granmer, strong-willed as ever, insisted she would go to live there as well, for she did not think the pair of them could manage on their own. Although she was not very spry she could still potter and cook, even if called upon to do so (as she was in this case) on an old-fashioned, coal-fired range.

Aunt Clara and Uncle George were upset, of course, but they had to accept these arrangements. It was a difficult time for everyone concerned, as the whole of Preston was agog with the news that the Greenwood family had split apart. However, there had been no actual row, only a difference of opinion. Uncle George supplied groceries to Uncle Fred and Granmer, Aunt Clara's helper, Audrey, still did their washing, and there was plenty of to-ing and fro-ing between Jackson's shop and Woodbine Cottage, as the tiny house was called. Whenever Mother and I went to Preston, we visited both establishments.

The name Woodbine Cottage puzzled me, for I assumed it must be associated with Woodbine cigarettes, until Mother told me it really meant Honeysuckle

Cottage. There was no honeysuckle to be seen by then, either on the front wall, which rose straight up from the pavement, or in the minuscule yard behind. The planked front door had an old-fashioned sneck, and Granmer's single bed was immediately to the right as we entered, under the window, and shielded from draughts by a wooden screen. It was a bed I remembered from the past, with a bamboo head-board, and a pale orange eiderdown bearing a geometric design in black. Until I started to write about it, I had not realised I remembered that eiderdown so well.

Against the left-hand wall as we walked into the cottage was a possession of Granmer's I would value now, though at the time it seemed a stuffy piece of Victoriana – a highly-polished, bow-fronted mahogany chest-of-drawers. In one of the drawers she kept photographs, and once I remember her producing some of my father. Why, oh why, did I not ask more questions about them, or beg that I might have some to keep, for I never saw them again.

We would sit together, she and I, before the glowing coals, and perhaps she would sip a milk-stout, and light the cigarette Uncle Fred had left for her as he went out to meet Ivy. Granmer was an amateur smoker, and usually indulged once every twenty-four hours, holding the fire-brand with awkward delicacy between stiffly-extended fingers, and puffing with the single-mindedness of someone who had been told it was a certain cure for jangly nerves.

A tiny passage, with shelves and a cupboard at one side, led from the living-room to a yard with a soil-closet, and the only water available for cooking and washing was from an outside tap. At the other side of the passage, a twisted wooden stair rose directly into the bedroom shared by Uncle Fred and Brian. This was rustic life with a vengeance, but I never heard Granmer complain about the conditions she had chosen to come to, and the rent for Woodbine Cottage was very low.

Sometimes Mrs Rawson would pop in for a word with Granmer. She was a friendly, rosy-cheeked farmer's wife who lived next door in a handsome, double-fronted house I longed to visit. I knew everything would be perfect, for Mrs Rawson was very fastidious, and dusted every day. Then she would wash out her duster, because she was a firm believer in the maxim, 'A Clean Duster Makes A Clean House'.

***

MY COUSIN GEORGIE (though he really preferred George) was fourteen in April, 1947, and his parents threw a party for him. I was invited, but for some reason I was unable to go. Though I was disappointed, there was a certain relief in not having to mix with a lot of people I didn't know. Annette went to the party, however, and had a very good time, so much so that when she answered my eager questions about it afterwards I felt decidedly envious.

Early in September, there was a glut of ripe fruit in the orchard behind the shop, and Georgie did some harvesting before leaving his mother and her helpers to their jamming and bottling, and going for a bike-ride with his friends. It had been a hot day, and Georgie was tired and complained of a headache on his return. He went to bed early, I think, and during the night roused his mother to say he was feeling worse. An ambulance was summoned, and Aunt Clara accompanied him to hospital.

They had a long way to travel, and as he lay on the stretcher he told her anxiously that he had lost the feeling in his hands. Auntie rubbed them, and tried to cheer him up, assuring him that he would be all right. They had made the same journey twice before in recent weeks because Georgie had suffered two bad nose-bleeds that had required hospital treatment. This new ailment did not seem particularly serious to Auntie, and she said afterwards that she had not really been worried as she kissed Georgie goodbye at the hospital, and set off for home. On the whole, past experience had given her a huge faith in doctors, and she felt she was leaving him in safe hands.

The shop had a telephone, and next morning Auntie rang the hospital to ask after Georgie, and was told that he had died. However gently this news was broken, the fact that it was relayed to her as she stood confidently at the end of the line is as horrifying to me now as it was when I first heard of it; and though all this happened sixty years ago, and my aunt and uncle are themselves long dead, I know I can never fully comprehend their grief, nor begin to imagine how my aunt felt at receiving such a message over the telephone.

I do not know how she told Uncle George. I do know that she was hysterical as she stumbled out of the front door and ran the few yards up Main Street to Woodbine Cottage, and Granmer. I suppose a telegram must have been sent to Mother at the Drum, for this was the only way bad news could travel quickly to people like us, who had no telephone.

I remember coming home from school that day, and Mother, with stricken face, choosing her words very carefully to tell me that Georgie had died. I heard her in a daze, for the idea that something like that could have happened to him was nothing short of preposterous.

Even when I was finally convinced, I did not burst into floods of tears, though I remember squeezing out one or two because I knew I ought to cry. Sorrow for him, and for his parents came later; but in those first moments, all I could feel was awe that Georgie had gone ahead into unknown territory, and now knew all there was to know about it.

Georgie had been a victim of poliomyelitis. An epidemic of it swept the country that summer of 1947, causing many deaths or cases of paralysis, for those were the days before the Salk vaccine. Aunt Clara said she had been told by the doctor who had treated Georgie that he would have had a better chance of recovery if the disease had not attacked the upper part of his body. As it was, his heart had been affected.

Georgie's was another funeral I stayed away from, but Mother went to Preston for it, of course, and described to me later how full the lovely old church had been, with many of Georgie's schoolfriends among the mourners. A choir had sung 'O For the Wings of a Dove', which she had found unbearably moving. Although I was not there, whenever I hear this piece of music now I think of Georgie, and the terrible waste of a life that had scarcely been lived.

Apart from my cowardly desire to avoid a harrowing service, I felt I could not bear to face Aunt Clara and Uncle George. But face them I had to at some stage, and not long after Georgie was buried, Mother said they needed to get away from Preston, and were coming to stay at the Drum.

I remember very clearly the day of their arrival, and how apprehensive I felt during lessons, knowing that they would be waiting when I got home from school. I remember picking my way slowly over the uneven ground towards the Drum after I had been dropped by the school bus at tea-time, and wondering how I should greet them; how they would look; what they would say to me; what I should say in reply. If they asked me the usual questions about how I was and what I had been doing, they might cry if I told them, because it was so cruelly unfair that I was still getting on with my life when Georgie could not.

In the event, my worries were groundless. Though he was the most good-natured of men, and never teased me, I had never had a proper conversation with Uncle George, for his formidable reputation as a wit had always made me feel inadequate. Privately, I regarded him as a quiet sort of person, so the brief smile and kiss he gave me now were just what I would have expected in normal circumstances.

Auntie hugged me as she always did, and seemed as pleased as ever to see me. No doubt there were tears, but I cannot remember anything about the rest of the evening, though I feel sure that when Mother went down to the bar, Auntie and Uncle made their way there as well. They had lots of friends at the Drum, and sitting chatting over a drink helped to dull the edge of their grief for a little while.

Uncle George lived for thirty more years, and Aunt Clara for more than forty, and the welcome they gave me whenever I called on them never varied. Uncle's rubicund face would break into a grin, which contented me; Auntie aimed for something more effusive. ('Oooh look George, JANET'S here!'). Her voice, no matter how recently she had seen me, would soar aloft in the wonder of surprise, just as it did whenever she greeted my cousin Brian, or my mother, or anyone else she was fond of.

Uncle was never the same man, though, after Georgie's death. It was as though the stuffing had been knocked out of him. He still cracked jokes, but his heart didn't seem to be in them, and during his silent spells it was hard to guess what he was thinking. He never discussed the past with me, but Aunt Clara did sometimes. I had not been as close to Georgie as Brian had, but I had known him pretty well, and she seemed to find this very comforting.

How unlucky it was, she would say, that just when Georgie appeared to have grown out of his childhood illnesses, and she had begun to stop worrying about him, polio had struck him down. And how even more unlucky it was that it had been the sort to kill him, for if he had simply been paralysed she could have looked after him.

This line of thought was poignant enough, but when she added that it was not just losing Georgie which was so hard, but losing all hope of a daughter-in-law and grandchildren as well, the devastation caused by his death assumed an even more startling bleakness.

***

LIFE IN THE village lost its savour for Auntie and Uncle after their bereavement, though they carried on as bravely as they could for two or three years. Granmer mourned this loss of a fourth grandchild in her own gentle way. If she and I talked about Georgie, she would recall how Aunt Clara had run screaming along the pavement and flung herself against the door of Woodbine Cottage when she came bearing the news of his death. 'Poor Clara and George,' Granmer would sigh, and dab her red eyes with a hanky. But even though she was still anxious about us all, my grandmother had reached the stage where, once a disaster had actually occurred, she was able to accept it calmly and philosophically. This seasoned approach to life's real catastrophes must be part of the ageing process, even for people like Granmer, who was a born worrit (though not usually for herself).

It was probably around this time that Granmer went to hospital for an operation on a big mole which had long troubled her, and had now grown to such a size that it almost half-covered the back of one of her hands. I had never seen anything like it, and would press my index finger softly against the strange, purplish-black cushion to feel its springiness. Granmer said this did not hurt, but when she eventually started to knock the mole and make it bleed as she went about the house, it did become a great nuisance.

So into hospital she went to have it removed, and replaced by a flap of skin taken from her thigh. Though she must have been in her late seventies, she made a good recovery, but while the sore place on her thigh was healing, she would sometimes confide, in a fit of helpless laughter, that it was far more painful than her hand.

When she was better, Granmer continued to take her holidays in Doncaster, first with Uncle Jack and Aunt Elsie, then with Mother and me. Aunt Clara and Uncle George often came to stay, too. Just as their home had become a haven for us after Dad died, so now the Drum provided a refuge for them.

Not long after Georgie's death, they came to Bentley at the same time as Aunt Nancy. She had lost her little boy, Michael, to diphtheria, so she above all people knew how Aunt Clara and Uncle George must have been feeling.

As the two aunts stood before our living-room mirror one evening, combing their hair and powdering their faces before descending to the bar, they talked about the pain of losing a child. Suddenly, to my great surprise, Aunt Nancy asked gently, 'Why don't you have another one, Clara?'

Aunt Clara, taken aback, gave a startled laugh and cried, 'What, at our age?' Little more was said on the matter, and the conversation turned to other things. But this brief exchange stuck in my mind, because I was so amazed that Aunt Nancy considered Aunt Clara, who must have been about forty, young enough to have another baby.

***

MY VISITS TO Preston were fewer after that tragic autumn of 1947, and indeed I only remember one in any detail. There was to be a dance in the village hall for which Uncle George would be Master of Ceremonies, and Aunt Clara thought it would be a treat for me to go. Superficially at least, she had recovered enough of her optimism to paint a glowing picture of what the 'do' would be like, and so I packed my best frock and took the train. I had hoped Annette might meet me in Hull and go to Preston with me, but she must have been otherwise engaged, because I ended up a lonely wallflower, though I am sure Aunt Clara had expected me to spend most of the night on the dance-floor.

She came late to the event, but Uncle of course was there from the start, bow-tied and gleaming like a country gentleman. Dear man, he had a couple of dances with me, but otherwise he was kept busy: being kind to other ladies (many of them his customers), introducing musical numbers, urging on the menfolk with frequent cries of 'Take Your Partners PLEASE', supervising the Ladies' Excuse-Me and the Paul Jones, whipping up interest in the raffle, and generally keeping the ball rolling. Meanwhile, his face never lost the bright smile it always wore on public occasions.

I was fourteen, and very self-conscious, but I really tried hard to show I was enjoying myself, and Aunt Clara was convinced of it, even though not a single boy had invited me on to the floor. It was not a bit like the gatherings back home in the Drum's concert-room, where some of the kind old men might get me up if they saw my foot tapping. Even more did I enjoy whirling around with George Henry, if he could be coaxed to leave the bar and partner me, for he was an excellent old-time dancer. My best chance of persuading him was to rush up with the news that they were playing 'Just For A While' or 'The Gold and Silver Waltz', because those were his favourite tunes.

Things warmed up that night at Preston during the Hokey-Cokey and the Palais Glide, for everyone got to their feet for these, including me. I was welcomed into a group of strangers, and we all linked arms across our backs, and started the side-to-side motions of 'Horsey, Horsey, Don't You Stop', when suddenly I spotted in a line of people moving towards us the figures of Uncle Fred and Ivy.

Although I had seen them together in the Nag's Head once or twice, I had never had any direct contact with Ivy, so to be suddenly confronted by the pair of them was a bit awkward. Now, cavorting on the dance-floor, and standing in the same circle to perform the Hokey-Cokey, it was impossible for us not to smile at each other.

I have one other clear memory of visiting Aunt Clara and Uncle George at Preston after Georgie died, though whether this was at the time of the village dance, or on an earlier occasion, I have no means of telling. All I can remember is walking along the upstairs corridor and passing the bedroom that had been Georgie's.

I peered in fearfully, and it looked very bare. Aunt Clara had told me that it had had to be fumigated in case anyone caught polio from it. I felt like an interloper and shut the door quickly, even though now it was just another bedroom, with no signs of Georgie anywhere.

***

TONGUES STARTED TO wag again in Preston when it became rumoured that Ivy was expecting a baby, and Uncle Fred was the father. The shock that ran through the Greenwood family can readily be imagined, for at that time, the late 1940s, it was considered scandalous to give birth to a child out of wedlock.

Ivy must have found it hard to hold up her head in that small village, while for Aunt Clara, Uncle George, Granmer and Brian the news was devastating. The child was born, a boy, and was called George, although he took his mother's surname, and not Greenwood. Surrounded as they were by memories of their own son, Aunt Clara and Uncle George found life in Preston more difficult for them than ever, and when Jackson's, their employers, offered them the chance of managing a shop in Doncaster, they leapt at it.

The shop, a recent acquisition for Jackson's, stood in Nether Hall Road, close to the town centre, and was being altered to accommodate an off-licence, for which Uncle would be responsible, and a confectionery department, which would be Auntie's province. Auntie was eager to take up any fresh challenge, because she had reached the point where she could not wait to shake the dust of Preston off her feet. I expect Uncle George was not sorry to leave either, although his opinions were never expressed as openly as Auntie's. It was obvious, though, that they were both glad to be coming to live nearer to Uncle Jack and Aunt Elsie, and Mother and me, and Aunt Clara added excitedly that now I was a newspaper reporter in Doncaster, I would often be able to pop in and see them (which turned out to be true).

Once the new premises were ready, in 1950, they made their move. Granmer must have missed them terribly after they left Preston, but she stayed on in Woodbine Cottage for another five years. Looking after Uncle Fred was still her fond aim, but it became increasingly obvious that he was looking after her.

I have no real knowledge of what happened in those months and years after my new cousin George was born, only the sense that, over time, the breach between Granmer and Ivy gradually healed. From snippets of information passed on to me, it seems that my proud, but increasingly frail, grandmother did in the end accept Ivy's help. I think, too, that Granmer grew to know her latest grandson, though how well I cannot be sure.

***

THERE CAME A time when Granmer developed pneumonia. She was very ill, and spent several weeks in the bed beneath the living-room window at Woodbine Cottage. A nurse came in to wash her, but she needed more constant care, and could not be left alone at night, so to help Uncle Fred and Ivy the family rallied round to a remarkable degree. A rota was organised, and Mum, Aunt Clara, Aunt Elsie and Uncle Jack travelled by train and bus between Doncaster and Preston at various times, in order to sit up all night with Granmer. Mrs Dunn, a stalwart friend if ever there was one, volunteered to accompany Mother, and George Henry took charge of the Drum during Mum's absence. It was a difficult and exhausting time, for I don't suppose any of the watchers managed to get much sleep, propped up on chairs in the tiny living-room at Woodbine Cottage. So the Greenwoods were enormously grateful when Aunt Nancy and Uncle Bob, who really had no need to offer, shouldered some of the burden by joining the roster too.

No-one expected my help. At twenty-one, I was old enough to share the responsibility of looking after Granmer, but, even had I not been working all sorts of unpredictable hours for the newspaper, the idea would never have crossed my mind.

I did go over to see her, of course, but by this time she was only half-conscious, and making painful efforts to breathe. She had always been small, goodness knows, but now there seemed scarcely anything left of her. She moaned when we raised her to give her a drink, flopping back like a little rag doll.

Mother, always careful to shield me from unpleasantness if she could, would have been unlikely to want me by her in the sick-room during the long watches of the night. All the same, perhaps I should have offered, though from what I gathered, the vigils at Woodbine Cottage were uneventful, and Granmer's wants were few.

A development that Mother did find rather disconcerting was when the nurse arrived one morning to give Granmer a bed-bath, and started to fill the washing-up bowl. Mother protested weakly, 'That's the washing-up bowl', and Nurse's reply was something along the lines of, 'Never mind, it's only soap and water.'

Mother thought she could understand why a busy nurse might seize the first receptacle that came to hand, but honestly, who could fancy pots washed in it now? As soon as she was able, she slipped out to buy another bowl; of course she had no guarantee that it would be kept just for dishes, but at least it stood a chance. When she mentioned the episode to me on coming home, we laughed and rolled our eyes at each other, for we knew what a bugbear our fastidiousness could be.

***

EVENTUALLY GRANMER BECAME so ill that she was taken to hospital in Driffield. When we visited her, she did not seem to recognise us, and soon afterwards she died. Arrangements were made for her to be buried in Hull, and this was one funeral I really did need to be part of, because I had loved her very much, and wanted to say a proper goodbye to her. So Mother and I went together by train, and made straight for the funeral parlour where Granmer was laid out in her coffin.

She was the first person I had ever seen dead, and she looked just as though she was carved out of wood. I forced myself to gaze at her face, and was surprised by the redness of her cheeks, for they had always been very pale. Perhaps the undertakers had rouged them? Mother bent down and kissed her, but this was something I could not bring myself to do.

I remember nothing of the funeral except watching the coffin being lowered into the ground at Northern Cemetery, with 'Eleanor Greenwood' engraved on a brass plaque on the lid. Granmer had been a good age, eighty-seven, and now she had gone to join Grampa.

Afterwards, Mother, Aunt Clara and I caught a late train back to Doncaster. Uncle George, Uncle Jack and Aunt Elsie must have taken an earlier one, because we were the only three people in the narrow corridor compartment. Mother and I sat on the long plush seat on one side, with Aunt Clara facing us on the other. Thus disposed, with blinds pulled down against the solid blackness of a winter's night, we relaxed in the heat of the carriage, and talked about the old days.

Mother and Aunt Clara spoke of the Granmer I had never known, the Granmer who had once exercised an influence over her husband, sons and daughters-in-law far greater than her gentle, accommodating manner would ever have suggested to anyone outside the family circle. Mum and Auntie had each spent the first year of her married life under Granmer's roof, and both had felt their strings being pulled rather too tightly at times by that controlling hand. Mind you, though Granmer loved having her family around her, so many of them had crammed into her little home in Pendrill Street that it would have taken a saint with the wisdom of Solomon to please everybody.

In any case, Mother and Aunt Clara had forgiven her long ago, and the picture they painted of her that night was a very affectionate one. I had heard most of their stories before, but it was no hardship to hear them again. As for the laughter that rang through the compartment when they recalled the wonderfully happy times they had known in Granmer's house, what finer tribute could they possibly have paid her?

But where was my beloved Grampa in all this? It had been his house, too, of course, and Mother and Auntie always referred to him as 'the loveliest old man'. Aunt Clara never tired of describing the relief she and Uncle George had felt when, struggling to pay the instalments on a pram for their first baby, Little Harry (the smallest resident in the Pendrill Street household), they had been given a lump sum by Grampa to clear the debt.

Mother's and Auntie's recollections of Grampa echoed my own dim memories of his generous, kind and tolerant nature. The only criticism I ever heard them level against him, if it could be called a criticism, was that he had been far too easy-going.

***

AFTER GRANMER'S DEATH, I did not go back to Preston. Uncle Fred moved in with Ivy, and eventually they married. We exchanged Christmas cards, and when Uncle entered hospital at one stage, I wrote to him and received a reply in his beautiful, curly writing. But the only time I ever saw him again was at Uncle George's funeral in Doncaster in 1976. Despite the sad occasion, he still managed to crack a few jokes over the sandwiches and sausage rolls afterwards, and it was then that he surprised me by claiming what wonderful dinners Granmer used to cook.

His son, my cousin Brian, who had served abroad with the Coldstream Guards, returned to Preston after his discharge, and exchanged one uniform for another, becoming a fireman. He married a local lass called Stella, and they have a daughter and grandson, and have lived in the village ever since. We have kept in touch over the years, and after Uncle George's death, Aunt Clara used to spend a holiday at Brian and Stella's home each summer, renewing old acquaintances from her Preston days, and even, on one occasion, being reunited with Brian's mother, Aunt Gwen, after a lapse of some fifty years. There were meetings, too, with Uncle Fred and Ivy.

When Uncle Fred died, Aunt Clara and I went to Preston for his funeral. After a service in the parish church, he was buried in the village cemetery, and due to a mix-up at the undertaker's, the flowers I had sent went missing, and turned up a day later on someone else's grave. This caused me consternation, but I could imagine how the fiasco would have amused Uncle Fred. Whereas Uncle George had been renowned for quick-fire ripostes, Uncle Fred's brand of humour had been slower, more deliberate. He used to preface his remarks with a rub of his hands, an upward tilt of the chin, a glance at us down his nose (mysteriously longer than his brothers' noses) and a drawn-out 'Well...'

Aunt Clara and I went back to the family home for a cup of tea, and for the first time I met Ivy's two daughters and my other cousin George. We chatted amicably, and I thought him the spitting image of Uncle Fred.

Photographs were produced of Uncle, some taken at a Butlin's Holiday Camp. Ivy, who looked ill and found it difficult to move from her armchair, spoke quietly of the life he and she had built together, and said that sometimes my uncle used to say, 'I don't suppose I'll ever see Janet now.'

I was pierced by this revelation, and the realisation that, had I only taken the initiative, Uncle Fred would have welcomed a visit from me, and perhaps, if I had pressed him, would have talked about his childhood, and told me things I wanted to know about my father. He was the youngest, and last, of Dad's brothers, and had been the only person still alive who remembered him as a very young man. I said to Ivy that I had sometimes thought of suggesting I might call on them; but of course I had left it far too late, just as I had missed any chance of exploring the past with Uncle Jack and Uncle George.

For years, Uncle Jack had called at the Drum every Friday night. His visits had a purpose, because when cigarettes were in short supply, he used to buy his from Mother. I always made a bee-line for this affable uncle of mine whenever I saw him enjoying his glass of beer in the lounge, for I was very fond of him, and found him easy to talk to; it was immaterial that he always brought us a big bag of toffees from the Radiance sweet factory where he was the supervisor.

He would have been the ideal person to tell me about my young father, because there had been only sixteen months between their ages. But I never introduced the topic, partly because I was shy of trespassing on the past for fear I might appear over-curious, or over-sentimental; mainly because, at that stage of my life, I simply wasn't curious enough.

***

IVY DIED SOON after Uncle Fred, and I lost touch with George and his half-sisters. The shop premises called Francis Myers, where Uncle George and Aunt Clara held sway, and which for years had been my second home, were eventually knocked down, and the site used for house-building. 'Owd Woman's', the strange old pub where Cousin Georgie and I kicked our heels in the dark parlour as his parents consumed their nightcaps, has been converted, as is the way with old pubs, into a modern eating establishment. Nowadays it offers a wider choice than 'Owd Man' Dunstan's 'crud cheese-cake' ... and so the world moves on.

CHAPTER TWENTY-THREE

– SCOT LANE

ON AUGUST 1ST, 1949, at the age of fifteen, my childhood ended. Face clarted with Atkinson's Beauty Products, I caught a Bentley trackless to town, and made my way to the newspaper office in Scot Lane, and up its battered old stairs. Bob Walker, the Editor of *The Doncaster Chronicle*, showed me into the battered old Reporters' Room, where I was welcomed with brief hellos by a small group of preoccupied people.

Everything about the building was old and battered, and the Reporters' Room especially so. There was no desk for me, but then there were no proper desks anyway, apart from the News Editor's, which was an ornate, high-fronted, Victorian affair. Everyone else sat around mug-ringed, ink-stained tables that all looked as though they had started out in somebody's kitchen. There were five or six vintage typewriters lying around, of various makes — Corona, L.C. Smith, Royal, Underwood — and when any member of staff blew in with a story, as they frequently did, they would seize whichever machine was idle, bear it off to an empty space, wind three sheets of paper into its roller with two 'blacks' (pieces of carbon paper) sandwiched between, consult their shorthand notebook, and type at a rate of knots, with one eye on the wall-clock.

The room contained three telephones, including one on the News Editor's desk, which was regarded as chiefly for his use. The only other facilities were an arrangement of metal shelving bearing back copies of *The Yorkshire Post*, *Yorkshire Evening Post*, *Yorkshire Evening News*, *Doncaster Gazette*, *Doncaster Free Press* and *Doncaster Chronicle*; a filing cabinet containing newspaper cuttings; and an enormous rubbish bin.

The News Editor was Bill Marshall, a lumbering figure with an unusually large head, a fringe of white hair, and a shiny pink crown, which he patted in times of stress. He also had a most distressing habit of blowing his nose and hawking into sheets of copy-paper, which he screwed up and dropped into his wastepaper basket. The reporters' diary stayed on his desk during working hours, but he locked it away in a drawer at night. In the margin on the left-hand side of every page of the diary, Mr Marshall, as he was respectfully addressed by his staff (they came to refer to him as 'Clunk' behind his back, which apparently signified a rush of excreta to the brain) entered reporters' names opposite assignments, or 'jobs'. Some of these were routine enough to be set in stone.

'Early Duty 8 a.m.' meant arriving then (most of the staff came in at nine o'clock) in order to comb through a pile of morning papers looking for follow-up stories. Many of their titles, such as *The Daily Dispatch, Daily Sketch, Daily Herald, News Chronicle* and *Sheffield Telegraph* have long since disappeared. 'Telephone Duty 8.30 a.m.' entailed making calls to fire, police, ambulance, and Doncaster Royal Infirmary and asking hopefully, 'Anything doing?' Reg Hancock, a nervy chap who became known as 'The Peppermint Kid' when he started to crack mints all day in an effort to stop smoking, would set off on foot to visit the town's two police stations, Doncaster Borough and West Riding, on a similar errand. The Borough Magistrates sat at the Guild Hall on weekday mornings at ten, and the West Riding magistrates presided over as many as four courts in a building near West Laithe Gate.

Inquests were other staple news stories, conducted sometimes in distant villages by the Doncaster District Coroner, W.H. Carlile, whose clerk wrote every scrap of evidence down in long-hand. Often there would be an inquiry into a sudden death at Western Hospital. Formerly the Workhouse, it retained, despite a reassuring entrance hall with a welcoming vase of flowers, the smell of institutionalism: boiled sheets, boiled cabbage, and sick old bodies. Sometimes an ancient inmate would shuffle by, as if to make the point, and once I glanced sideways up a corridor and saw an old woman on her knees, scrubbing the floor. We hated going there.

The next regular assignments marked on the diary were 'Telephone Duty 12 — 1' and 'Telephone Duty 1 — 2.45', when incoming calls often included reams of copy from some of *The Evening Post's* numerous correspondents which, if the regular copy-takers were busy, had to be typed out by a reporter wearing earphones. Repeating the names of these contributors now is as emotive a mantra as the Shipping Forecast: 'White, Sheffield. Hacking, Mexborough. Strike, Retford. Tomlins, Worksop. Mozley, South Elmsall. Bridgewater, Barnsley. Plowright, Scunthorpe'. If you had to give precedence to other people's stories instead of concentrating on your own, the rich, convivial tones of Mr Plowright (his daughter, Joan, became the famous actress) made the task bearable. But it was less agreeable to 'take' from Mr Bridgewater because of the stress detectable in his hurried, anxious bark.

Scrolling back now through microfilmed pages of those old broadsheet newspapers we worked for is a reminder of how even the most minor event received exhaustive coverage. It is still true today, of course, that where the provincial Press is concerned, and especially in the case of weekly newspapers, names and faces boost circulation: hence the need, especially in the 1950s, for group photographs (usually with a couple shaking hands at middle front), and lists of people who might be anything from bazaar stall-holders or triumphant competitors in music, speech and drama festivals, to flower and dog show prize-winners, or mourners at important funerals.

Council minutes were scanned for 'follow-ups', and many a cracking story was scavenged from sheaves of bureaucratic jargon. Parish councils, though usually given to trivia, were rewarding if fur started to fly.

On the cultural front, Doncaster boasted two successful amateur operatic societies, the Amateurs and the Thespians, as well as a number of established drama groups whose productions merited serious treatment by senior reporters. Village music and drama groups staged regular shows as well, and expected appreciative 'crits' from the local Press; so Mr Marshall would order a lowly hack (even, in course of time, a greenhorn like me, who had never heard of Whitehall Farces or Gilbert and Sullivan) to catch a bus out to the sticks, and do the right thing.

I remember my first attempt to give an opinion on a musical (staged by the amateur operatic society in the mining village of Stainforth) which began, 'The worst thing about *The Country Girl* ... ' Shortly after I handed it in to the *Chronicle* office, Mr Walker sent for me, and waved the typewritten sheet under my nose despairingly. The cast were drawn from a small community, he said, people who deserved credit for putting on such an ambitious show. It was the *Chronicle's* job to encourage them, yet here was I, decrying their efforts with my opening sentence. Any criticism ought to be kept to a minimum, wrapped up a bit, and put well down the report.

Smarting because I felt I should somehow have realised all this (how well I remember my chagrin) I bore my rejected 'crit' away to work out a kinder approach. But I had had a narrow squeak, for I could see now that, had I been less cautious, and expressed even subtle doubts about the suitability of the lady who played the heroine, I would have provoked an even stronger reaction from Mr Walker. (She had sung well enough, but was enormously fat.)

There was much to be learned. At that time, in 1949, no formal training scheme for journalists existed, and it was a matter of picking up tips as you went along; accompanying experienced colleagues when they went out on jobs; listening in to interviews; marvelling how good reporters could worm facts out of even the most reluctant people; studying their confident telephone techniques; looking over their shoulders as they typed out their stories, and noting what actually appeared in print; admiring how they handled our half-friends, half-enemies, the subs in the next room, who were responsible for fitting stories into pages, writing headlines, rewriting copy, covering it with blue pencil-marks, cutting it up and sticking it back together in a different order, or, worst of all, spiking it as rubbish.

Douglas ('Daddy') Clayton, as Chief Sub-editor, sat at the top of the long table, with his son, Jack, among the other six or seven subs further down the line. Jack's brother, Michael, had achieved great things, for he was a sub in the Manchester office of *The Daily Express*, at that time not only the most popular broadsheet national daily, but also revered by journalists themselves for its scoops, columnists, features, layout, catchy headlines, snappy 'intros' (opening paragraphs) — in fact, its entire style. Daddy Clayton held the *Express* constantly before us as an example of what a newspaper should be, and we imitated it as best we could.

A news story should have an 'angle' — a striking intro which made the reader want to know more. Then should come a meaty middle section with 'a fact in every line', and preferably a punchline at the end. With space at a premium, our copy was written to an accepted format, and ruthlessly pared. The subs could usually be relied on to kill off most adjectives and adverbs as a matter of course, though writers of feature articles, known as 'specials', were permitted to develop their own style, and allowed some flights of fancy. Thus encouraged, Ian Skidmore, who joined the staff eventually, produced consistently brilliant pieces, being a fey and gifted writer who was frankly wasted on bread-and-butter reporting.

It was important to remember that *The Yorkshire Evening Post* was a family newspaper, which could, indeed, be said of all the provincial Press. We knew Daddy Clayton expected us to produce 'good tea-time reading', and that references to anything vulgar or sexual (the word 'sexy' was still uninvented) would be excised from our copy, but even so, we could be caught out.

Daddy Clayton personally once cut a court case of mine because it mentioned a lavatory seat. This was fair enough, but I often failed to spot ambiguities, and ended up looking foolish. One such instance occurred when I was asked to write an amateur drama column, and put forward my mother's suggestion of 'First-Nighter' as a byline. I was mystified when Jack Siddle, the Deputy Chief Sub, screeched 'You can't call yourself THAT!' and the Sub-editors' and Reporters' Rooms dissolved in laughter.

Both these incidents took place after I had completed my apprenticeship in my early twenties. When I had begun my training, I had been given the duty of making weekly Church Calls for the *Chronicle*. Each Thursday the paper published a column about events at all the local churches, and I was told it was no good just ringing up the clerical gentlemen to ask for information, I must visit them at home, because there was no substitute for personal contact. Consequently, I walked or caught the trackless to most of their houses, and presented myself to people like the Rev E.B. Bacon, Minister of Hall Gate Congregational Church, who made leather handbags in aid of his church funds, and the Rev W. Hartley Totty, Minister of Spring Gardens Methodist Church, who had a most fruity voice. It seemed to be a peculiarity of Methodist ministers that they nearly all used their second Christian name, preceded by an initial. Perhaps they thought this imparted a greater air of authority.

One cleric I did not ever visit at home, and did not need to, was the Rev G.W. Parkinson, Minister of Doncaster Free Christian Church. Mr Parkinson was eager for publicity about his church, and would stump upstairs to the Reporters' Room once a week to impart to whomsoever would listen the latest news about its various organisations, including the P.M.A. These letters stood for Pleasant Monday Afternoon, when a group of ladies would meet for discussion and tea. Mrs Cuffling, Joy's mother, was one of their number, so even had I not been weighed down by the responsibility of Church Calls, I would have taken the P.M.A. seriously.

On the face of it, the Church news was the easiest part of the paper to write, which was why I was doing it, but it could be challenging. At my first bazaar, as I tried to gather the names of all the stall-holders, I was asked by some of the ladies, 'Would you like my own initials, or my husband's?'

This was a teaser, for I had not been given any guidelines about the correct procedure. It seemed sensible to answer, 'Whichever you prefer.'

But, at a Zenana Missionary Society Sale of Work (Zenanas, I gathered, were sort of Arab harems) I encountered a lady with a much more determined idea of how I should style her. She absolutely refused to give me her initials. 'I am Mrs Kingsley-Brown. You don't need my initials. I am the only Mrs Kingsley-Brown in the telephone directory. Everybody in the town knows me as Mrs Kingsley-Brown, so that will be quite sufficient.'

It was useless for me to bleat that the *Chronicle* always insisted on printing everyone's first names or initials. She swept me away with an imperious wave, and I trudged back to Scot Lane wondering how to confess my failure to Mr Walker. Salvation came when I nervously broached the matter with one of the older, more cynical, reporters (I think it was Dennis Laxton, who used to come into the office at night to write a novel). He advised me to stick a J in front of Mrs Kingsley-Brown's name. In similar circumstances, he said, he had always found that a J was a good bet, because most women's names began with J, though M ran it a close second. I did as he suggested, and jumped every time the office phones rang for the next two weeks, fearing Mrs Kingsley-Brown might be on the warpath, voicing her indignation.

***

THE NEXT JOB I was given at the *Chronicle* was the 'Around the Youth Clubs' column. By the early 1950s, youth clubs had sprung up everywhere, and were very popular. Meetings were held in the evenings, and sometimes at weekends, in various halls and schools. Coffee and soft drinks were available, and activities usually involved snooker, table-tennis, listening to records, discussions, dances, team sports, and, occasionally, drama. As an answer to restless adolescence, it all seemed to work quite well.

Uniformed organisations were a reliable source of copy, too. I could usually squeeze at least a paragraph out of the Girls' Friendly Society, Girls' Life Brigade, Boys' Brigade, Church Lads' Brigade, Air Training Corps, Sea Cadets, Army Cadets, Scouts, Guides, Brownies and Wolf Cubs. I also popped into the Y.M.C.A. and Y.W.C.A. and rang up the Young Farmers and various church groups. But while I had no trouble raking together enough news items to fill half a page, the column's lead story had to be strong enough to justify a bit of a spread and a decent headline, and Mr Walker thought 'Insider' (my nom-de-plume) should introduce a personal touch by visiting a different organisation each week, and giving it a write-up.

All went smoothly until I accepted an invitation from the Sea Cadets to accompany them on a trip down the canal. The officer in charge, whose name was Raper, duly handed me into the boat, a *Chronicle* photographer took a picture, and the vessel put off with a very self-conscious 'Insider' sitting in the stern. To try to overcome my diffidence, I remembered as we floated how much I had enjoyed reading *Treasure Island,* and later secretly blamed Long John Silver, Jim Hawkins and the rest for putting me in a fanciful frame of mind.

When it came to writing the story, now that my descriptive powers were being tested I was eager to do full justice to the events on the canal. How best to convey the flavour of that brief voyage, and the disciplined response of the cadets as they sprang to obey the orders of Chief Petty Officer (or was he Lieutenant?) Raper? Quotes always looked good in an intro, and I could think of no better way of setting the scene than to depict him instructing the boys to hoist the sails.

'Up mains'l! Up tops'l!' were my opening words, and they still burn in my brain. Why I chose them I now have no idea. I suppose I must have believed they were, if not the ones Mr Raper actually used, at least an acceptable translation, for they sounded suitably seaman-like, the kind of orders that had rung across the deck of the 'Hispaniola'. I completed the piece to my own satisfaction, and was gratified to see it appear exactly as I had written it the following Thursday, accompanied by a photograph of us all setting off in the boat.

A day or two afterwards, a letter arrived from Mr Raper, addressed to the Editor of *The Chronicle*, complaining that 'Insider' had made him and his crew look foolish. What on earth did I think I was doing, using such a ridiculous form of words about hoisting the sails? He would never employ such phrases, nor anything like them; they were a sheer invention on my part. From my report, the general public would get the impression that the Sea Cadets did not take their training seriously, or know the correct terminology for putting up sails. He ended by demanding that *The Chronicle* set matters straight, and print an apology.

The first I knew of this bombshell was when Mr Walker sent for me and told me to take it away and read it, mildly adding that I appeared to have upset Mr Raper. I was relieved that Mr Walker was not angry, too, but it was with a sinking heart and very red face that I made my way down the corridor back to Reporters, and showed the letter to Ray Bower. Ray was a charming, whimsical fellow in his late twenties who, if asked for advice, dispensed it lightly. But on this occasion he said very firmly, 'I'll show you what I'd do with THAT!', tore the piece of paper into fragments, and threw them in the bin.

I felt a bit nervous, but hoped that might be the end of the matter. Then Mr Walker sent for me again and asked for the letter back, as he intended to print it. I could only manage a nod of acquiescence, and staggered back to Reporters in a state of extreme distress; whereupon Ray, realising he had overreacted, tipped the big metal rubbish bin upside down and helped me to search for the bits of letter. It took us some time to find them all and glue them together on a sheet of copy-paper.

Mr Raper's remarks were still legible, but it was perfectly obvious what had happened, and I would be thought the culprit. Heart sinking even further than before, I returned to Mr Walker and presented him with the sticky jigsaw, murmuring something about an accident.

All he did was give a wry smile and take it from me. The following Thursday, *The Chronicle* carried Mr Raper's letter in full, with a footnote from the Editor saying that 'Insider' wished to apologise, and would in future remain a land-lubber. My incompetence and shame were public knowledge, but even as I squirmed I had to admire Mr Walker's way with words.

***

SUCH INCIDENTS HAVE their amusing side in retrospect, but I have other, much starker memories. On September 26th, 1950, a year after I started work, there was a coal-mining accident at Creswell in Derbyshire, resulting in an underground fire. I was sent off in a car with two senior reporters (as far as I can remember they were Reg Hancock and Ray Bower) and after quite a long journey we arrived at the pithead to join a crowd of distressed relatives waiting for news of trapped miners.

As the events of that terrible day unfolded, and Reg and Ray set about their task of interviewing pit officials and afflicted families and piecing a story together, I did what I had been sent to do, locating a phone-box, running to it at frequent intervals, and phoning snatches of their hastily-scrawled copy back to the office. One would think such a major disaster would have etched itself on my memory in sharp detail, if only because of the sight of those distraught people gathered near the pit cage, hoping against hope to see the lift ascend, and rescued loved ones being brought to the surface. But though I struggle to remember, I have retained only two impressions of those anxious hours; firstly, of running and phoning and running and phoning; and secondly, of my alarm when I got back to Doncaster, and saw from the *Evening Post's* front-page headline that the subs had believed Creswell was spelt 'Cresswell', and had inserted an extra 's'.

I blamed myself for not spelling out the name of the colliery over the phone to the copy-taker, and went cold with dread, assuming I would have some explaining to do, for this was surely an error of the first magnitude. But no Editor came storming down the corridor demanding to know who was responsible for giving Creswell two 's's when other newspapers had rightly given it one. Nobody regarded the mistake as mine, and no repercussions shook the building, but I think someone in subs must have felt the edge of Daddy Clayton's tongue.

The full horror of the Creswell Colliery disaster did not strike me until I came to write about it now, fifty-eight years later. To confirm my vague memories, I looked it up in a book entitled *Great Pit Disasters* (Helen and Baron Duckham, published by David and Charles). Buried among a chronological list of mining accidents dating from the year 1700 are the bare details of Creswell: 'Underground fire resulting from a damaged conveyor; 33 bodies had to be sealed in the workings. Death roll 80.' Thus, in a few short words, the anguish of an entire community is tacitly conveyed.

Mining accidents used to be disturbingly common, though normally, thank goodness, on a much smaller scale. As Doncaster was encircled by collieries, the area had its share of fatalities, and reporters grew used to calling at the home of some unfortunate victim and asking his widow or other relatives for a few personal details about him, and the loan of a photograph to go with the story. A delicate task it was to be sure, but a necessary part of working for a newspaper, and amazingly, we were rarely turned away by grieving families. Questions about the dead man's life would be willingly answered, and drawers full of photographs diligently searched for his best likeness. These intrusions on private grief were a humbling experience, no matter how frequently we had to make such visits, or how automatic our approach to them inevitably became.

Because I had gone to Creswell with a definite role to play, and the accident had happened underground, nothing I had seen or heard there had prepared me for a major disaster I witnessed six months later. On the morning of March 16th, 1951, a London-bound express train, the 'Cock of the North', crashed at Balby Bridge, a short distance from Doncaster Railway Station. Thirteen people, including an eleven-month-old baby and her parents, were killed, and one man died later in hospital. Five of the train's fourteen coaches were derailed, and it was three-and-a-half hours before all the bodies were recovered. Many people were injured, and doctors rushed to the scene with morphine, one crawling under the debris to reach a little girl who was trapped, but still alive.

All this I know now because I have before me a copy of the *Evening Post's* final edition, which appeared the same night. I needed to refresh my memory because, although I had actually been involved, I could recall very few details, catastrophic as the incident had been. Now I read that as the third coach of the train was passing under Balby Bridge, it 'wrapped itself round a bridge support and splintered like matchwood', and four other coaches were derailed.

The blurry pictures on the print-out show a horrifying sight, with carriages sprawled across the line and rescue-workers clambering over them in a desperate attempt to free trapped victims. The report says that railway-men working nearby rushed to help, using axes and saws to cut through to those inside, and oxyacetylene equipment was brought to the scene. Such details faded from my memory long ago, and all I can recall is walking dazedly through an area of utter chaos, and peering into empty carriages, which appeared to have jumped from the track like Cousin Georgie's Hornby train-set used to do. But this was a derailment with devastating consequences, for from these full-sized compartments people were emerging with bloodstained clothing.

Every available reporter and photographer had been scrambled, and experienced journalists, having assessed the situation, were snatching interviews, jotting down whatever bits of news came to their ears, and rushing to the nearest phone to ensure a steady stream of information reached the excited subs.

Was I asked to send any of their copy? I have a vague memory of finding a phone and ringing the office, but whether to assist a colleague, or transmit some feeble impressions of my own, I have no idea. Nothing in the *Evening Post's* graphic account is identifiable to me now. Sub-editors come into their own in a crisis such as this, and ours rose to the challenge that day, stringing together disjointed facts to create a powerful story. At the railway station, certain reporters were coaxing eyewitness accounts from passengers who had managed to make their way back along the line. But as a seventeen-year-old girl at the scene of the crash, I felt I lacked the authority to plunge into the mêlée, and feared if I started asking questions I might impede the rescue operations.

The rest of the team at *The Evening Post*, reporters, photographers, copy-takers, subs and printers, had done a terrific job, for the paper's last edition could hardly have furnished its readers with a more gripping or comprehensive story. Everybody had turned up trumps but me. A day or so afterwards, Mr Marshall beckoned me over, saying someone had told him I had appeared at a loss, and emphasising that if ever I was faced with a similar crisis, I must pull my weight and make a contribution.

I protested faintly that I had done something – though what it was is now beyond me. But I was grateful that his reproof had been so mild, for in my heart I felt I had let the side down, and deserved a more rigorous telling-off.

***

THOUGH I NEVER again experienced a disaster of such proportions, covering deaths, fires, road-accidents and similar events became part of my working life. While newspaper reporters have the reputation of being hard-bitten and ruthless, and their pulses cannot help but race at the prospect of a good story, it is detachment more than cynicism that helps them to do their job.

Learning how to be dispassionate is not easy, but as my training progressed I began to take things more in my stride. I recall being sent to an incident where a young man had apparently committed suicide by jumping from a bridge on to a railway line, and arriving in time to see the corpse being borne away on a stretcher, and an ambulance-worker walking behind with the poor chap's innards in an enamel bucket. Though shocked, I managed to call a cheery greeting to Ken, the man with the bucket, whom I happened to know, and we exchanged a few words as he made his way up the embankment. Having established that the dead person seemed to have deliberately jumped off the bridge, I wrote a story to that effect.

As soon as I saw Brenda Mitchell, one of the senior reporters, grimacing disapprovingly as she read my account in the *Evening Post* that night, I realised I must have done something wrong. She pointed out, kindly but firmly, that I should not have said the young man had jumped, simply that his body had been found on the line. Whether or not he had committed suicide was a matter for the coroner to decide.

In those days, newspapers were more cautious about giving the cause of injuries or death, or apportioning blame before an inquest or court case had been held. Rather than claim someone had been 'knocked down' by a vehicle, we would say only that they had been 'in collision' with one, or had been taken to hospital 'as a result of an accident involving' one. Knowing all this had not prevented me from making a rash assumption about the young man under the bridge, and I lived in fear of another angry phone call, this time from the coroner's office. But none came.

Brenda, who was twenty-four, was my role model. She had moved to Doncaster from Head Office in Leeds, and was vastly experienced. There was no subject she could not write about, from amateur theatre to local connections with the Pilgrim Fathers; from political rivalries in Warmsworth Parish Council to ambiguities she unearthed while combing through the minutes of even more authoritative bodies. No person breathed, it seemed, whom she could not coax into giving her an interview. Sent to face a group of militant miners on strike at Bentley Colliery, Brenda asked their spokesman, Henry Huckerby, if they were looking forward to a proposed visit from Wilfred Pickles and his radio programme, *Have A Go*. By drawing from him the answer, 'What we want is beef, not pickles', she got herself not only a terrific headline, but a story repeated to this day in doddery old journalistic circles.

When it came to typing her copy, Brenda called herself a 'hunt and pecker', a phrase she had found in a novel, and I became one, too. Not many of the staff could touch-type, and it seemed pointless to start again when I was already using the office machines, albeit ham-fistedly. But shorthand was a necessity, and after learning the rudiments of Pitman's from Reg Hancock in his spare moments, I asked Mother if she would pay for me to have weekly lessons at Doncaster Commercial School. When I left some months later, I had achieved a respectable speed of ninety words a minute under the no-nonsense regime of a lady called Miss Roffe.

My decision to stop dithering and get down to learning shorthand was triggered by an embarrassing encounter with Ray Gunter, the prospective Socialist candidate for the marginal Parliamentary seat of Doncaster. It was 1950, a General Election was imminent, and both Mr Gunter, an impassioned Welshman, and his Conservative opponent, Anthony Barber, were touring the constituency giving speeches.

The local Press tended to cover political meetings at length, and to make life easier, Reg Hancock asked for an advance copy of a speech Mr Gunter proposed to deliver that night, and sent me round to collect it. But horror of horrors, when I arrived at the local Labour Party headquarters, Mr Gunter met me with the news that, alas, no copy of his speech was available. However, if I cared to follow him into his office and take a seat, he would happily give me a quick run-down of what he intended to say.

I reached for my notebook, wondering how to confess I couldn't do shorthand, but even as I pondered he launched into his speech, and I felt myself sinking beneath a great tide of oratory. At this rate I would be lucky to get even one sentence down on paper! Warming to his theme, he began to pace the floor, which made me afraid he might look over my shoulder and catch sight of my desperate scribbles. Once or twice he paused to ask if I would like him to slow down (he was a kind man). By this stage it seemed too late to break the news that he had been wasting his time, and that, due to my incompetence, scarcely any of his visionary words had been recorded.

When at last the ordeal was over, I thanked Mr Gunter and slunk ashamedly back to Scot Lane. I remember being on the verge of tears as I blurted out my admission of failure to Reg and Mr Marshall, who took the news in a spirit of surprising calmness. Reg immediately rang the Labour Party office to explain the situation, and I can see him now on the end of the phone, having a rueful laugh with Mr Gunter before donning his overcoat and trilby, and setting off to repair the damage. Mr Gunter said he quite understood why a young reporter who had come expecting to pick up a draught of his speech had been too shy to tell him she couldn't do shorthand, and he was perfectly willing to go through it all again with Reg. So Reg saved my skin with his fast, impeccable Pitman's, and I, grateful to be rescued, resolved to follow his example and master it myself. That was not quite the end of the story, though, for when, much later, I was sent to cover a political meeting at which Mr Gunter was speaking, he spotted me on the front row ... and winked.

In the General Election of 1950, he emerged triumphant, securing the Doncaster seat by a margin of 878 votes; but another General Election was held the following year, and this time Tony Barber won with a majority of 384. Later Ray Gunter became M.P. for Southwark, and in the Wilson Governments of the 1960s held the posts of Minister of Labour and Minister of Power. On his part, Tony Barber, an equally agreeable man, became a Tory Chancellor of the Exchequer, and was subsequently elevated to the House of Lords.

***

WHILE I WAS writing the 'Around the Youth Clubs' column in 1950, Mr Ben Robinson, the father of one of my school friends, told Mother he was having trouble arranging accommodation for a party of young Germans who were coming to Bentley. Members of the youth club which he ran had already stayed in the homes of German families, but now there was a shortage of hosts for an exchange visit. Mother said she would be happy to take two of the girls, which is how Ingrid and Inge came to spend a holiday at the Drum.

Ingrid was twenty-two and blonde, Inge twenty-one and dark-haired, and both were dazzlingly pretty, and spoke charming English. It was amazing how quickly we were all at ease with one another, especially as the war between our two countries had ended only five years before. They spoke of the war matter-of-factly, but when Mother and I were invited back to their homes, first to Ingrid's in Iserlohn in 1951, then to Inge's in Gütersloh in 1953, we saw what terrible damage the R.A.F. had inflicted on cities like Cologne and Düsseldorf. We were also shown the rebuilt Möhne Dam, famous for having been breached by our 'bouncing bombs'.

Ingrid's father had been a German Army Officer, and at first he greeted us with reserve. One evening, however, to the great surprise of Ingrid and her mother, he invited Mum and me into his study, handed us tiny glasses of Vermouth, and engaged us in rather stiff, but friendly, conversation. By Inge's family, too, we were treated as honoured guests; and although I eventually lost touch with her, Ingrid and I corresponded for more than fifty years, until, sadly, she became too ill to write. Now her son sends me a Christmas letter instead.

***

IF EVER WE were short of copy in Scot Lane, and scratching around for something to fill the paper, we could always ring up to ask if anything was happening at the Dogs' Home. We did not usually need to ask, because Mrs Elsie Morrison, Chairman of the Doncaster branch of the R.S.P.C.A., which ran the home, knew the value of publicity, and kept in regular touch with the local Press. While we might at times regard her phone calls as a nuisance, stories and pictures of animals were good for circulation. What reader's heart would not be touched by the sight of an abandoned litter of kittens, or a dog with only days to live unless a new owner came forward?

The cavernous premises of the Dogs' Home, tucked away under the arches of North Bridge, were decked with bunting at Christmas-time, and the staff arranged special treats for their charges. One year Mrs Morrison invited Doncaster Borough Police Choir to put on a carol concert. They were willing enough at first, but changed their minds when they learned they would actually be expected to sing at the Dogs' Home. We heard on the grapevine that they were afraid it might make them a public laughing-stock; perhaps they also feared a rival chorus of canine howls.

Another person who devoted her life to animals was Mrs Edith C. Williams of the Our Dumb Friends' League, a small, white-haired lady who specialised in rescuing donkeys. She frequently came into our front office asking to see a reporter, and whoever obliged needed little shorthand, for she spoke slowly and deliberately, as if to a half-wit.

Mrs Williams looked as mild as milk until she fixed you with her faded blue eyes, and you saw in them the unsettling glint of missionary fervour. A much louder and more colourful campaigner was Mrs Rachael Surtees, a miner's wife from Dunscroft, who every so often got a fresh bee in her bonnet, and tried to enlist the help of the Press in promoting her latest crusade.

Once she became concerned about the welfare of lorry-drivers, and rang the office on Coronation Night to suggest a scheme for protecting these vulnerable men from the wiles of wicked young women who displayed their charms at the roadside. The only reporter left on duty (everyone else was out covering street parties) listened patiently to Mrs Surtees, but I don't think anything came of it.

On another occasion, she had an idea for a new piece of apparatus that could assist trapped householders to escape from a fire. In order to demonstrate its possibilities, she summoned local dignitaries, reporters and members of the Fire Brigade to witness her descent from her front bedroom window, and laid on tea and sandwiches for the expected crowd. Alas for Mrs Surtees, she was unable to work the equipment and got jammed in the window, displaying her bloomers as she was rescued by the firemen, according to Brenda Mitchell, who covered the story. There were not many takers for her tea and sandwiches, and I can't think her method of leaving a burning building was ever patented.

But Mrs Surtees was not one to be put off by failure, scorn or disappointment. She was of the same kidney as Mrs Morrison and Mrs Williams. Across a distance of fifty years and more, I salute them now, those indomitable women, even though I regarded them askance when they were at their zenith. Mad? Perhaps they were a little. Obsessive? Certainly. Eccentric? That goes without saying. But Doncaster would have been a poorer place without them.

CHAPTER TWENTY-FOUR

– GETTING ON

NOT ALL THE eccentrics were on the outside. We in the Scot Lane office had a few colourful characters of our own, not least Jack Dibb, the Editor, usually referred to by his initials, J.R.D. Regular as clockwork, at 3.30 p.m. and 4.30 p.m. every weekday, a possible outburst from this large, red-faced man put fear into the heart of every reporter in the building. (Thankfully he was usually off on Saturday afternoons.)

It was the junior's job (for a long time mine) to obtain copies of the 3.20 p.m. and 4.20 p.m. editions of *The Yorkshire Evening News* from a vendor who stood at the end of the street, and carry them straight back to J.R.D. Bill Marshall, the News Editor, was always on tenterhooks in case our rival had scooped us, and was grateful if I could arrange for him to have a quick glance at the paper before I took it up the corridor. Sometimes all was well, but on bad days this secret glimpse allowed Mr Marshall time to get on the phone before the frightening figure of J.R.D. came storming in, brown eyes bulging, arms aloft, if the Evening News had a really big scoop, as he waved the paper furiously around his head. He would slap it down on Mr Marshall's desk, point to some story we had missed, which he had helpfully outlined in heavy blue pencil, and demand, 'WHY HAVEN'T WE GOT THIS?' And Mr Marshall, still on the line as he tried to confirm the salient facts, would break off to say penitently, 'Just on to it now, Mr Dibb, just on to it now.'

One never-to-be-forgotten afternoon J.R.D. was so incensed that, in an impressive feat of strength, he picked up a thick file of newspapers, raised it above his head, and flung it across the room, narrowly missing one of the reporters. Yet his very fearsomeness made J.R.D. a good editor, for it kept us on our toes, and we could not afford to be complacent because we were in the midst of a circulation battle. As well as *The Yorkshire Evening Post* and *The Yorkshire Evening News*, the town was served by two morning newspapers (*The Yorkshire Post* and *The Sheffield Telegraph*), three weeklies (*The Doncaster Gazette*, *The Doncaster Free Press* and our own *Doncaster Chronicle*), and another evening paper (*The Sheffield Star*). In addition, our stamping-ground might earn a visit from Peggy Robinson of *The Daily Express*. One sight of her short haircut and trousered legs and we would know something was afoot, supposing we hadn't known about it in the first place. She was always very friendly, though, in spite of her formidable reputation as a newshound.

In complete contrast to Peggy was our own Annie Higson, whose reputation, though huge, was at a more parochial level. *Jocelyn's Social Round*, her weekly column in *The Doncaster Chronicle*, was an institution occupying at least a full page, so large and loyal was her circle of women readers, and so copious the gossip (in the best sense of the word) that poured unceasingly into her ready ear.

We all loved kind-hearted Annie, yet sometimes, if we could, we avoided her, because she was apt to engage you in long conversations when you were just about to dash off somewhere, and she was so amply-proportioned that it was difficult to squeeze by her. This was particularly true in the Ladies, where I sometimes encountered her in the tiny space before the mirror, combing her grey hair or dabbing powder on her nose before going off to conduct an interview, open a bazaar, or speak at a women's meeting. She was short-sighted, despite wearing thick lenses, and stood up close to you in order to see your face, oblivious to the fact that two inches nearer and you would be pillowed upon her bosom.

Although she had a nose for news, a sense of urgency was not one of her strong points. I was once sent with her to cover a big fire, because her new Ford Popular, the pride of her heart, was parked just up the street, and no other car was available. It was rare for Annie to be assigned a hard news story, and as she drove us the considerable distance to the scene of the fire, and I tried to concentrate on working out the quickest route, and catching the next edition, she kept leaning towards me, beaming and chatting, as if no more haste were required of us than if we had been heading for a Women's Institute talk on flower-arranging.

As well as being the doyenne of the *Social Round*, Annie ran *Aunty Jocelyn's Children's Corner* in the *Chronicle*, which every week published a letter from her, photographs of new members, and encouraging messages about saving foil milk-bottle tops and bringing them to our office, where they would be welcomed as a source of charity fundraising. (I think it was for Guide Dogs.)

So responsive was the *Children's Corner* to this appeal that Annie's desk was permanently surrounded by large sacks of milk-bottle tops; and although she frequently reminded her young readers that their contributions should be washed before dispatch, alas, in many cases her pleas fell on stony ground, and the stench of sour milk filled the small room, being especially strong in Aunty Jocelyn's own corner.

Consequently, whenever Annie had one of her increasingly frequent asthma attacks, and was unable to come to work, whoever was chosen to fill her shoes and sit at her desk felt overwhelmed not only by the responsibility of writing her column, and disappointing those who rang asking to speak to her personally, but also by the effluvium from the milk-bottle tops. I was one of those who deputised, and although I begged and begged Mr Jarman, our independently-minded janitor,

278

to take the sacks down to the basement, he was very dilatory. In any case, by the time he got around to the task, more parcels of smelly foil were already piling up.

Annie was a great friend of Daddy Clayton and his wife, and for years she drove them down for a holiday in St. Ives, a long journey in those days, necessitating one, if not two, overnight stops en route. Though she could sweet-talk the men, and was inclined to simper and flutter her eyelashes as she did so, she never married, but lived with a widowed cousin, and died well after retirement age, corresponding with me on every birthday in the early years of my marriage. She wrote several plays for women and children, at least one of which was performed on BBC radio; she was a skilful pianist, and a Cordon Bleu cook. When Bob Walker won a competitive one-act play festival with a skit on the supposed invention of the first Yorkshire Pudding, Annie was convincing in the role of a Stone Age wife and mother. (I was cast as her daughter, and Brenda Mitchell made me a costume from an old plush table-cloth.) Annie is also still remembered for a tradition she established of taking a party of young reporters to the St. Leger Fair every September, and watching gleefully from the sidelines as they whirled and screamed on dizzying rides like the Waltzers and Octopus.

***

IT HAD TAKEN Annie years to save up for her Ford Popular, and when at last she could afford it, a rash of other new vehicles was appearing in Scot Lane. Only one other reporter, Eric Hobson, a gentlemanly ex-R.A.F. officer, who wrote stories about the Air Force under the byline of 'Griff', already owned a car, a perky little coupé. Jack Dibb was given a new Hillman by Head Office; Dougie Guest, one of our two photographers, and an ex-flier who had been a bomb-aimer during the war, treated himself to a Ford Prefect, and pleaded with me not to bang the passenger-door so hard when we were out on a job together. Horace Wright, the other photographer, clung on to his old Flying Standard, and continued to stick his right arm through the gap between body and roof when signalling to turn or slow down.

We also suddenly had the luxury of an office Ford, PUB 85, for taking journalists out on assignments, as well as delivering papers. Previously, unless we went with a photographer we would travel by van, sitting alongside the driver on a pile of newspapers tied up with string. It was a precarious business because, when turning a corner sharply, the van's sliding doors were inclined to glide backwards, and we were in danger of falling out through the yawning gap. Sometimes we still had to use the vans, and I always hoped my chauffeur would be Old Tommy, a small, patient man in a cap, with very bony knees, amazingly long yellow fingernails, and often a dewdrop on the end of his nose. We had very satisfactory conversations, Tommy and I, and although he steered with one hand on the gear-stick, he went more slowly than most of the other drivers.

***

NEW CARS WERE not the only things that helped to make life more agreeable at Doncaster Office in the early 1950s for, a few years after I joined the staff, the premises were refurbished. Builders arrived, knocking down the wall between Reporters and J.R.D.'s room, and improving the toilets. J.R.D. moved up the corridor to a grander office with a much bigger desk, a transfer made possible by the retirement of a quiet old man who had sat there for years without appearing to do anything, though I think he was supposed to be the General Manager. The dignity imparted by his new surroundings must have pleased J.R.D., for his previous den had been quite poky.

The Reporters' Room received new desks and chairs, and what excitement when they were allocated! We were also given an extra typewriter or two, and a telephone kiosk was erected in one corner, which we named 'The Box'. The switchboard was moved upstairs to join us, and there, in her own special box, Bessie, its operator, would sit all day, puzzling over the Daily Telegraph crossword in quiet periods. If she was absent for a short time and I was free, I used to enjoy taking her place, and, if one of the board's silver eyelids descended to indicate a call, inserting a metal plug on its long red cable into the hole beneath and cooing, 'I'm putting you through now' in my best telephone voice.

The biggest improvement of all was to *The Evening Post* itself, which, due to wartime conditions, had shrunk to a tabloid, but, now that there was no shortage of newsprint, went back to being a broadsheet in October, 1952. I remember how eagerly the first print-run of the new-look paper was awaited, and how, when early copies were rushed up to Reporters, hot off the press, my knowledgeable colleagues spread their arms to accommodate the pages, and made comments which I took to signify approval.

A great deal of work had been necessary to bring about the change, not least in the Case Room, where some dozen Linotype machines buzzed and clicked under the supervision of their veteran overseer, Roland Bentley. Despite his pronounced limp, oil-stained overall, green eye shade, and habit of stomping up and down at times of stress with a piece of copy in each hand and one between his teeth, Mr Bentley wielded such power that even J.R.D. and Daddy Clayton had to bow to his jurisdiction where newspaper production was concerned. I was afraid of him at first, but then I was afraid of quite a number of people, even Sally Snowden, who kept a check on the basement store-room, and begrudged handing out extra envelopes, glue or toilet-paper.

But fiercer by far was Jack Siddle, the Deputy Chief Sub, who, until I got to know that his bark was worse than his bite, sometimes embarrassed me by bursting into Reporters, waggling one of my stories under my nose, and yelling, 'Now then, Fairyfeet, what's all this b****y rubbish?' His criticisms were deserved, and once I stopped sending him quite so much rubbish, we got on famously.

One of our new office desks, though careful ownership had been laid to it, was seldom filled for long. It had been specially selected by Hughie Goodall, our Sports Editor, and was near the door, perhaps because this made it easier for him to dash in and out. Hughie practically lived at Doncaster Rovers' Football Club. He would breeze in, make a phone call or two, then breeze out again on his way to the ground. His long reports appeared in *The Evening Post* under the non-de-plume of 'Red and White' (the club's' colours) until he eventually got his own byline. But though he helped to popularise the Rovers with his exhaustive coverage of their fortunes, and had a large and loyal readership, Hughie was always deferential when he spoke on the phone to Peter Doherty, the Rovers' charismatic player-manager.

If he happened to be at his desk, and not rushing to meet a deadline with his four-fingered typing, Hughie might entertain us with his favourite song, which had an unlikely lyric, and began, 'A, you're adorable, B, you're so beautiful, C, you're a cutie full of charms ...' and proceeded in similar vein right through to Z. On other occasions, he would reel off what he claimed was a complete list of Red Indian tribes, which he had memorised as a boy.

We dreaded those Saturday afternoons when the Rovers were playing at home, for then Hughie took his lunch at the office. He would carve himself a slice off his Sunday joint, cook it on a tin dish, which he heated on an apparatus used for melting lead in the plate-making department, and bring it upstairs to eat at his desk, filling the building with a stife that bore no relationship whatsoever to prime steak.

Oh, what laughs we all had, what 'in' jokes, what teasings, what anecdotes, what Christmas parties! We helped one another out of holes, commiserated if things went wrong, and made admiring noises if the subs gave somebody star-spangled treatment (known as 'a good show') for a specially fine article or story. Rubbing shoulders with rival reporters who turned up on the same jobs could be illuminating, for no-one enjoys a gossip more than one journalist with another. They, too, had their eccentrics, distinguished by nick-names like The Laughing Hatter, The Gnome, Silent Jim, The Senator, National Angle, and Duty Coconut (who, as the only reporter on *The Doncaster Free Press*, apart from the Editor, was always on duty, and whose hair stuck up like coconut-fibres). These sobriquets had been bestowed with uncanny accuracy by Nobby Clarke of *The Sheffield Telegraph*, who had a gift for such things. Nobby himself was known as The Great Nobrowski, but this particular epithet was not of his devising.

Life was great. Who would really want to work anywhere but on a newspaper? Reporters departed for better jobs, usually on the national Press in Manchester, and others would come to replace them, fitting in awkwardly at first, then suddenly becoming accepted, as though they had been part of the team for years. Personalities did clash from time to time, inevitably; but my overriding memories of that tightly-knit office are of hard work, strong support, good companionship, and fun. And if ever one of my male colleagues patted my bottom, commented on my appearance, or even propositioned me, I would simply laugh, or walk coolly away, and never dream of complaining to a higher authority. The Women's Liberation movement was unheard of then, and in any case, I felt flattered.

Occasionally I heard rumours of romantic escapades. When one journalist's affair was discovered by his wife, she threw him out, so the lads at *The Sheffield Telegraph* took pity on him, and let him sleep on the newspaper files in their cramped branch office. Then the erring one's wife marched round to complain to his boss. I wonder what advice he gave, for it transpired that he, too, was having an extra-marital fling.

***

A MAJOR EVENT on Doncaster's social calendar was the annual Press Ball, organised by the local branch of the National Union of Journalists in aid of the union's Widows' and Orphans' Fund. It was planned by a committee along ambitious lines, and tickets went like hot cakes, not least because the occasion offered chances to win some wonderful prizes. For several years I shared the task of sending out begging letters, and sometimes a British film company would be one of the generous donors who answered our appeal.

Once we were sent a lilac satin house-coat worn in a recent movie by the glamorous star Mai Zetterling. Another time, it was decided to adopt a maritime theme, and as a film about a mermaid called 'Miranda' had been all the rage, with Glynis Johns in the title role, someone persuaded the studio to lend us her fish-tail. One of the reporters whose girlfriend was a model said if we liked he would ask her to recline in the foyer wearing the tail (and not much else) to welcome people arriving for the ball.

At first the young lady agreed, and hopes were high. But alas, when the big night came, she got cold feet, and changed her mind. There was no time to find a replacement, and nothing to be done but swallow the disappointment of her sudden withdrawal, and greet the guests with an empty tail. Even with no girl inside, though, Miranda's bottom half was a splendid object in its own right. Connotations with Glynis Johns, and a successful film in which it had played such a vital role, imbued it with special magic, and it drew many awed comments in the foyer.

***

MY SOCIAL LIFE was bound to suffer because of the uncertainty of diary engagements. Though some jobs were entered up in advance, often we had no idea until we arrived at the office in a morning whether we would be working that night. Once I started having boyfriends, I could rarely make a firm date, and sometimes had to cancel arrangements, or else take the young man with me, if the occasion allowed; perhaps to a Sunday night concert by the Yorkshire Symphony Orchestra at the Ritz Cinema, a foreign film at the Arts Centre, a musical at the Grand Theatre, or a performance by an amateur dramatic society. (It was a tight squeeze out at Finningley, because the venue was a converted bus, parked in a field.)

When I was sixteen, before I started going out with boys, I often spent a free Tuesday or Thursday evening polishing up my ballroom-dancing, and meeting members of the opposite sex at either Berry's or Buller's in town. The atmosphere at these small dancing clubs, which were both run by professional husband-and-wife partnerships, was sufficiently anodyne for a girl to arrive alone, change her shoes with the rest of the giggling group in the cloakroom, patronise the soft-drinks bar, and perch herself on one of the gilt chairs around the ballroom without feeling out of place. She would be bound to feel shy, though, and her heart would start to pound when the next Victor Sylvester record was switched on, especially if it happened to be 'The Blue Tango', for tangos were hard to dance. But far, far worse was being a wallflower, pinned to a golden chair with no-one to talk to, so I was glad if Annette was staying at the Drum, and came with me. The last waltz was at ten o'clock, I think, and we felt perfectly safe as we walked back through the town to catch the trackless home. Annette enjoyed the dances, but was less happy about accompanying me to amateur theatricals, because she said she would die of embarrassment if an actor dried up on stage, or part of the scenery fell down, crises which were not unknown.

Days, weeks, months and years flew by, and as I gradually became a more competent member of the *Chronicle* and *Evening Post* reporting team, and grew more familiar with the formulaic requirements of newspapers, the spectrum widened. Courts, inquests, council and political meetings, accidents, campaigns, innovations, achievements, official openings, traffic jams, deaths, plays, cattle and sheep prices, coal-production figures, epidemics, flower-shows, lectures, art exhibitions, strikes, fires, concerts, dog-shows, dinners, dances, sporting fixtures, advertising articles, charity events, school prize-givings, agricultural shows ... almost anything that happened in our large circulation area, which took in parts of Nottinghamshire and Lincolnshire, was grist to our mill.

In addition, there were certain jobs that only a woman could handle: social gossip, weddings, sales-of-work, describing the fashions at race meetings and the Yearling Sales, compiling twice-weekly lists of the prices of fish, meat, vegetables, fruit and flowers at Doncaster Market, and writing the shopping notes with gift ideas in mind ... all these were solely my concern once I became the only female remaining on the *Evening Post's* Doncaster staff.

Provincial journalism could be a grinding occupation. Given the thousands of words that were strung together, mistakes could happen, and though these were usually of a minor nature, complaints sometimes reached the Editor. This was where J.R.D. showed his true metal. If someone objected to the slant of a story, or a factual error, and rang him in an angry mood, he would try to calm them by adopting a tone of rueful sympathy. But if the caller grew obstreperous, Jack Dibb would spring to the defence of the reporter concerned like a tiger protecting its cub. Of course, some corrections did get published, but I cannot remember any instance of an actual apology being printed, apart from when my own bungled version of the Sea Cadets' sail-hoisting technique was so deftly excused by Bob Walker in the *Chronicle*. I think it unlikely, however, that this was the only apology to appear during the nine years I worked in Scot Lane.

For some reason, women reporters were occasionally asked to open or judge things. At various times I was expected to choose the most attractive young lady at a village fair by mingling secretly with the crowds; open a new section of a youth club (when I made a hash of cutting the ribbon); appear on a quiz panel organised by Don Valley Conservative Association (a terrifying experience); present the prizes at a Coronation Night street party (it was rained off); and, to my mother's vast amusement and incredulity, help to judge a sewing competition on the stage at the Co-operative Hall.

Why such trust was placed in my judgement simply because I a) wrote for the local paper, and b) was a woman, I had no idea. But two reporters, both men, who at different times occupied desks in our office, did become real celebrities, though the first, the now-famous novelist, playwright and columnist Keith Waterhouse, called in only briefly, and sprawled on the desk rather than sat at it. He was on our Leeds staff in those days, and had set off to walk from Yorkshire to London. The bulletins he sent back to the paper were hailed as triumphs of eventful progression and literary style, but legend has since had it that the man who went on to write *Billy Liar* got more stories by propping up bars than pounding the beat.

One day, while I was compiling the *News From Our Doncaster Office* column for *Postscript*, our company house magazine, J.R.D. dictated a paragraph about a reporter who was soon to join us after completing his National Service. His name was Michael Parkinson, and when he arrived we found him a genial fellow. A Barnsley lad, he knew a lot about cricket, enjoyed throwing parties, and showed flair as a drama critic, so it was usually Michael who covered the first night of any play that came to the Arts Centre. If a comedy tickled his fancy, he often used to describe it as 'zany'. This was a new word for me, and I liked it, but it was Michael's special adjective, and borrowing it would have seemed like plagarism.

Not only did Mike stand out as a reporter, his enthusiasm for the job was enormous (though he was sometimes a bit quiet on a Monday morning, when over-enthusiastic weekend partying was possibly to blame). Then came a day (a Monday, maybe) when his *joie-de-vivre* entirely deserted him.

I was not there, but the apocryphal tale runs thus: Clunk (Mr Marshall), in his capacity as News Editor, marked Michael down to cover the funeral of a certain Mr Machin, President of the local Newsagents' Federation. The last rites of so important a figure would be sure to attract a large congregation, and publishing their names would boost our circulation. Michael must attend the service, and make a list of all the mourners.

Michael, indignant at being given such a long, boring and menial task, refused point-blank, whereupon Clunk went along the corridor to inform J.R.D., who ordered Michael along to his office. When Mike still declined to collect the mourners' names, J.R.D. grew angry, and threatened reprisal. Loud recriminations were heard coming from the room, then Michael marched out, slamming the door so violently behind him that he broke a pane of glass in it. Whether he had resigned or been fired is a moot point, but what is certain is that as he left the building, J.R.D. flung up the window and yelled down to him and everyone else in Scot Lane, 'YOU'LL PAY FOR THAT OUT OF YOUR WAGES!' These were not idle words, either, for when Michael received his final wage-packet, the cost of repairing the door had been deducted.

Michael shook the dust of Doncaster off his feet, joined *The Manchester Guardian*, went on to review films for television, became 'Parky', the celebrity chat show host with his own international fan club, is now one of the biggest names in

T.V. history, and has earned himself a knighthood. Of course, he would have done great things anyway, without the help of a dead newsagent; but timing, they say, is everything, so perhaps Mr Machin and his catalytic funeral merit a passing nod.

***

ONE EVENING, WHEN I was about twenty, Daddy Clayton paid a surprise visit to the Big Drum. I cannot remember whether I had been out, and arrived home to find him in the bar as I passed through the lounge, or whether I was upstairs and he sent a message for me to join him. All I recall is seeing him standing in Doctors' Corner, ramrod-straight, with the familiar walking-stick, pipe, glasses, trilby, grizzled sideburns, and wolfish smile. I was appalled. Why was he here? What had I done? Had he come to sack me? I was aware that I owed my apprenticeship entirely to him.

He spoke spasmodically between puffs at his pipe, sometimes pausing in mid-sentence, as if considering the next link in his train of thought. The gist of his brief lecture was this: the time had come for me to think about moving on. I should send my best cuttings to *The Daily Express* in Manchester, and ask for a job.

I agreed without daring to show my reluctance. Truth to tell, I had lost my appetite for becoming a foreign correspondent, like Sylvia Starr in that childhood comic, and I no longer had my sights set on Manchester or Fleet Street. I felt comfortable in my niche in Scot Lane, I was fairly confident about coping with its demands, and I had a romantic interest in my life, and did not wish to leave my home, my mother or my boyfriend. But I could not say all this to Daddy Clayton, who obviously thought I had reached the stage where I would be eager to depart for pastures new.

He drank up his half of bitter, gave one of his throat-clearing harrumphs, said goodbye, and left. My mother, who had been as startled as I by his appearance, went rather quiet when I told her why he had come. I suppose she must have felt torn between the prospect of my leaving home and the exciting possibility that I might be going to work on *The Daily Express*, her favourite morning paper.

I was too stunned to wonder how Daddy Clayton had made his way to us, or how he would get home, for he had no car, and faced a long bus-ride up the Great North Road to Skellow. Maybe on impulse he had dropped off his homeward-bound bus as it passed the end of Watch House Lane, and walked along to the Drum. Of course, his visit might have been partly due to curiosity, but the more I think about it, the stranger it seems.

Over the next week or two, I assembled a few of my cuttings and, as directed, posted them to the Editor of *The Daily Express* in Manchester with a request for an interview. I could not do otherwise, but it was a relief when, a few days later, I received a reply thanking me for my interest, but informing me that they had no vacancies at present. They would always be glad, however, to look at any stories I might send them.

I showed Daddy Clayton the letter, and he acknowledged the contents with a nod and a harrumph. He never mentioned the matter again to me, nor I to him, and I sent no more job applications. So much for high ambition!

***

IN JANUARY 1952, a shy lad called Malcolm Barker came to join the reporting staff at Scot Lane. He was twenty, two years older than I, and had just completed his National Service in the R.A.F. Because he lived in Whitby, and had been snowed-in there, his arrival had been postponed for a couple of days, a source of amusement to some of us in the office. Malcolm withstood all the teasing, but, although he had worked for a short time on *The Whitby Gazette*, where his father was Editor, he seemed rather unsure of what was expected of him in his early days in Doncaster.

His first job was to interview Mrs Maria Tuke, a nonagenarian who had previously been the subject of one of my own inquiries. He came back to the office, sat at a typewriter, and was obviously floundering, so I helped him to write the story.

Very soon, however, Malcolm began to emerge from his chrysalis. The gawky probationer who, during his first weeks in Scot Lane, sometimes rang up his father to ask for help (as, for example, when covering the political in-fighting at Barnby Dun Parish Council, where street-lighting and unadopted roads were emotive topics) gradually found his wings. It did not seem long before he was running a quirky column in *The Doncaster Chronicle*, sniffing out exclusives on Retford calls, showing a distinctive turn of phrase as a feature-writer, and taking control if reports of a disaster came in. He had the ability to draw the threads of a major story together while it was still happening, and weave them into a front-page spread, even with Jack Siddle breathing heavily down his neck.

Nicknamed 'The Gangler' by Nobby Clarke because of his height, awkwardness, and annoying habit of hanging over other people's typewriters to see how their stories were shaping, Malcolm once mistakenly picked up and drank somebody else's beer in the Saracen's Head. From then on, any similar faux pas was referred to as 'gangling', although, according to tales filtering out from that stronghold of male chauvinism, Malcolm was never known to shirk his round. He could be a brooding presence in the corner of the office after a night on Barnsley Bitter, though even under such trying circumstances his ironic sense of humour did not wholly desert him. He was never at a loss for ideas for *Chronicle Page One Leads* (a dreaded weekly chore that Clunk marked on the diary), and took over as Sports Editor for a time after Hughie Goodall blew himself up with a Primus stove while camping.

We worked together for five years, Malcolm and I, time enough to get to know each other very well. Though we liked one another, at first it did not seem our destinies would fuse. But then fate, and love, took charge.

This is why, when Malcolm left Doncaster to try his luck in Leeds, and became, first the Deputy Editor of *The Yorkshire Post*, then the Editor of *The Yorkshire Evening Post*, I was the one riding on his coat-tails.

Chapter Twenty-Five – Catharsis

MY MOTHER LEFT the Big Drum the day before her fifty-ninth birthday, on November 6th, 1956, and married George Henry at St. Peter's Church, Bentley, five days later. She had managed the Drum for fourteen years, ever since my father died, and though she and George Henry had been talking of marriage for quite some time, they had decided to wait until they were sure of my intentions.

I was aware they were holding back, but not convinced that my mother was ready to give up her independence. Fifty years on, their reluctance seems much more like self-denial, certainly on George Henry's part. This makes me ashamed of my selfishness, for at the time I was so preoccupied with my own interests that it never occurred to me to encourage them to change the status quo. And yet, if I am honest, I would not have had things any other way.

Malcolm was on the scene now, and there was no longer any reason to put off their wedding, so, after looking at a few older properties and being unimpressed, they took out a mortgage on a semi-detached house in Sandall Park, Wheatley Hills, a new estate on the east side of Doncaster.

At last Mother would be the mistress of her own house, for all her life she had either shared someone else's, or lived on business premises. They calculated they could afford to pay the mortgage on the £2,000 price of Number 18 Sandall Park Drive if George Henry, by now a railway lorry-driver, worked an extra shift for double pay on Sunday mornings, something that, despite his bad smoker's chest, he was very willing to do. For the first eighteen months they also had a contribution from me of four pounds a week 'board', for after Malcolm had moved to Leeds I continued working at Scot Lane and living at home until our wedding.

Even as I laid my own exciting plans for the future, separating myself from the Drum required a strong anaesthetic. As the day of our departure drew near, and I walked through the familiar rooms committing them to memory, I was seized by a kind of fatalism that helped to deaden the pain of impending loss. Latterly I had tended to ignore the garden, especially since the bottom end had been sold by John Smith's to a construction company. Now I walked in it for one last time, sensing perhaps how, in its happiest guise, it would continue to haunt me.

Farewell presentations were made to Mother and George Henry: a mantel clock with a Westminster chime from the customers, and a canteen of cutlery from John Smith's. When removal day came, I went to work as usual, catching a Wheatley Hills trackless to our new home at tea-time, which felt very strange. On arrival, I found

Mother and George Henry trying to make space for her furniture (thank heavens George Henry had none to bring), for although she had left certain items behind, including the huge mahogany sideboard and two fireside-chairs that hailed from the Station Inn, what furniture she had brought looked far bigger in this small house than it had at the Drum. Eventually, though, all natural laws being suspended, the quart was got into the pint pot, a miracle unknown in the licensed trade.

Mrs Dunn declared she would be Mother's matron-of-honour, George Henry's eldest brother, John, was best man, and about forty relatives and close friends were invited to the wedding. Mother wore a green dress and jacket with bronze accessories, and her friend Mrs Mullen, who ran the dear old Red Lion in Doncaster Market Place, put on a traditional sit-down lunch.

The honeymoon was in Saltdean, near Brighton, and Mrs Dunn insisted on moving into Number 18 during Mother's absence in order to look after me. I was perfectly able to take care of myself, but I think she enjoyed holding sway in a shiny new house.

We were fond of each other, in an undemonstrative way, and she had long forgiven me for asking 'Have you been married two or three times, Mrs Dunn?' if, indeed, she had ever held it against me. I was only about ten at the time, and did not realise I was being impertinent until Mother cried out in horror, and made me apologise.

On her return from honeymoon, Mother set about the business of becoming a full-time housewife: sewing curtains and clothes, laying lino, painting, papering and cooking. George Henry took pride in the garden, and had astonishing success with sweet peas and hollyhocks. Mother planted parsley, which grew so prolifically down the side border we joked that it was obvious who wore the trousers, if any truth could be attached to the old wives' tale. She joined Doncaster Conservative Association and the Townswomen's Guild, and fulfilled a long-held wish to be confirmed. She listened to (and took) advice from younger neighbours about the latest trends in home-making: painting the walls of a room different colours, papering recesses, positioning the clock to one side of the mantelpiece, buying a pierced plastic shade for the standard-lamp, and learning how to make prawn cocktails. Among the children round about, she cut a grandmotherly figure, and was known for her jam and lemon tarts, Victoria sponge and chocolate cake. One day she hoped to have grandchildren of her own, and bought a doll at a church bazaar with this in mind.

I threw a farewell party at the Red Lion one Saturday lunch-time, and Malcolm and I were married at St. Aidan's Church, Wheatley Hills, Doncaster, on Thursday, April 24th, 1958. To Aunt Clara's huge delight, I was given away by Uncle George, a role he had been anticipating ever since my father died. I wore white lace, and carried an all-white, mainly rose, bouquet. 'Too pale!' cried Daddy Clayton's wife, and tried to introduce some colour as Dougie Guest took the photographs by ramming red rose-petal confetti down my neck.

Malcolm's sister, Elizabeth, and Cousin Annette were bridesmaids in delphinium blue and cyclamen pink, with anemone headbands and posies, and Harry Green, Malcolm's schoolfriend, was the best man. He had calmed the groom during the morning by taking him to a barber's for a scrape with a cut-throat razor, for the very good reason that, fearful of my bridegroom turning up at church with a blood-stained collar, I had issued firm orders: on no account must he cut himself, as he often did, whilst performing his pre-wedding shave.

These and similar word-pictures help to give substance to my dream-like impressions of my wedding-day. It was blustery, showery weather, and I remember hearing rain beating on the roof of the church during the service. But as we left, the sun came out, and a puff of wind blew my short veil straight up above my head, giving Dougie an unusual picture for the front page of *The Evening Post* that same afternoon. Copies were for sale at the reception, for J.R.D., who was one of the guests, naturally looked upon the gathering as another chance to sell papers, and had arranged for a bundle to be rushed to the venue, the Green House Hotel.

After our honeymoon at Hawkshead in the Lake District, Malcolm and I took up residence in Larkfield Crescent, Rawdon, near Leeds. We had secured a mortgage on 'Fairbourne', a rather dreary-looking house, drawn to it because it was on top of a hill, with panoramic views of the Aire Valley, and a long garden backing on to a field where horses grazed. But the garden was overgrown, and the house, though it cost £1,900, slightly over the odds for a two-and-a-half-bedroomed semi, had been built in the 1920s, and was in a poor decorative state.

Even though we were wildly optimistic about our capabilities as home-makers, we knew it would take us years to achieve all the improvements we planned. This was one reason why I decided not to apply for the post of Women's Editor of *The Yorkshire Evening Post* when the paper's Editor, Alan Woodward, invited me to Head Office for a chat. There were other reasons, too: I lacked confidence in being able to handle the job, and felt 'written out' after spending my last months in Scot Lane working all hours as the only woman reporter. I was looking forward to a change of pace, and starting a family, and writing solely on women's topics had never appealed to me. Of course, the money would have been useful, but Malcolm was earning seventeen pounds a week, enough to support us, and held charmingly old-fashioned views about being the only breadwinner.

We survived happily at first without a car, a fridge or a television set. I could drive, and a car would have been useful when Malcolm succumbed to an overactive thyroid five months after our wedding, and spent a fortnight in Leeds General Infirmary. Visiting him involved a fourteen-mile bus journey there and back, and at the time I was plagued by swollen joints, which turned out to be a symptom of rheumatic fever.

I had kept my problems from Malcolm, but when I collected him from hospital he noticed there was something wrong, and walked me down to the doctor's that same evening. After blood tests, I was ordered to bed, so Malcolm, who was still not allowed to return to work, became nurse, cook and housemaid, helped by both mothers at different times. A month later, I, in my turn was admitted to the Infirmary, and found myself at the end of a huge, ground-floor women's ward, in a bed immediately below the one Malcolm had occupied while upstairs in Men's Medical. Such a coincidence did not escape notice: even Matron commented on it when she made her rounds.

Because my heart was playing tricks, I remained there for a month, and when Christmas arrived Malcolm refused to spend it in Whitby or Doncaster, despite my urgings. He had tinned chicken for dinner, then came to visit me. In mid-January, pumped full of penicillin, cortisone and aspirin, I was sent to Doncaster by ambulance, and spent five months convalescing with Mother and George Henry. Malcolm, by now back at work, lived at Rawdon from Monday to Friday and joined us at weekends.

In late spring he and I spent a holiday in Whitby, and because his mother had recently undergone gynaecological surgery, Elizabeth was in charge. With her customary kindness, she ran me a bath, not realising it would be the first I had had for months, and without demur I took it – and survived. His father booked seats at a local cinema (an unheard of luxury) for the latest American blockbuster, *The Big Country*, and we trooped in *en famille*. Not only were we enchanted by the film, Malcolm's mum and I felt sure that seeing it had hastened our recovery.

On a glad day in June, six months after had I left in an ambulance for Leeds, Mother took me home by train and bus to 'Fairbourne'. There, Malcolm, who had spent his lonely evenings working secretly on the house, welcomed us with a liver dinner.

That summer of 1959 was memorably hot, and I spent most of it sitting in the garden, soaking up the sun. By September, a year after the onset of the fever, I was well again, thanks to all the care I had received, and the long, long rest bestowed on me.

When I was young, *The People* newspaper used to run a feature about a family called The Neverwells and their G.P., Doctor Goodenough. Every week one of the Neverwells either succumbed to a new ailment or was injured in an accident, and no sooner had the poor man soothed their fears, prescribed appropriate treatment and put away his stethoscope than up would pop another Neverwell with an entirely different set of symptoms (which the good doctor promised to deal with the following Sunday).

Though our family was not quite so consistent, various health worries surfaced in the fifties and early sixties. Elizabeth broke a leg in an accident in the school gym, and needed major surgery. Brother David had a kidney operation in 1957. In 1962 Malcolm submitted thankfully to surgery on his fractious thyroid after a protracted course of drugs had failed to stabilise his condition. (The attempts to balance it had reminded us of Alice nibbling opposite sides of the mushroom during her visit to Wonderland, though in Malcolm's case the effects were horizontal rather than vertical, sending his weight see-sawing up and down, and requiring him to have three different sizes of suits in his wardrobe.)

But there were many lulls, many happy times: weekends spent at Whitby or Doncaster, and return visits made by Malcolm's family or Mother and George Henry to us. One sunny Saturday, Mother and I caught a bus from Rawdon to Harrogate, marvelling at the impressive houses as we passed along Leeds Road. We alighted at the Co-op, walked down to the Valley Gardens, tried to get lunch in one café along Royal Parade, left in disgust after a long wait without any service, and had more luck at another a few doors away. What a lovely place Harrogate was, said Mother, in spite of the disappointment at the first restaurant. It never crossed our minds that one day Malcolm and I might live in the town.

While we were enjoying our day out, George Henry remained at 'Fairbourne' with the Awful Pym and watched football on television. The Awful Pym was Mother and George's rumbustious, highly excitable dog. If you asked what breed he was, George Henry would tell you proudly that he was 'a first cross', mainly Manchester Terrier. But whatever Pym's genealogy, he had a personality disorder, and was given to tantrums which his doting master regarded as natural canine spirit, and made few attempts to curb.

Although Mother spoiled Pym too, she was less adoring. Her patience was tested if anyone arrived at their home, for the little dog set up a barking and whining that could last throughout the visit. As he grew more hysterical with the passing years, he had to be shut in a bedroom when callers came, though the noise went on unabated, scarcely muffled by the thin walls.

If Malcolm and I were spending a weekend at Number 18, Pym could detect when we had got halfway down our cups of bedtime coffee. This was the signal for him to plant himself in front of us, and bark and bark, eyes flashing green, until we had no option but to leave the room. His wilful ways cast a blight on our visits to Doncaster, though he calmed down if he came to stay at Rawdon while Mother and George Henry went on holiday, perhaps because we tired him out with long walks. On these occasions he could be great fun, although it was embarrassing when he indulged in another of his peculiarities: backing up against a fence or a post to empty his bowels, and parking his faeces as high as he could, so they hung there like Catherine wheels.

***

THERE CAME A day in 1961 when, soon after Elizabeth's wedding to Malcolm Frost, I made one of my frequent flying visits to Doncaster, and Mother told me she had found a lump in her other breast. She had known about it for some weeks, but had decided to not to say anything before the wedding. She had kept hoping she was mistaken, or that the lump was harmless, for it was sixteen years since her mastectomy. Now, as I hugged her, she said tearfully, 'I can't go through all that again.'

In fact, she did not need to, for when she saw a consultant shortly afterwards he made no mention of cancer, and advocated no operation, no radiotherapy, just a regular injection. Following some weeks of this treatment, the lump appeared to have softened and flattened – surely a hopeful sign that the drug was working, and it wasn't cancer?

Malcolm and I spent Christmas that year at Whitby, and on Christmas Night he developed terrible stomach pain and was rushed to Scarborough Hospital for an appendectomy. Elizabeth and I went with him in the ambulance, praying his appendix would not burst as we bumped along the wintry coast road, with the poor sufferer rolling in agony on the stretcher. After a week or more in hospital, he spent two weeks in a convalescent home, but when he returned to work his thyroid trouble flared up again, and this was when the medics admitted defeat, and surrendered him up for surgery.

Throughout all this time, George Henry had soldiered quietly on, beset by a terrible, phlegmy cough that was particularly troublesome first thing in a morning before he left for the yard to collect his lorry. Because he knew a lot about cars, Malcolm and I asked for his opinion on one we had found at a Doncaster garage, and were thinking of buying. It was an old Standard 10, costing £200, and although our bank balance would not stretch to such a sum, Mother offered to lend us the money, which we arranged to repay at ten pounds a month.

George Henry inspected the Standard, and approved, and David, though not yet a driver himself, accompanied me on the train to Doncaster when I went to collect it. Nervously I drove our amazing acquisition to Sandall Park Drive, pulling up outside the house just as George Henry was returning from work. In response to my invitation, he got behind the wheel, and propelled us ever so smoothly around the block, coaxing the gear-stick gently into place, for he had never shed the habit of double de-clutching.

This was to be the last time he drove the car. Days later, he fell ill with what seemed like a severe bout of bronchitis, and had to stay off work. Eventually, as his condition worsened, he took to his bed, and Mother learned from the doctor that X-rays had shown his symptoms were due not to bronchitis, but inoperable lung cancer. George Henry himself was never told this, though I think he must have guessed: he gave up smoking, but by then it was too late.

Mother tried to tempt his palate, but he grew gradually weaker. Still, he never complained, accepting the situation with his customary patience and cheerfulness, touchingly appreciative of all that was done for him. The only time I remember him showing any real concern about himself was when he confided to me that he had coughed up some blood – 'but don't tell your mother, she might be worried.'

That winter of 1962-63 was one of the worst on record, and plunging temperatures and heavy snowfalls challenged our inexperience during frequent trips to Doncaster in the brave little Standard. Malcolm, though still on L-plates, did much of the driving. Since his thyroid operation, which had taken place a few weeks earlier, he had been unable to work, as the scar on his neck refused to heal. This was lucky in a way, because it meant we could spend time at Sandall Park Drive, playing cribbage with George Henry, and exercising the Awful Pym, who knew no loyalty, and refused to go near his master's bedroom, despite appeals to his better nature. George Henry laughed at his reluctance, though I think he felt hurt about it.

But if the Awful Pym shunned the sickroom, there was a regular stream of human visitors. One of them was Mrs Dunn, whose pragmatic devotion bore us up, and lasted to the end. When George Henry reached the final stages of his illness, drugged into quiet sleep, she came to stay and share the nursing. When he died, she was there in the room with Mother and me. He slipped away in character, without distress or fuss.

The date was January 6th, 1963, the day after David's twenty-first birthday, which had been celebrated with a family party at Sleights. I had opted to stay in Doncaster, so Malcolm had travelled to his parents' house alone. There was no phone at Number 18, so I rang him with the news of George Henry's death from a coin-box, and he came back on the earliest train.

After the funeral, Mother decided to move back to Hull, to the same little house in Bethnal Green which my father had bought for his parents more than thirty years before. Because Dad had died intestate, the house belonged to me now, and when the tenants left I made it over to Mother for a peppercorn payment. There was no bathroom, so she had one built, extended the kitchen, and had all the rooms redecorated. It seemed a promising retreat, a short bus-ride from the city centre, handy for local shops, a stone's throw from Cromer Street and Inglemire Lane, where she had lived as a young woman, and about half-a-mile from the Station Inn. Three of her old friends were within strolling distance, and Pearson Park lay conveniently close for walks with the Awful Pym. I clung to the belief that Mother would spend many contented years in Bethnal Green, with me popping over in the car to see her, and sometimes bringing her back for holidays at 'Fairbourne'.

Four months after George Henry died, Malcolm and I had driven her south in the Standard for a holiday in Torquay. Knitted suits were all the rage, and she had made one to take with her, which I still have tucked away. We had asked for a ground-floor bedroom for Mum, as she seemed to tire more easily, but she was well enough to sunbathe on the sands, and go sight-seeing, and we all enjoyed a night at an old-time music hall. It had begun to puzzle her why she could no longer reach the high notes when singing hymns at St. Aidan's; but here in the theatre stalls, egged on by some renowned but ancient entertainer whose heyday she remembered, she seemed to have no trouble with 'On Mother Kelly's Doorstep, Down Paradise Row'.

It was clear to us, though, that her health had started to deteriorate since she had moved to Hull. When the builders dismantled her outside water-closet in order to build her a new bathroom, she was without a lavatory for many days, and had to run a hundred yards or more to the one in Aunt Bel's back yard. This was not just an embarrassment, but a source of great anxiety; the disruption occurred at a time when her need was often pressing, but because she could not leave her home in an insecure state, she was unable to come to Rawdon, or stay at Aunt Nancy's.

Taking the train back to Doncaster for periodic check-ups at the Infirmary became more and more of a dread as advancing illness took its toll, though she was able to stay overnight with Mrs Dunn and her daughter. As far as I could gather, nothing much was said at the hospital confrontations. The injections continued, but she became so thin her stockings would not stay up, and started to wrinkle round her ankles; and though she had always been taller than I, now she seemed to be shrinking into herself, 'growing downwards like a cow's tail', as she put it.

We had always joked and chattered, but nowadays her conversation was quieter, more reflective, as though her thoughts were elsewhere. Because her right thumb had grown painful, she started to cradle it in her left hand, catching her breath now and then when it 'jumped'. Pity and tenderness welled in me whenever she turned her back, for the tired slant of her shoulders, and the delve where her shingled, iron-grey hair tapered down to a darker V in the nape of her neck, somehow seemed the focal point of all her vulnerability.

During all this time, the Awful Pym had become more and more of a handful. He seemed to hate living in Bethnal Green, and the building of the bathroom unsettled him so much he kept running away. On one occasion he was found at a kennels where he had briefly stayed, but mostly he ran to Aunt Nancy's, and had to be brought back by Uncle Bob. At night, after Mother had gone to bed, he whined and barked in the sitting-room, and she feared he would disturb the neighbours. When she took him for a walk, he strained so much on his lead he almost pulled her over.

Once the building work had been finished, Mother moved in for a time with Aunt Nancy and Uncle Bob, helping to look after my aunt, who had developed a serious heart problem, and Pym only added to the household's troubles. In late December I went over to Hull expecting to put the crazy, mixed-up little beggar in kennels again so Mother could accompany Malcolm and me to Sleights for Christmas.

It was a shock when Mother told me she had decided to have Pym put to sleep because he had become too much to cope with. She did not think he would ever settle, and giving him away in his nervous condition, even to us had we been willing to take him, was out of the question. Perhaps she was also preparing for what lay ahead.

Beyond asking her if she was sure this was what she wanted, I did not try to dissuade her. We piled up his plate for one last time with his favourite Pal Meat For Dogs, and after he had devoured it we put him on his lead. Then, feeling like traitors because he trotted along so excitedly, we walked him down Clough Road to the Dogs' Home, where, after brief formalities, he was placed in a gas chamber.

Pym was eight years old, but because he looked such a fit and handsome dog Mother was afraid the Home might have a change of heart, and pass him on to somebody else who might be cruel to him because he was so naughty. So we sat in the waiting-room until the melancholy business was over, and then I did as she had asked and went to take a peep at him to make sure he was dead. As we linked arms to walk back to Bethnal Green, she sighed, 'Eh Janet, you and I have come through some times together.'

We had a glowingly happy Christmas with Malcolm's family at Sleights, and after her return to Hull Mother began to seem quite settled; closely in touch with Aunt Nancy, my cousins and their large brood of children, and able to call on Uncle Bob if she needed help around the house and garden.

But though she insisted on holding a house-warming party, her vitality was ebbing, and arrangements were made for her to see a consultant in Hull so that she need no longer make those wearisome trips to Doncaster. It was while I was driving her back to Bethnal Green from one of these Hull appointments that she said bleakly, 'I know it's cancer'.

This there was no gainsaying, for her appearance alone confirmed it, but perhaps something had been said at the hospital to make her confront the truth at last. Or perhaps she had always known, but did not wish to acknowledge it. As her condition worsened we begged her to come to stay in Rawdon, and once she had completed a course of radiotherapy she came to us with a quiet acceptance unusual in her.

We did not speak much about her illness during those first uneventful days, but once when she referred to her cancer I tried to rally her by saying, 'We've beaten it before, and we'll beat it again.'

'Not this time', she said.

After she took more or less permanently to her bed, the number of her visitors increased. Aunt Nancy was one who made the journey, and encouraged me enormously by saying I was looking after her sister very well.

'Yes', said Mother, 'it's as though she's the mother now, and I'm the child.'

Aunt Elsie came from Doncaster, transported by my cousin Dennis and his wife, and Aunt Clara, as determinedly cheerful as ever, brought Uncle George. Mrs Dunn arrived armed with a bouquet of red roses so big it had to be arranged in a bucket. Someone else brought arum lilies, but after they had left Mother asked me to remove the flowers because the smell of them reminded her of funerals. And yet her own was on her mind, because one day she said, 'I want you to take me to Hull and cremate me.' It was an instruction for which I was grateful later, though at the time I could not think about it.

Another of her instructions was, 'Don't remember this, remember the happy times.' I have tried to do so, and am grateful for the mercies that helped to make her last weeks bearable. The greatest mercy of all was that, though she was weary, she assured her visitors that she felt no actual pain, thanks, no doubt, to the radiotherapy and our wonderful Doctor Riley, whose frequent visits came to mean as much to us at 'Fairbourne' as Doctor Outwin's had meant to Mother and George Henry when he befriended them at Sandall Park Drive.

When I asked if she would like the Vicar to call, Mother said no, and murmured something about having made her own peace. She was not afraid of dying – 'I just don't want to leave you.'

It is more comforting to bring to mind other fragments of conversation that passed between us. She said once, as she brushed her hair, 'I've had a wonderful life.'

'You've had a very hard life,' I remember interjecting.

'Oh no I haven't, I've had a wonderful life. A wonderful family, two wonderful husbands, wonderful friends, a wonderful daughter ...'

And when I sobbed, 'Oh, but there've been times when I've given you such trouble,' she smiled at me, and lied as she said, 'You never ever did.'

Towards the end, her lungs became congested. Dr Riley said that while they could be drained in hospital, the benefit would only be temporary, and being hospitalised might distress her. I felt sure that it would, and decided to keep her at home. But I was never called upon to perform any difficult nursing duties, for to the end my mother was able to wash herself and reach the lavatory, which, especially from her point of view, were very positive blessings.

Malcolm was our doughty knight, our emissary to a wider world which, despite the fact that dreadful events occurred in it, represented normality. Welcoming him home from work in the evening brought the world back in to us. Having a big, manly presence around the house dispelled some of the fears that had accumulated inside our small capsule during the day, and made death seem, for me at least, a huge improbability. A tender husband, but not usually the most patient of men, now he schooled himself in patience, realising I needed to give rein to my emotions when we were alone together.

***

JULY THE FIFTEENTH, 1964, and quite hot, as I recall. Mother was in one of the twin beds in the guest room, and I made up the other and suggested I stay with her that night. But no, she said, not tonight – perhaps tomorrow.

The following day, more visitors came, and though she managed to talk to them, once they had left she seemed drained of all energy, and sighed, 'I feel a hundred.' This time she accepted my offer to stay in the room with her, and I gave her some of the morphine-based medicine that Dr Riley had prescribed.

He had told me that if she asked for a further dose, even if she had taken one quite recently, I should give it to her; so when she woke me during the night and requested more medicine because she couldn't sleep, I put a spoonful of the pinkish liquid into a glass and diluted it as usual.

'It looks a lot', she said.

I explained it was mainly water.

I lay for a long time listening to her talking in her sleep. She seemed to have returned to the far-off days when she was married to my father, and to be among a crowd of people, possibly enjoying one of those motor bike trips that she and Dad used to take with his brothers and their wives or girlfriends. Once she murmured

'Harry', and another time, ' George', though whether she was referring to George Henry or my Uncle George I do not know.

Much of what she voiced was unintelligible, but I did hear her say very clearly once or twice, 'Let's all go to our house.' Then she said, 'We all love our homes.' I wondered which home she meant, though wherever her memories had taken her, she sounded very happy. But before I fell asleep she had started to say 'Oh dear, oh dear ...' over and over again, which Aunt Nancy told me later was something people often did when they were dying.

Death has its own silence, and as soon as I awoke I knew before I opened my eyes that my mother was dead. Knew, but did not believe. I rushed screaming into Malcolm, and he rang Dr Riley, who came immediately, still in his pyjama-jacket. I was hysterical, borne down not only by grief, but by guilt, for I thought I might have used the wrong spoon, and given Mother more morphine than he had prescribed. When I told him this, he assured me that I had done nothing wrong, and that, had he been there, he would have done exactly the same.

Anguished as I was, I did become more rational. My mother's end had been painless, dignified, peaceful, happy, and though I had been asleep, I had been with her. But I could not forget how she had said, 'It looks a lot.'

Now the grim wheels of disposal had to be set in motion. How could the earth still spin when my mother no longer breathed upon it? But practicalities must be dealt with, rituals observed. We arranged a service at St. John's, our family church in Hull, before cremation, and afterwards my cousins organised a gathering at the little house in Bethnal Green. It was amazing how many were able to cram in, and how almost a party atmosphere developed as people relaxed over tea, and sherry, and whisky, and sandwiches, and sausage rolls, and Thirsk's ham-and-egg slices, and Cousin Dorothy's mince pies, and remembered all the happy times they had shared with Mother. While part of me thought how glad she would have been to see so many people there, and hear their merry chatter, part of me thought such a display insensitive. Now I know better, of course.

***

OUR DAUGHTER, DOROTHEA, was born nine months later, in April, 1965. Her expected date of arrival made it seem likely that her conception occurred around the time of Mother's death. But Thea took her time, and was eleven days late, because she is her own person: which is as it should be.

Twenty months later, another miracle: Patrick was born, our bonny, blue-eyed boy.